MEDIA, FEMINISM, CULTURAL STUDIES

Stepping Forward: Essays, Lectures and Interviews
by Wolfgang Iser

Liv Tyler
by Thomas A. Christie

The Cinema of Richard Linklater
by Thomas A. Christie

Walerian Borowczyk
by Jeremy Mark Robinson

Wild Zones: Pornography, Art and Feminism
by Kelly Ives

'Cosmo Woman': The World of Women's Magazines
by Oliver Whitehorne

Andrea Dworkin
by Jeremy Mark Robinson

Cixous, Irigaray, Kristeva: The Jouissance of French Feminism
by Kelly Ives

Sex in Art: Pornography and Pleasure in Painting and Sculpture
by Cassidy Hughes

*The Erotic Object: Sexuality in Sculpture
From Prehistory to the Present Day*
by Susan Quinnell

Women in Pop Music
by Helen Challis

Detonation Britain: Nuclear War in the UK
by Jeremy Mark Robinson

The Sacred Cinema of Andrei Tarkovsky
by Jeremy Mark Robinson

Jean-Luc Godard: The Passion of Cinema / Le Passion de Cinéma
by Jeremy Mark Robinson

Julia Kristeva: Art, Love, Melancholy, Philosophy, Semiotics
by Kelly Ives

Luce Irigaray: Lips, Kissing, and the Politics of Sexual Difference
by Kelly Ives

Helene Cixous I Love You: The **Jouissance** *of Writing*
by Kelly Ives

MARVELOUS NAMES

IN LITERATURE AND CINEMA

MARVELOUS NAMES

IN LITERATURE AND CINEMA

P. ADAMS SITNEY

CRESCENT MOON

Crescent Moon Publishing
P.O. Box 1312, Maidstone
Kent, ME14 5XU, Great Britain
www.crmoon.com

First published 2023.
© P. Adams Sitney 2023.

Set in Book Antiqua 10 on 14pt.
Designed by Radiance Graphics.

The right of P. Adams Sitney to be identified as the author of this book has been asserted generally in accordance with sections 77 and 78 of the Copyright, Designs and Patents Act 1988.

All rights reserved. No part of this book may be reprinted or reproduced, stored in a retrieval system, or transmitted, in any form or by any means, electronic, mechanical, photocopying, recording or otherwise, without permission from the publisher.

British Library Cataloguing in Publication data available for this title.

I.S.B.N.-13 9781861718044
I.S.B.N.-13 9781861719119

CONTENTS

Preface ◆ 13
Sources ◆ 17
Introduction ◆ 20

1 Ahab's Name ◆ 38
2 Called Ishmael ◆ 58
3 The Sonnet That Names Itself ◆ 88
4 The Autobiography of a Metonomy ◆ 116
5 Naming the Evasive Heart ◆ 128
6 Calling Judy Madeline ◆ 140
7 Nomen Est Omen: Stan, Georges, and Harry ◆ 157
8 Dropped Names ◆ 176
9 Dubious Terms and Names: Structural Film Redux ◆ 196

"Nous leur donnerions un nom." – "Ils en auraient un." – "Celui qui nous leur donnerions ne serait pas leur vrais nom." – "Tout de même, capable de les nommer." – "Capable de faire savoir que, le jour où ils se reconnaîtrient prêts, il y aurait un nom pour leur nom." – "un nom tel qu'il n'y aurait pas lieu pour eux de se sentir interpellés par lui, ni tentés de répondre, ni même jamais dénommés par ce nom." – "Pourtant, n'avons-nous pas supposé qu'ils en auraient un qui leur serait commun?" – "Nous l'avons suppose, mais seulement pour qu'ils puissent plus commodément passer inaperçus." – "Alors, comment saurions-nous que nous pouvons nous addresser à eux? Ils sont loin, vous savez." – "C'est pour cela que nous avons les noms, plus nombreux et plus merveilleux que tous ceux dont on use habituellement." – "Ils ne sauraient pas que c'est leur nom." – "Comment le sauraient-ils, ils n'en ont pas."

Maurice Blanchot: *Le pas au-delà* (Paris: Gallimard, 1973), pp. 16-17.

[*"We would give them a name". – "They would have one". – "The one we would give them would not be their true name". – "All the same, capable of naming them". – "Capable of making it known that when the day came that they would realize they were ready, the name would be there for their name." "A name such that it wouldn't occur to them to feel questioned by it, or that they were tempted to answer to it, nor even that they were ever designated by this name" "Yet, have we not supposed that they would have one in common?" – "We supposed it, but only so that they could pass more easily unnoticed." – "Then, how can we know that we might contact them? They are far away, you know." – "That's why we have names, more numerous and more marvelous than those we use habitually" – "Then, they wouldn't know it's their name." – "How would they know it; they don't have one."*]

Maurice Blanchot: *The Step Not Beyond*, trans. Lycette Nelson (Albany: State University of New York Press, 1992), p. 8.

Conquest of the North Pole (Géorges Méliès, 1912).

Vertigo (Alfred Hitchcock, 1957).

Preface

The advantage (or the curse) of old age is the capability of seeing the patterns of one own fascinations and how narrow one's interests have been over a whole life. As I reach the middle of my Seventies, I can see that literary onamastics has always been near the core of my writing and teaching.

I must have read Stéphane Mallarmé for the first time in the late Fifties, before I knew any French, or Latin or Greek for that matter. My copy of Angel Flores's *Anchor Anthology of French Poetry: From Nerval to Valéry in English Translation* was frazzled with wear. But it did not contain either of the two sonnets in yx. I don't remember when I first encountered them. At the Yale Graduate School I took a superb seminar on Mallarmé, conducted in French by Paul de Man. I remember being disappointed that he never reached "Ses purs ongles", although it was on his syllabus; so, I wrote my term paper on it. Elements of the research I conducted then have found their way into the third chapter of this book, nearly forty years later.

My reading of Luigi Pirandello's *Si Gira* preceded that seminar. I had been teaching it at NYU before I entered graduate school. I began to explore the relationship of nicknames to metonymy then. Tom Gunning, who must have heard me talking on the book back then, asked me to provide an introduction to his republication of it for the University of Chicago Press. It turned out to be not what he had in mind, or remembered. He wrote the Introduction himself and used my essay as an Afterword. It was a win-win event all around.

My late wife, Marjorie Keller, founded a journal for the Collective For Living Cinema in the Seventies, called *Motion Picture*. She asked me to write up a lecture I had given on Hart Crane's "Chaplinesque" for its premier issue. Much later Rani Singh lured me to the Harry Smith symposium at the Getty Research Institute in Los Angeles. I write 'lured' because I have avoided symposia whenever I could, and successfully eschewed joining or attending the meetings of all 'learned' societies throughout my fifty years in academia. At the Getty I presented, in 2001, the nucleus of the chapter on Harry Smith's reading, which she published nine years later (after a second Smith symposium) with lavish illustrations in *Harry Smith: The Avant-Garde in the American Vernacular*.

The year of the Getty's first Harry Smith symposium Daniel J. Leab requested an essay on Alfred Hitchcock's *Vertigo* from me, for the journal *Film History*. Quite uncharacteristically, I acceded and sent him a text. He screwed up – later claiming that he was out of the county and his email was hacked as an excuse for neither publishing it nor remembering to acknowledge I sent it. Happily, a much better publishing opportunity soon presented itself. Mary Beth Bandy and Antonio Monda were editing a book for the Museum of Modern Art, *The Hidden God: Film and Faith* (2003). They had already solicited a text on Tarkovsky's *Nostalghia* from me when I offered them the *Vertigo* essay as well. I was proud to have it in that volume.

Long after I left graduate school, I ran into Harold Bloom in a bookstore in New Haven. 'What do you have for my Chelsea House series of essays on major authors?' I told him I had a good piece on Hart Crane's "Chaplinesque". 'Too late' he said, 'the Crane volume is already published. Do something new.' Tentatively, I suggested that I might be able to write something on *Moby-Dick*. He refused to hear the qualifications and commanded me to get it to him in three weeks. I knew I had the germ of a good essay when I had been asked to elaborate on Ahab's name in a class I was conducting at the School of the Art Institute of Chicago. I wrote that up in a frenzy to fulfill Bloom's deadline. He used it in his Melville collection and again in the volume devoted to *Moby-Dick* alone.

I was happy with that essay but I was nagged by the feeling that I ought to do a more thorough reading of *Moby-Dick*. When I retired in 2016 after teaching thirty-five years at Princeton University, I imagined I would complete my project of editing an elaborately footnoted, critical edition of the first book with my name on it – Stan Brakhage's *Metaphors on Vision* – and give up writing, or rather trade that energy into reading through all the dialogues of Plato in the original Greek.

When Jon Aumon of the British annual *Hotel* wrote asking me to contribute any unpublished piece of writing I may have lying about, I was pleased to answer I had nothing, and was working on nothing; there would be nothing more coming from me. Yet, his letter left an itch in my brain. The typical day of a retired professor living in a dull Rhode Island town is long. One morning, after I completed my daily Stephanus page of Plato, I scribbled the outline of an argument about the narrative voice of *Moby-Dick*. A couple of weeks later, I sent more than thirty pages on that subject to Aumon.

Then in a furious effort to cleanse my mind of the backed-up detritus of my Princeton seminars, I wrote an essay on Stan Brakhage and Deleuze; then another on Brakhage's long sound film, the enigmatic *Passage Through: A Ritual*. Tony Pipolo took advantage of my Bacchic energy, saying I could no longer use the excuse of retirement to refuse to contribute to his journal, *The Psychoanalytical Review*. For him, I wrote about a scene in Antonioni's *Il deserto rosso*. At Aumon's suggestion I made a new book by placing these recent texts in the context of my other writings on landscape and film music. That required yet another new chapter on the way Brakhage and Deleuze theorized film sound.

I thought I was finally through when I sent off the manuscript of *Melodic Landscapes: Visual Sound and Natural Beauty in Cinema* to Aumon. Fat chance! My friend, Daniel Heller-Roazen, had given me photocopies of essays by Jean-Claude Milner on Mallarmé. The brilliance of those essays ought to have made me abandon any notion of writing on the "Sonnet en yx" again. Instead, I decided to jot down my accumulated observations on the two versions of the poem since publishing a few paragraphs on it in *Modernist Montage*.

It was a short step from that rash act to the realization that most of my writing on literature and many of my texts on cinema devolved from the intrigue of names. By the time I completed the new study of Mallarmé in the light of the naming process of poetry, I had selected the other chapters of this book. Only the two on *Moby-Dick* have hardly been revised. The extensive revisions of all the others brought me to reflect on my long enthrallment to names in books and films. That reflection generated the Introduction to this volume.

I was still bugged by something missing, but I didn't know what it was. Eventually, I realized that I needed to write more on the films of Michael Snow, or rather on his use of names in them. When I had finished that chapter, I thought the volume was as complete as I could make it. However, several months later in the prolonged lull of a pandemic, I kept thinking about the controversy I sparked when I gave the name "Structural Film" to the new sensibility I found in the American avant-garde cinema in 1969, when I returned from a year in Europe. The discussion of that term and his criticism now ends this book.

Sources

"Ahab's Name: A Reading of 'The Symphony,'" in *Herman Melville* (Modern Critical Views) edited by Harold Bloom, Chelsea House, New York, 1986. Reprinted in *Herman Melville's Moby Dick* (Modern Critical Interpretations) ed. Harold Bloom, New York, 1986.

"The Narrating Voice of *Moby-Dick*," *Hotel* no. 5, Winter 2019 (UK), pp. 153-175.

"Introduction" to *Modernist Montage: The Obscurity of Vision in Literature and Cinema*, Columbia University Press, 1990, pp. 5-10.

"Poet as Film Viewer: Hart's Crane's 'Chaplinesque'," *Motion Picture* Vol. 1, No. 1, 1986.

"Luigi Pirandello's *Shoot!*" in Luigi Pirandello, *Shoot!: The Notebooks of Serafino Gubbio, Cinematograph Operator*. Introduction by Tom Gunning. Cinema and Modernity Series, University of Chicago Press, 2006.

"I Want To Go Into the Church Alone: Alfred Hitchcock and Religion" in *The Hidden God*, ed. Mary Lea Bandy and Antonio Monda, Museum of Modern Art, New York, 2003.

"Harry Smith, Bibliophile, and the Origins of Cinema," in *Harry Smith: The Avant-Garde in the American Vernacular*, ed. Andrew Perchuk and Rani Singh, Getty Publications, Los Angeles, 2009, pp. 103-113.

Introduction

...the thing worth trying to get to do, is to heave out of oneself a proper noun, or more than one, which is both so recapitulatory and so intensive that it CAUSES the past, which means makes the future.

(Charles Olson to Robert Creeley [Vol. 9, of their *Complete Correspondence*]).

Exodus 3:13-15 is the primal scene of heaving out a name. I understand it as establishing the horizon of the naming process towards which a vatic poet, such as Mallarmé or perhaps Hart Crane, looks. Since I know no Hebrew, I shall cite the passage in the Septuagint:

> kaì eîpe Mouses pròs tòn THeón. idoù ego exeleúsomai pròs huioûs Israel, kaì ero pròs autoús. ho THeòs ton patéron emon apéstalké me pròs humâs. erotesousí me: tí ónoma autoi: tí ero pròs autoús. kaì eîpen ho THeòs pròs Mousen légon: ego eimi ho on. kaì eîpen. oútos ereîs toîs huioîs Israel. ho on apéstalké me pròs humâs. kaì eîpen ho THeòs pálin pròs Mousen. oútos ereîs toîs huioîs Israel. Kúrios ho THeòs ton patéron emon, THeòs Abraám kaì THeòs 'Isaàk kaì THeòs Iakob apéstalké me pròs humâs. toûtó moú estin ónoma aionion kaì mnemósunon geneon geneaîs (And Moses said to God, Behold I shall go to the sons of Israel and I will say to them, the God of our fathers sent me to you. They will ask me. What is his name? What will I say to them? and God spoke to Moses saying, I am the being [in Jerome's Latin Vulgate "ego sum qui sum" – 'I am who I am'], and he said Thus you shall say to the sons of Israel, The being ['who is' "qui est

misit me"] sent me to you. And again God said to Moses, Thus you will say to the sons of Israel, the Lord God of our fathers, the God of Abraham, the God of Isaac, and the God of Jacob sent me to you this is my eternal name and a memory of generations of generations.)[1]

In the Gospel of Luke 2:21, Jesus is given his name as it was conveyed to Mary by the angel of the Annunciation:

> Kaì hóte eplesthesan hai hemérai okto toû peritemeîn to paidíou, kaì ekelthe. tò ónoma autoû Iesoûs, tò klethèn hupò toû aggélou prò toû sullemphthenai autòn en teî koilíai.
> (And when the eighth day came for his circumcision, and his name was proclaimed Jesus, which he was called by the angel before he was conceived in the womb.)

In Matthew 1:21 an angel appears to Joseph in a dream commanding him to name the child Jesus [kaléseis tò onóma autoû Iesoûn]. An earlier text, Paul's letter to the Philippians 2:9-11, apparently citing a liturgical hymn, speaks of the magical power of that name:

> diò kaì ho THeòs autòn huperúpsosen, kaì echarísato auto ónoma tò hupèr pân ónoma, hína en toî onómati Iesoû pân gónu kámpse epouraníon kaì epigeion kaì katachthoníon, kaì pâsa glossa exomologesetai hóti Kúrios Iesoûs Christòs eìs dóxan THeoû patrós (Because God lifted him up and he bestowed in him a name beyond every name that at the name of Jesus every knee should bend in the heavens and on earth and under the earth, and every tongue would acknowledge the lord Jesus Christ for the glory of God the father.]

In Acts 3 and 4, Peter cures a lame man in the *name* of Jesus, who is the only path to salvation (he claims) (dià toû onómatos toû hagíou paidós sou Iesoû)

In the Gospel of John, Jesus repeatedly plays on the ego eimi ('I am') of the Divine Name but he does not say directly ego eimi ho on. From the very start John alludes to him as both the Logos

---

[1] These and subsequent transliterations of ancient Greek quotations suffer from the impossibility of printing Greek orthography here, or using longmarks over 'e' and 'o' to distinguish the Greek vowels, 'eta' from 'episilon' and 'omega' from 'omicron'. Nor can iota subscripts be printed.

and the Christ, but he enters the narrative as 'Jesus,' without any account of how he was named. When he says 'Before Abraham, I am' (8:58) (eîpen autoîs Iesoûs: Amen amen légo humîn, prin Abraám genésthai ego eimí) he might be merely reaffirming that there was God, who named himself ego eimi, before Abraham; then, again, he might be asserting that he – Jesus – was before Abraham (and therefore divine). In the same Gospel he predicates ego eimi repeatedly as the bread of life (6:35), the light of the world (8:12), the door for the sheep (10:7), the resurrection and the life (11:25), the good shepherd (10:11), the way, the truth and the life (14:4) and the true vine (15:1). But if it is Jesus, not the God of Hebrew scriptures – whom Jesus calls the father – who speaks in Revelation 1:8, he assumes the Divine Name:

> Ego eimi tò 'Álpha kaì tò Ö[mega] légei Kúpios, ho THeós, ho on ho en kai erchómenos kaì ho Pantokrátor
> (I am the Alpha and the Omega, says he Lord God, the Begining and the Coming One, the power over everything.) (King James Version translates ho on kaì ho en kaì ho erchómenos – 'which is, and which was, and which is to come')

Yet, when he first appears in a blinding vision to Paul on the road to Damascus, he answers the question of the future Apostle simply: 'I am Jesus [Ego eimi Iesoûs hòn sù diokeis] whom you are persecuting.' (Acts 9:5). However, as literary readers, we may be more likely to remember the powerful double vocative of the previous verse: 'Saul, Saul, why are you persecuting me?,' itself an echo of the way God addressed Abraham, Jacob, Samuel (Genesis 22:11; 47:2; Samuel 3:10) and Moses: 'the Lord called to him from the bush, saying Moses, Moses. And he said, What is it?' (Exodus 3:4). The double vocative seems to be a prerogative of divinity, since Jesus utters it twice in the Gospels without using a personal name, and another three times, addressing Jerusalem, Martha, and Simon Peter. The exception to the use by a divinity would be David, in his intense paternal grief, addressing the corpse of his son, 'Absalom, Absalom' (2 Samuel 14:25).

The New Testament never mentions Jesus's Hebrew name. Presumably, it was Joshua (meaning 'Yahweh saves') the very name that Moses bestowed upon his favorite, the spy Hosea, when he commissioned him. Under the name of Joshua, he became Moses's chief assistant, and the leader of the children of Israel after the departure of Moses; thus, his heir. Genesis records several occasions of similar ceremonial re-namings: Abraham for Abram; Sarah for Sarai; Israel for Jacob. Those Hebrew names were designations of meaning, before names became conventionally recycled.[2] 'Saul' too seems to have his name changed to 'Paul' but in Acts 13:9 when Saul – himself *named after* the tragic first king of the Hebrews – confronted by a Jewish magician, excoriates him, we learn that he had another name – presumably his Greek name was Paul all along, as the *ho kai* indicates: Saûlos de, ho kaì Paûlos... By the time of the New Testament, Jews had adapted the Greek tradition of using a traditional first name followed by a patronymic.

Melville's use of Biblical names carries the connotations of the actions of the men who bore them in Hebrew scriptures even though Ahab, Bildad, Peleg, Elijah, and Gabriel received their names from the conventions of recycling. (In *Moby-Dick*, Ishmael seems to have nicknamed himself.) The reader of Melville's novel cannot evade the connotations of Biblical names; the opposite is true of *Vertigo* (1958). Alfred Hitchcock, a slyer allegorist than Melville, smuggles the names of Mary Magdalen and Judith, the daughter of Merari, into *Vertigo* as 'Madeline' and 'Judy,' without deliberately alerting his viewers to the religious undertones of the film that connect the former to the good prostitute who befriended Jesus and the latter to the heroic, castrating slayer of Holofernes. The crime novel, *D'entre les morts* by the pseudonymous pair, Thomas Narcejac and Pierre Boileau, from which the film was freely adapted, used the even more suggestive names of

---

2 Heller-Roazen, yet again, pointed me to Philo's PERI TON METONOMAZOMENON KAI ON ENEKA METONOMAZONTAI [*Concerning those with changed names and why they were changed*], where the Hellenistic Jewish author provides theological interpretations of God's names and the changes he made in the names of his prophets.

Madeleine [sic] and Renée (Reborn Woman). The filmmaker's change of Renée to Judy suggests an effort to hide the symbolic value of the name without utterly effacing it.

Although there may be nothing in Western literature to match the magical power of God's name or Jesus's in Scripture, there are at least three monumental focal scenes of speaking names with overwhelming effects: in the earliest of them, Odysseus brings disaster on himself because he cannot resist teasing the blinded Polyphemus with an elliptical variant on his name; 'Oútis' may be an infantile mispronunciation of his actual name, deliberately delivered in baby-talk to mock the slow-witted cyclops, but it is also the negative pronoun meaning 'no one.' Polyphemus takes it as a Proper Name (as we might be tempted to understand *ego eimi ho on*) when he calls the curse of *his* divine father, the god Poseidon, on the man who blinded him. An even more powerful instance of uttering a dramatically delayed name occurs in the Thirtieth Canto of *Purgatorio* when Beatrice addresses Dante (the first and only sounding of his name in the whole *Commedia*). Even more pages of text must be read before Albertine calls the narrator of Proust's *A la Récherche du temps perdu* 'Marcel' in *La prisonnière*, the fifth of the seven-volume series.

Dante's *Commedia* is all about naming. As the Pilgrim explores the three realms of the afterlife, he wants to know whom he encounters. He recognizes few figures by sight; some Virgil (later Beatrice) names for him; some tell him their names or give an autobiographical account that explicitly reveals their identities, while most of those few in *Inferno* who refuse to identify themselves are spitefully named by their damned companions. At the very start, the shade of Virgil gives the Pilgrim enough clues that he knows to call him Virgilio. A little later, in Canto 6, Ciacco names himself at Dante's request; Virgil supplies the name of Farinata in 10; Brunetto Latini names himself (Canto 15); in Canto 33 the dreadful Conte Ugolino answers who he is and names Rugghieri as the spirit he cannibalizes.

Purgatorio 21 mirrors the initial encounter of the Pilgrim poet and his mentor, but there neither Statius nor Virgil offer up their names. In fact, Virgil signals to Dante to keep his identity secret when Statius confesses his adoration of the author of the *Aeneid*. Yet in the next canto, Dante uses both names in his narration. The sixty-three previous cantos may have prepared us for the inevitable meeting of Dante and Beatrice, but still the poetics of naming in *Purgatorio* 30 exceeds all expectations. Dante scholar, Rachel Jacoff, wrote: 'Canto XXX is commonly regarded as the structural and emotional center of the *Comedy*, its kernel or nucleus.... Names, in fact, are of [its] essence...' It begins with the seven stars of Revelation 1:20, symbolizing its seven Churches, although there is an academic argument about whether Dante's 'settentrïon' refers to the Big or the Little Dipper. The name Virgilio occurs three times in a row to underline his disappearance by alluding to the Orpheus's triple cry of 'Eurydice' at the conclusion of his own *Georgics*. That tripling is matched by 'ben' in Beatrice's self-identification: 'Guardaci ben! Ben son, ben son Beatrice (30:72). Then, finally, we hear her call out his name, 'Dante.' The poet even apologizes for allowing himself to be named in his poem:

> quando mi volsi al suon del nome mio
> che di necessità qui si registra (30: 62-63)
> (when I turned at the sound of my name
> which of necessity I register here)

Proust entitled a section of the opening novel of À *la recherche du temps perdu, Du côté de chez Swan,* "Noms de pays: le nom." One of his recurring characters, the Sorbonne professor, Brichot, is obsessed with the etymologies of names. Above all, the author must have had Dante's hyper-dramatic moment in mind when, after some thousand pages of his masterpiece, he ventriloquized Albertine to name the narrator:

> L'hésitation du réveil révélée par son silence, ne l'était pas par son

> regard. Dès qu'elle retrouvait la parole elle disait: «Mon» ou «Mon chéri» suivis l'un ou l'autre de mon nom de baptême, ce qui en donnant au narrateur le même nom qu'à l'auteur de ce livre eût fait: "Mon Marcel", "Mon chéri Marcel". (Proust *Pléade III*, p. 75.)
>
> (The hesitation of awakening was revealed by her silence, not by her glance. Once she recovered her speech she said, 'my' or 'my darling' followed one way or the other by my baptismal name, which, giving the narrator the same name as the author of this book, would have been 'my Marcel,' 'my darling Marcel.')

Here the gerund clause followed by the subjunctive pluperfect verb has the force of a conditional. Marcel would be the hypothetical name of the narrator, *if* the narrator were to have the same name as the author of the book. I take it to reflect, indirectly through a grammatical mood, Dante's more explicit apology for allowing his baptismal name into the *Comedia*.

Italo Svevo does not delay the self-identification of the protagonist of his masterpiece *La Conscienza di Zeno* (1923) quite as dramatically as Proust. The protagonist rarely has an occasion to insert his name into the fictive manuscript that he has prepared under the instructions of his psychoanalyst. After the title page, it doesn't occur until the second, long chapter when a servant calls to him 'È lei, signor Zeno?',[3] but the significant self-introduction and clarification of his name occurs only later, in the fourth chapter, when he is considering marrying one of his business mentor's daughters:

> Portava un grande rispetto alla sua casa e forse non tutti coloro che sedevano a quel tavolo gli sembravano degni di saper ne qualche cosa. Colà appresi soltanto che le sue quattro figliuole avevano tutti i nomi dall'iniziale in A, una cosa praticissima, secondo lui, perché le cose su cui era impressa quell'iniziale potevano passare dall'una all'altra, senz'aver da subire dei mutamenti. Si chiamavano (seppi subito a mente quei nomi): Ada, Augusta, Alberta e Anna. A quel tavolo si disse anche che tutt'e quattro erano belle. Quell'iniziale mi colpí molto piú di quanto meritasse. Sognai di quelle quattro fanciulle legate tanto bene insieme dal loro nome. Pareva fossero da consegnarsi in fascio. L'iniziale diceva anche qualche cosa d'altro. Io mi chiamo Zeno ed avevo perciò il sentimento che stessi per prendere

---
[3] Italo Svevo, *La Conscienza di Zeno* (Milan: Einaudi – dall'Oglio, 1976), p. 37.

moglie lontano dal mio paese. (p. 69-70.)

([Giovanni Malfenti] had great respect for his family and probably not all [his colleagues] who sat at that [Stock-Exchange] table struck him as worthy of knowing anything about them. There I learned only that all four of his daughters had names beginning with the letter A – according to him a very practical measure since any [garment] bearing the initial could be handed down from one to the other without alterations. Their names were: Ada, Augusta, Alberta, and Anna (I memorized them right away). At that table it was also said all four were beauties. That initial struck me more than it ought to have. I dreamed that those four girls were tightly bound together by their names. It seemed as if I might take them in a package. The first letter also meant something else. My name is Zeno, and because of that I had the feeling that I was about to choose a wife far from my own land.)

'Iniziale' is the noun, indicating first letter of the names (and of the alphabet). It resonates through this passage about cognition and presentiments (sembravano degni di saper... appresi...i nomi dall'iniziale... era impressa quell'iniziale potevano passare... Quell'iniziale mi colpí... Sognai... Pareva fossero da consegnarsi... L'iniziale diceva... il sentimento...) The very word 'iniziale' bears both Z and A.

Although the putative 'author' eventually declares his psychoanalysis a failure – because it does not cure him of smoking cigarettes – *La Coscienza di Zeno* remains the greatest novel directly representing psychoanalysis. Freudian discourse, with its goal of revealing initial causes, permeates it, down to the level of the letter.

Melville placed a discussion of Ahab's name rather early in *Moby-Dick* (chapter 16), but the Captain does not actually make an appearance for another twenty chapters (in "The Quarter-Deck"). The white whale, Moby-Dick, is first named there – and he is the only whale that has a name in this novel of whaling, – but he is first sighted and enters the action only at the end of the book. The use of a name here makes the delayed entrance more dramatic.

In a minor mode, even *Si Gira* delays the identification by name of the first-person narrator of Pirandello's novel until the second of the seven putative notebooks Sarafino Gubbio wrote. Names, of course, play a major role in Pirandello's fiction and drama because of the enigma of identity at the heart of his enterprise. Famously, the six characters 'in search of an author,' in the eponymous play of 1921, all lack the names they would require to complete them as living beings. The opening sentence of *Il fu Mattia Pascal* (1904) – 'Una delle poche cose, anzi forse la sola ch'io sapessi dicerto era questa: che mi chiamavo Mattia Pascal' (One of the few things that I know for sure that I can say is this: my name is Mattia Pascal) – is an irony: the novel will reveal that he has twice passed for dead. The name is the only thing that survives of him.

Even more emphatically, in the eighth book of *Uno, nessuno, e centomila* (1926), the protagonist, Vitangelo Moscarda, meditates on the gap between his *nome* and his *vagabond* identity :

> Nessun nome. Nessun ricordo oggi del nome di jeri; del nome d'oggi, domani. Se il nome è la cosa; se un nome è in noi il concetto d'ogni cosa posta fuori di noi; e senza nome non si ha il concetto, e la cosa resta in noi come cieca, non distinta e non definita; ebbene, questo che portai tra gli uomini ciascuno lo incida, epigrafe funeraria, sulla fronte di quella immagine con cui gli apparvi, e la lasci in pace non ne parli piú. Non è altro che questo, epigrafe funeraria, un nome. Conviene ai morti. A chi ha concluso. Io sono vivo e non concludo. La vita non conclude. E non sa di nomi, la vita. Quest'albero, respiro trèmulo di foglie nuove. Sono quest'albero. Albero, nuvola; domani libro o vento: il libro che leggo, il vento che bevo. Tutto fuori, vagabondo.[4]
>
> (No name. No memory today of yesterday's name; of today's name, tomorrow. If the name is the thing; if a name is our concept of everything situated outside us; and without a name the concept doesn't exist, and the thing as if blind, undistinguished, undefined stays within us; then, every man should carve the one I bore among them, a funeral epitaph, on the face of that image as I appeared to him, and then leave it in peace without another word. That's right for the dead. For those who have come to an end. I am alive and I am not coming to the end. Life does not end. Life doesn't know any names. This tree, a quaking breath of new leaves. I am this tree. Tree, cloud; tomorrow book or wind: the book that I read, the wind that I drink

---

[4] Luigi Pirandello, *Uno, nessuno e centomila* (Milan: Mondadori, 1967), p. 223.

in. All outside, wandering.)⁵

Rather than postponing the revealing of a name, many novels and plays use aliases, disguises, epithets and titles to intrigue or delight readers. Take *Don Quijote* as a paradigm: the protagonist, Alonso Quixano, calls himself El Caballero de la Triste Figura (the Knight of the Rueful Countenance); and he renames Aldonza Lorenzo, his imagined mistress, Dulcinea of El Toboso; Zoraida chooses the name María when she converts from Islam to the Roman Catholic Church. The other name changes are aliases created to deceive Don Quijote by stressing his insane gullibility: Sansón Carrasco gives himself the epithet the Knight of the White Moon; the doleful Duenna Rodríguez pretends to be the Countess Trifaldi; the criminal Ginés de Pasamonte passes himself off as Maese Pedro and Ginesillo de Parapilla; Dorotea takes on the role of the Princess Micomicona.

Shakespeare's disguised and renamed characters are abundant: In *As You Like It*, Rosalind cross-dresses as Ganymede; Viola in *Twelfth Night* does the same as Cesario. Kent becomes Caius, and Edgar Poor Tom, for *King Lear;* Vincentio, in *Measure for Measure*, is disguised as Friar Lodowick, just to cite the major instances. French fiction too abounds in aliases. When Jacques Colin is unmasked as a criminal mastermind in *Père Goriot*, we learn his real name is Vautrin. Later in the *Comédie humaine* he disguises himself as l'Abbé Carlos Herrera in *Illusions perdues* and again in its sequel, *Splendeurs et misères des courtisanes*. In prison, he acquired the nickname *Trompe-la-Mort*. Edmund Dantès hides as the eponymous Count of Monte Cristo. Jean Valjean, the hero of Hugo's *Les Misérables*, is also known as Monsieur Madeleine, Ultime Fauchelevent, Monsieur Leblanc, and Urbain Fabre. Even Proust's painter, Elstir, is called M. Biche in the Verdurin clan; in turn he tries to hide his portrait of another clan member, Odette de Crécy, by calling her 'Miss Sacripant.'

No writer in English has more fun with names than Charles

---

5 *One, No one, and One Hundred Thousand,* trans. William Weaver, Samuel Puttnam (Venice: Marsilio, 1992).

Dickens. Aliases and nicknames are just a fraction of the humorous and suggestive nomenclature of all his novels: (John Rokesmith and Julius Handford for John Harmon (in *Our Mutual Friend*); Nemo (Latin for 'nobody') for Captain James Hawdon (in *Bleak House*) and the Artful Dodger (of *Oliver Twist*); Mr. Dick (in *David Copperfield*); and Tattycoram (of *Little Dorrit*).

The majority of the significant literary biographers eschew the novelistic tradition and call their protagonists by their surnames. Richard Ellman writes of 'Joyce,' Joseph Frank of 'Dostoyevsky,' Richard Holmes of 'Shelley,' David Bellos of 'Perec,' although they might refer to the author's family members, friends, and associates by a first name. Hershel Parker, an exception, alternates between Melville and Herman in his massive two-volume biography. Psychoanalytic studies tend to take a different tack: Sigmund Freud felt the need to protect his patients' anonymity by using a first name alias – such as 'Dora' or 'Anna O' – a nickname – 'Little Hans' – or he simply wrote 'the patient' for the characters we have come to know as "The Rat Man" or "The Wolf Man". He used the surname only for the paranoid Dr. Daniel Schreiber, who was never his patient and had died before he undertook to analyze him from his writings.

In filmmaker Stan Brakhage's lectures on other filmmakers, he practiced a form of psycho-biography, imagining the type of childhood that would have eventuated in the making of their films. He regularly refers to his subject by first name in order to keep the idea of infantile formation in the foreground. Generally, he related these fantasy childhood narratives to fairy tales. In so doing, he may have taken a cue from Freud's 1918 study "From an History of Infantile Neurosis" (or *The Wolf-Man*) where the father of psychoanalysis tells he probed beyond his patient's claim that an obsessive dream image of seven wolfs in a tree came from 'Little Red Riding Hood' or 'The Wolf and the Seven Little Goats.' Freud was led from his recognition of the patient's expressions of intense fear to repressed memories of his father in his uncovery of primal scene traumas underlying the fairy tale memories. (*Three*

Case Histories pp 216-17). Conflating Freud's case studies with Gertrude Stein's imaginary biographies of George Washington (as a religious leader), Ulysses Grant (as a painter), Wilbur Wright (as a novelist) and Henry James (as a military hero) in her *Four in America* (1947), Brakhage embroidered his focus on the filmmakers' first names with versions of *nomen est omen*. Following both Freud and Stein, he viewed the great filmmakers as psychological types. I find his typology more convincing than his biographical speculations. Therefore, in demonstrating the influence of Georges Méliès on Harry Smith's cinema and following Smith's reading of psychoanalytical texts, I shall read a key passage from Brakhage's 'biography' of Méliès as if it were about Smith, substituting 'Harry' for 'George' (*sic*) in Brakhage's tale.

Lyric poetry tends to suppress personal names. Of course, there are significant exceptions. Hymns and prayers invoke and evoke divine names; ballads human names. Most of Catullus's poems have an addressee. Wallace Stevens hyperbolized Robert Browning's predilection for naming the speakers of his dramatic monologues with his fecund invention of Blanche McCarthy, Peter Quince, MacCullough, Nanzia Nunzio, Mrs. Alfred Uruguay, General Du Puy, the Canon Aspirin, Bawda, Mrs. Pappadopoulos, Mr. Burnshaw, Old John Zeller, Madame La Fleurie, *et al*. Yet, in one of his grandest moments of lyric vision he elevates Mallarméan namelessness into the American Sublime. Thus, he concludes the sixth section of "Auroras of Autumn":

> This is nothing until in a single man contained,
> Nothing until this named thing nameless is
> And is destroyed. He opens the door of his house
>
> On flames. The scholar of one candle sees
> An Arctic effulgence flaring on the frame
> Of everything he is. And he feels afraid.

Hart Crane's version of that sublimity occurs in the section of

The Bridge entitled "Southern Cross":

> I wanted you, nameless Woman of the South,
> No wraith, but utterly – as still more alone
> The Southern Cross takes night
> And lifts her girdles from her, one by one –
> High, cool,
> wide from the slowly smoldering fire
> Of lower heavens, –
> vaporous scars!
>
> Eve! Magdalene!
> or Mary, you? […]
>
> I wanted you… The embers of the Cross
> Climbed by aslant and huddling aromatically.
> It is blood to remember; it is fire
> To stammer back… It is
> God – your namelessness. […]

Unlike Stevens's practice, the rare given names in Crane's poems are well-known mythological or historical figures, with the crucial exception of the pun on 'heart' to work his own name into "Chaplinesque." Although personal names are scarce in modern lyric poetry, astral phenomena abound. So, Crane writes:

> but we have seen
> The moon in lonely alleys make
> A grail of laughter of an empty ash can

In the name of Charlie Chaplin – displaced to the title of the poem as an adjective – the light of the moon transforms a trash can into a quest object (grail), but in Crane's fine catachresis it holds laughter for its communion, not panis angelicus or blood. Likewise, by condensation Mallarmé transforms an asterism (le Septuor) into music. But his seven flickering stars do not chant of the mysterious founding of the cosmos in their very distant connotation of Job 38:6-7:

Who laid the cornerstone thereof;
When the morning stars sang together,
And all the sons of God shouted for joy?

In the lyrical tradition as well, Mallarmé never attached a proper name to 'le Maître,' the shadow-hero who hovers between life and death.[6] We infer it is both himself and Gautier in "Toast funebre," and in addition to himself, Socrates, Hugo, Baudelaire, Jesus, Homer, Pindar, and Ovid lurk in the penumbra of the two sonnets in -yx. Behind his self-conscious awareness of the historicity of French words, lay a view of poetry as a quixotic quest to recover the primal magic of a divine language in a cosmos without divinity. In French, 'nom' means both name and noun; 'nommer' is to name and to assign a word to a substantive or a process. Thus, in French texts names and nouns are conflated, so that all discussions of naming reach beyond the questions of the proper noun; they go straight to the mythos of the origin of language.[7]

✦

Some of these chapters were first formulated more than forty years ago. Only the final two, "Dropped Names", and "Dubious Terms and Names", were written entirely for this book. It turns out that names, along with ancient words, allusions, and types in

---

[6] If, elaborating on the principle of *Les anagrammes de Ferdinand de Saussure*, we might find all the letters (ignoring the acute accent on é) of the poet's surname hidden in 'le Maître'. The leftover letter, î, could even stand for the foreign first person pronoun "I" in the anagrammatic wit of the poet and English teacher. Of course, Mallarmé would have known that the acute and circumflex accents in French represented the loss of letters – allegories for the loss of names.

[7] Daniel Heller-Roazen posed the following philosophical/linguistic problem to me in an email of 2/20/2020:

'There is a general question that you don't address directly… *ónoma* (as you say of the French pendant): one grammatical tradition, deriving from Aristotle, takes them to belong to a single genus; thus in the Romance languages, *nom propre* and *nom commun* are specifications. Another grammatical tradition, deriving from the Stoics, takes them to belong to different genera: thus English *noun* vs *name*. The philosophical consequences of the difference are evidently far from minor. It is striking that both reach back to the Greek name (noun?) *ónoma*.'

films and books, have been my preoccupation for more than sixty years. My Ph.D. dissertation of 1980 focused on Maurice Blanchot and Charles Olson, a prose writer and a poet. The former was obsessed with the act of naming; the latter with what he called 'the Proper Noun' as the origin of poetry. In the final chapter of *Modernist Montage: The Obscurity of Vision in Cinema and Literature* (1990), I quoted the start of the following reflection on Narcissus by Blanchot:

> The water in which Narcissus sees what he shouldn't is not a mirror, capable of producing a distinct and definite image. What he sees is the invisible in the visible – in the figure the unfigurable, the unstable unknown of a representation without presence, which reflects no model: he sees the anonymity that only the missing name could keep at a distance [l'anonyme que le nom qu'il n'a pas pourrait seul maintenir à distance]. It is madness and death. (But *for* us, who name Narcissus [qui nommon Narcisse] and establish him as a doubled Same – as containing, that is to say, without his knowledge – and knowing it –, receiving the Other in the same, death in life: the essence of the secret: a schism which in fact isn't one, and which would give him a divided self without an I [lui donnerait un moi divisé sans je], while also depriving him of all relation to others.)... we recall what Schlegel is said to have claimed: 'Every poet is a Narcissus.' We should not be content simply to recover in this statement the superficial mark of a certain romanticism for which creation – poetry – is absolute subjectivity and the poet a living subject in the poem that reflects him, just as he is a poet by virtue of poetizing his life by incarnating in it his pure subjectivity [de telle manière qu'il la poétise en y incarnant sa pure subjectivité], one ought, no doubt, to understand Schlegel's statement in another way too: it is that in the poem, where the poet writes himself, he does not recognize himself, because he does not become conscious of himself, rejected from this easy hope of a certain humanism according to which, by writing or 'creating,' he would transform into an even greater consciousness the obscure part of his experience that he would suffer: on the contrary, rejected, excluded from what he writes, from even being present by virtue of his non-presence to *his own* death, he must renounce all conceivable relations of a self (living or dying) to the poem which henceforth belongs to the other, or else will remain without any belonging at all. The poet is Narcissus, to the degree that Narcissus is anti-Narcissus: the one who, turned away from himself, bearing and supporting the detour, dying of not recognizing himself, leaves the trace of what did

not take place. (*The Writing of the Disaster*, Ann Smock's translation modified, literally, to reflect Blanchot's syntax, [Lincoln: University of Nebraska Press, 1995], pp. 134-35)

The ubiquity of narcissism, according to Blanchot, can be gauged by the transformation of the name into an adjective: 'It suffices to form the adjective from the name (nom): what is there that isn't narcissistic?' Yet, it was only as I was finishing this book that I realized that the second part of the passage – Blanchot's 'correction' of Schlegel – might be a synopsis of the narcissistic movement of Pirandello's *Si Gira*, where the traumatized cameraman, Serafino Gubbio, writes himself into his *quaderni* in order to project the confrontation with death by the movie *diva* La Nesteroff, who regularly failed to recognize her own image on the film screen.

For Blanchot the nameless and unnamable force that Narcissus faces is death, but not merely the biological death that awaits him. In one of his first long theoretical texts, "Literature and the Right to Death" (1949), he described the very act of naming things and phenomena as killing them and resurrecting their substanceless ghosts. Mallarmé had said as much of poetry in "Crise de vers" (1897):

> Je dis: une fleur! et, hors de l'oubli où ma voix relègue aucun contour, en tant que quelque chose d'autre que les calices sus, musicalement se lève, idée même et suave, l'absente de tous bouquets.
> ('I say: a flower! And, beyond the oblivion where my voice banishes any contour, in so far as it is something other than known calyces, musically the sweet idea itself emerges, the lack of all bouquets.)

Near the end of "Literature and the Right to Death" Blanchot rephrases Mallarmé and aligns "Crise de vers' with Hölderlin and Hegel – the philosopher central to all three of them:

> I say, 'This woman.' Hölderlin, Mallarmé and all the poets whose theme is the essence of poetry have felt that the act of naming is disquieting and marvelous. A word may give me its meaning, but first it suppresses it. For me to be able to say 'This woman,' first I

must take her flesh-and-blood reality away from her, cause her to be absent, annihilate her. The word gives me the being, but it gives it to me deprived of being. This word is the absence of that being, its nothingness, what is left when it has lost being – the very fact that it does not exist. Considered in this light, speaking is a curious right. In a text dating from before the *Phenomenology*, Hegel, here the friend and kindred spirit of Hölderlin, writes: 'Adam's first act, which made him master of the animals, was to give them names, that is, he annihilated them in their existence (as existing creatures).' Hegel means that from that moment on, the cat ceased to be a uniquely real cat and became an idea as well. The meaning of speech, then, requires that before the word is spoken, there must be a sort of immense hecatomb, a preliminary flood plunging all creation into a total sea. God had created living things, but man had to annihilate them. Not until then did they take meaning for him, and he in turn created them out of the death into which they had disappeared.[8]

Blanchot's radicalism particularly illuminates my chapters on Mallarmé and Pirandello. The American works – I would include the American-made *Vertigo* among them – stemming from Ralph Waldo Emerson rather than from Hegel, configure the linkage between onamastics and death differently. In "The Poet" Emerson defined language as 'fossil poetry':

Language is fossil poetry. As the limestone of the continent consists of infinite masses of the shells of animalcules, so language is made up of images, or tropes, which now, in their secondary use, have long ceased to remind us of their poetic origin.

Fossils, too, are ghosts or mummies, retaining the visible form of the living entities whose substance has been transformed utterly. For Melville, the Bible was a fossilized museum of potent names and allegories. The pun in Hart Crane's name was a pliant fossil, the trope by which he could pirouette into Charlie Chaplin's persona. In his filmmaking Brakhage, a persistent Vitalist, believed he could evade Blanchot's Hegelian view of naming as embalming, but in his writing, he subscribed to Charles Olson's favored trinity: 'topos, tropos, typos,' where the

---
[8] *Work of Fire*, trans. Charlotte Mandrel (Stanford, Ca.: Stanford University Press, 1995), pp 322-323.

Proper Nouns of personal names were 'types.' Hitchcock seems to have viewed the Emersonian fascination with archetypes and circles of regeneration as a collective American mania through which a manipulative villain might get away with murder. The Canadian filmmaker, sculptor, and musician Michael Snow played with naming himself – through anagrams and a rebus – and incorporated the given names of cast members into the fabric of allusions and meaningful evasions in several of his greatest films. Although Snow never shared Harry Smith's conviction of the immanent *signatura rerum* by which objects could not be separated from their unstated names or from their range of unmentioned references, his films take advantage of the full gamut of associations open to a viewer, both explicit and unstated.

In many ways this book is an extension or elaboration on themes from my *Modernist Montage*. In that book too Exodus, Mallarmé, Blanchot, Stein, Brakhage, and Olson are central players, although the quarry is their concepts of modernism not their use of names. Its chapter on Stein treats the influence of cinema on her. I have contended throughout my career that the insights of great writers were more cogent to the theory of cinema than most of the contributions of academic film theoreticians. Here the poem of Crane and the novel of Pirandello will exemplify that polemical argument.

I

Ahab's Name

In "The Symphony," the one hundred and thirty-second chapter of *Moby-Dick,* the captain's dialogue with his first mate, Starbuck, drifts into a soliloquy in which he questions his control over his acts:

> What is it, what nameless, inscrutable, unearthly thing is it; what cozening, hidden lord and master, and cruel remorseless emperor commands me; that against all natural lovings and longings, I so keep pushing, and crowding and jamming myself on all the time; recklessly making me ready to do what in my own proper, natural heart, I durst not so much as dare? Is Ahab, Ahab? Is it I, God or who, that lifts this arm? But if the great sun move not of himself; but is as an errant-boy in heaven; nor one single star can revolve, but by some invisible power; how can this one small heart beat; this one small brain think thoughts; unless God does that beating, does that thinking, does that living, and not I.

In this context the tiny sentence 'Is Ahab, Ahab?' appears innocent enough. The force of fate makes the captain doubt his identity. For years I read this question ignoring the comma, supporting myself with the commonplace of editors that Melville was an ungrammatical punctuator, as if the sentence were the interrogative form of the tautology: Ahab is Ahab. But what might the question 'Is Ahab Ahab?' or 'Is X X?' when X stands for a proper noun, mean? In the form of a question doubt is raised about the *language* of the tautology. It asks if there is not something wrong with the naming of X that represents X as ontologically unstable. Then again, it could be a question about two different meanings of the proper noun. Does the first X correspond fully to the stable meaning of X represented by the second instance of the name? All three readings of the question are relevant to our interpretation of *Moby-Dick* as a whole: they correspond to ontological, epistemological, and typological investigations.

I would like to consider the alternatives posed by the problematic comma. If we read the second naming of Ahab as vocative, two interpretations of the sentence. 'Is Ahab, Ahab' are possible: either 'Is Ahab...?' questions his existence, or the sentence is incomplete, requiring reference to the previous one. In that case it asks if 'Ahab' is the answer to the previous question; is 'Ahab' the 'nameless... thing' that 'commands me.' In fact, the first English edition of *The Whale,* printed months earlier than the American, explicitly determines this reading. 'Is it Ahab, Ahab?' in the British text makes very good sense; for it fits all three opening sentences in this speech into a single form: 'What is it... Is it Ahab... Is it I, God, or who...'

We cannot conclude whether this is one of the many editorial intrusions to be found in *The Whale* or a genuine alternative from Melville's hand. Let's consider the consequences of accepting it as the superior reading. The ontological question posed by both 'Is Ahab Ahab?' and 'Is Ahab...?' disappears. Nevertheless, the repetition of the name in the vocative continues to underscore the potential ambiguity of the name which has both epistemological and typological consequences. It is this doubling of the *name,* consistent in both texts, which I take to be crucial; for it points up the relationship of the name to the dilemmas of identity and responsibility. Therefore, even though I prefer the richer ambiguities of the American version, what follows will not depend upon the choice of texts.

My conviction that 'Is Ahab, Ahab?' should be read as the questioning of a tautology rests on the echoing passage two chapters later in "The Chase-Second Day" when the captain refers back to his earlier encounter with the first mate:

> Starbuck, of late I've felt strangely moved to thee; ever since that hour we both saw – thou know'st what, in one another's eyes. But in this matter of the whale, be thy face to me as the palm of this hand – a lipless, unfeatured blank. Ahab is forever Ahab, man. This whole act's immutably decreed. 'Twas rehearsed by thee and me a billion years before this ocean rolled. Fool! I am the Fates' lieutenant; I act under orders.

'Ahab is forever Ahab, man' reasserts the ontological question of the earlier chapter in the rhetoric of bravado, taking the tautology out of the realm of time that had oppressed the captain, who feared that Moby-Dick would be taken by a rival whaler or that he would not live to finish the job. Now that he is in the midst of the 'fiery hunt,' he speaks as though he were reconciled to his relationship to Fate. But readers soon discover that he is haunted during this speech by hints of the fulfillment of Fedallah's prophecy of his death.

The paired lines 'Is Ahab, Ahab?' and 'Ahab is forever Ahab', do not dispel the ambiguities we found in the name, *Ahab*. The later speech proclaims that Ahab is an ontological entity, that his name is appropriate, and that he conforms to the model of the ancient, Biblical king.

The tone of these speeches is familiar enough. Melville wrote fresh from a reading of Shakespeare. The use of the name, instead of 'I,' in the mouth of the hero recalls a number of precedents in the plays:

> ...O Lear, Lear, Lear!
> Beat at this gate, that let thy folly in
> And thy dear judgment out!
> (King *Lear*, Act I, sc. iv.)

> Was't Hamlet wronged Laertes? Never Hamlet. If Hamlet from himself be ta'en away, And when he's not himself does wrong Laertes, Then Hamlet does it not, Hamlet denies it. Who does it then? His madness. If 't be so, Hamlet is of the faction that is wronged. His madness is poor Hamlet's enemy.
> (*Hamlet,* Act V, sc. ii.)

Shakespeare uses this substitution of the third for the first-person, of the name for I, here and in parallel speeches by Othello, Brutus, and Timon, to emphasize the machinations of fate or to dramatize the dislocation of selfhood in madness. Its illusion of objectivity indicates that the speaker has submitted to the language and the judgment of the world by renouncing his power to speak for himself. To make such a renunciation is to invoke the discourse of the victim.

Melville became excessively fond of this mode of self-address. It is a mark of Ahab's grandiosity. Interpreting the Ecuadorian doubloon he nailed to the mast as a reward for the first sighting of Moby-Dick, he repeats his name four times:

> The firm tower, that is Ahab; the volcano, that is Ahab; the courageous, undaunted, and victorious fowl, that, too, is Ahab; all are Ahab; and this round gold is but the image of the rounder globe, which, like a magician's glass, to each and every man in turn but mirrors back its own mysterious self.

As much echo as mirror, the coin reflects his name again and again.

In *Moby-Dick* calling oneself by name is not Ahab's exclusive privilege. Stubb does it with comic effect when he finds himself unfairly treated by the captain. The narrator calls himself by his pseudonym, Ishmael, three times in "A Bower in the Arsacides," as if, taking the side of his readers, he felt the need to demonstrate evidence of his authority for the whale lore he was about to expound. These whimsical versions of the discourse of victimization are not of the same order of frequency or dramatic intensity as Ahab's use of his own name. He embraces and sublimates his victimization, naming himself as if being called Ahab were an honor and a responsibility of which he was proud.

IS AHAB, AHAB WHO PROVOKED THE LORD GOD OF ISRAEL?

When we ask the question, 'is Ahab (of Nantucket) Ahab (king of Israel),' we are actually asking in what way the captain of the *Pequod* resembles the wicked king of the First and Second Books of Kings. In the sixteenth chapter, "The Ship," after first hearing the Captain's first name, Ishmael told of the peculiarity of Biblical names among Nantucket Quakers. He also speculated that such a name, coupled with the 'bold and nervous language' a man learns from solitude with nature, could fashion a being 'formed for noble tragedies.' Thus, as soon as we learn Captain Ahab's name in the novel, we are instructed to anticipate a tragic appropriateness to it.

The narrator had marshalled typology to give weight to his story in the very first sentence, 'Call me Ishmael.' He implies that the *ad-hoc* name is more relevant than the one given him at birth. No one in the novel ever addresses him as Ishmael, or by any other name. By stopping the flow of his narrative, as soon as Captains Peleg and Bildad are introduced and Ahab mentioned by name, in order to warn us of the importance of these names, he invites the reader to investigate Scriptural etymology and narrative.

In a useful note Willard Thorp pointed out that Peleg means 'division'; Captain Peleg divides the 'lays' of the ship's income. Bildad was one of Job's comforters; like him, the co-owner of the *Pequod* spouts warnings against wickedness. Neither of these men is 'formed for noble tragedies.' The manner in which Ahab will correspond to his Biblical type is not immediately apparent; only a reading of the whole novel will answer that question. "The Ship" whets our interest in Ahab, who will not appear for another twelve chapters. More is made of his name in this seductive chapter of intimations than of the other Biblical names. Captain Peleg's attempt to minimize the implications of Ahab's name only makes it more ominous:

> Captain Ahab did not name himself. 'Twas a foolish, ignorant whim of his crazy, widowed mother, who died when he was only a twelve-month old. And yet the old squaw Tistig, at Gayhead, said that the name would somehow prove prophetic. And, perhaps, other fools like her may tell thee the same. I wish to warn thee. It's a lie.

As an argument for Ahab's humanity, Peleg adds that he has a young wife and a son. These facts will play no role in the novel until "The Symphony."

The sudden appearance in chapter nineteen of a prophet, named Elijah, who curses Ahab, almost immediately confirms Peleg's warning. Yet the coincidence of two names from the First Book of Kings erodes the authority of his dismissal of the typological significance. Elijah cryptically refers to blasphemies the captain committed and to a prophecy that had been confirmed by his losing a leg. As soon as Ishmael learns Elijah's name, he repeats it with an exclamation mark.

Encouraged by the correspondence of names from the Scriptural narrative of Ahab's wickedness, the reader will look in vain for a Jezebel. Is Ahab Ahab without Jezebel? Certainly, in this novel virtually devoid of women, a moody leader, with a diabolical name, bringing himself and his crew to destruction would justify and fulfill the 'somehow' of Tistig's prophecy. Nevertheless, if we read "The Symphony" carefully we may find Jezebel haunting the chapter even though we never hear her name. I do not mean to suggest that the 'sweet, resigned girl' Ahab married is a figure for the Sidonian princess. On the contrary, her non-correspondence to the Biblical narrative seems to guarantee her ineffectiveness in *Moby-Dick*. "The Symphony" dramatizes the impossibility of Ahab's acting on her behalf.

In the chapter's opening paragraph Melville conflates two themes typical of *Moby-Dick*, the reduction of space to an undifferentiated plane and the domination of a single color, and introduces a third, the feminization of a part of the natural world:

> It was a clear steel-blue day. The firmaments of air and sea were hardly separable in that all-pervading azure; only, the pensive air was transparently pure and soft, with a woman's look, and the robust and man-like sea heaved with long, strong, lingering swells as Samson's chest in his sleep.

The reduction of the visible world to an undifferentiated monochromatic plane is the final version of a disorientation of spatiality that began in the dark of New Bedford with Ishmael's stumbling into a Negro church where he caught enough of the sermon to know it was about 'the blackness of darkness.' The Spouter-Inn's befogged oil painting, which poses the first puzzle for interpretation the narrator faces, and the crucial meditation on blankness in "The Whiteness of the Whale" would be the other moments in this series. "The Symphony"'s pervading blueness, then, completes the long-interrupted triad.

This is also the final instance of a more continuous play on color which progressed from the early passages on blackness and whiteness to the chromatic richness of silver ("The Spirit Spout"), yellow ("Brit"), and crimson ("Stubb Kills a Whale"), before reaching the lush blindness of blue on blue, a visual equivalent of the riddle of differentiation ultimately to be posed by the question, 'Is Ahab, Ahab?'

Against the backdrop of blueness Melville inscribes a parody of Genesis 1. In the opening paragraph the narrator mimes the work of God on the second day: he divides the firmaments. In the subsequent four paragraphs the work of the fifth, fourth, and sixth days, in that order, finds counterparts in the chapter as the creatures of air and sea, the stars, and, lastly, man are represented in the hitherto pervading blueness.

The world is remade in the first paragraphs of "The Symphony" in order to revise the place of woman in the scheme of Genesis. In the alternative cosmology nature itself is sexualized, and copulates. The feminine dimension appears benign and passive in the language of the chapter, but the metaphorical undercurrents suggest an active and destructive femininity. The simile of Samson's chest describes the latent power of the rolling ocean. However, crowding upon this image, comes the unstated allusion to his betrayal by Delilah. The only mention of Samson's sleep in the Old Testament is part of the narrative of her treachery: 'And she made him sleep upon her knees; and she called for a man, and she caused him to shave off the seven locks of his head; and she began to afflict him, and his strength went from him' (Judges, xvi, 19).

The subterranean logic of this passage contradicts the literal meaning. One day in the voyage of the *Pequod* brings to mind the first six days of Creation. The explicitly developed image of masculine sexual conquest of an innocent, gentle woman suggests erotic violence by the 'murderous' male; but the simile of Samson brings into play the erotic manipulations of a castrating female. Furthermore, I believe there is a silent symbolical equation of the unnamed Delilah with the unnamed Jezebel.

Melville renders Ahab's ambiguous position in this amorous spectacle with a verbal deviousness that deserves our attention. The fourth and fifth paragraphs postpone their grammatical subjects for seven and twenty-seven words.

In both cases retrospectively, it is possible to anticipate a different subject. First, we might read 'Aloft, like a royal czar and king,' as if Ahab himself were to be the subject. Instead, it is the sun. The previous paragraph, describing the identity of the air and the sea – 'it was only the sex, as it were, that distinguished them' – would lead the reader to expect a human agent to be introduced as the figure reading this sexual discrimination into the field of vision. Conversely, the fifth paragraph unreels a long series of past participles which can be read as a continuation of the description of the elemental love-making of the previous paragraph. The words 'Tied up and twisted; gnarled and knotted with wrinkles; haggardly firm and unyielding...' ambiguously fuse the delayed subject to the previous picture of copulation. The first four words could continue that primal scene unproblematically. Only after a fourteen-word description of his eyes, does the phrase 'untottering Ahab' specify at last the grammatical subject. We do not learn what he is observing, only that he faces 'the fair girl's forehead of heaven.' The paratactic construction permits us to read Ahab as alternately a participant and an observer in the primal scene of nature, until the grammatical meaning asserts itself, terminating the images of sexual intercourse.

The ambiguity of watching or participating in intercourse frequently characterizes the primal scene in psychoanalytical literature. It is important that Melville not only suggests this oscillation in his text, but he forces the reader into repeating this ambiguous situation in the process of discerning what is happening in the chapter. This strategy volatilizes the undersong of the text. As we focus upon the erotic representation, intimations of more than we can discern through the denotations of the descriptive language direct our attention to the repressed figuration of the narrative. Ahab even comes to represent the reader's problem here.

After a puzzling paragraph which I shall address shortly, Ahab finally directs his gaze to the sea. Therefore, he has looked at both participants in the sexual scene. But in looking at the sea, 'he strove to pierce the profundity.' The path to this 'profundity' is through his own reflected image. His narcissistic identification with the male half of the elemental coupling brings him into contact with the contradictory, but unreconciled, images of the female as innocent bride and castrating traitor. Although he cannot pierce this profundity, he is shaken by a feeling of the emptiness of his life, which is expressed first by a tear.

IS AHAB ISHMAEL?

In the preceding discussion I have been reading "The Symphony" as if the narrator, Ishmael, were identical with the author, Melville. The paragraph I mentioned, which comes between the introduction of Ahab and the scene of his gazing at the sea, makes that difficult.

In an apostrophe to the innocence of the air and sky, the narrator asserts his authority within the chapter by inscribing the pronouns 'us' and 'I.' However, the image he uses to personify the 'invisible winged creatures' of the air has eluded convincing interpretation:

> But so have I seen little Miriam and Martha, laughing-eyed elves, heedlessly gambol around their old sire; sporting with the circle of singed locks which grew on the marge of that burnt-out crater of his brain.

Charles Feidelson, the most discreet of the commentators, has noted that the reference to Miriam and Martha and their sire is not known. Mansfield and Vincent, at the other end of the editorial spectrum, fantasize that Melville has invented names for Lot's incestuous daughters here. Murray points to the description of Teufelsdroch in Carlyle's *Sartor Resartus:* 'as of some silent, high-encircled mountain-pool, perhaps the crater of an extinct volcano, into whose black depths you fear to gaze...' (Bk. 1, ch. 4), and identifies the innocent figures as Hawthorne's children under pseudonyms. In his fascinating and provocative annotations, Harold Beaver acknowledges some point to the private joke about Hawthorne, adding that Ishmael speaks as if he were Lazarus, recalling a scene of his two sisters. The variety and ingenuity of these glosses underscore the unresolved problem.

Not only is the allusion obscure, but the testimony of Ishmael seems unnecessary. None of the editors addresses the *strangeness* of Ishmael's intrusion here. Until "The Symphony," the narrator had not made his presence known by speaking in the first person since The Candles," thirteen chapters earlier. He will not utter 'I' again in the three concluding chapters of the chasing of Moby-Dick. The first-person reemerges, in the "Epilogue," with Ishmael himself as he accounts for his surprising survival after the whale wrecked the *Pequod*.

Only Beaver notices the presence of the narrator when he annotates this paragraph. If we understand Lot or Hawthorne to be the old sire, then, the declaration, 'But so have I seen...' only confuses the analogy to Ahab. Referring back to the third chapter, "The Spouter-Inn," Beaver suggests that Ishmael, who already knows the conclusion of the novel as he writes it, identified with Lazarus. But if that is true, who is the old sire? Why does he write 'their' not 'our' old sire? The New Testament tells us nothing of Lazarus' father. Perhaps the British editors saw the oddity of this passage; they omitted the whole paragraph from *The Whale*.

Although I have no superior reading for the 'laughing-eyed elves,' I dwell on this passage just because the narrator asserts himself here. Whenever the narrator writes 'I' or 'Ahab' in *Moby-Dick* he performs a straight-forward act of representation; a sailor or the captain comes into the reader's 'view.' Those same two words, in Ahab's mouth, are extremely problematic. Ahab's grandiose sense of his own name forecloses the possibility of his telling his own story. When Ishmael describes the world as he encounters it in his fictional persona, there is always a possibility that his neurotic obsessions, which he himself called his 'hypos' (slang for hypochondriac delusions) in the opening chapter, inflect or even distort his perceptions. The most massive of his 'hypos' is his reaction to whiteness. Perhaps we can read the chapters written in theatrical form as if they were marked off from the blinders of his 'hypos.' They begin to appear shortly before the meditation on whiteness.

Ishmael is almost as obsessed with blueness as he is with whiteness. In chapter thirty-five, "The Mast-Head," he attributes that color to the soul. He describes how the meditative sailor on watch in the mast-head endangers his life by losing himself in thought: he

> takes the mystic ocean at his feet for the visible image of the deep, blue, bottomless soul, pervading mankind and nature; and every strange halfseen, gliding, beautiful thing that eludes him; every dimly-discovered, uprising fin of some undiscernible form, seems to him the embodiment of those elusive thoughts that only people the soul by continually flitting through it.

Furthermore, in "Queequeg in His Coffin," he portrays the pagan's idea of heaven in terms of blue and white: 'for not only do they believe that the stars are isles, but that far beyond all visible horizons, their own mild, uncontinented seas, interflow with blue heavens; and so form the white breakers of the milky way.'

The opening of "The Symphony" is not only a description of a day in the Pacific. It is implicitly a representation of how Ishmael reacted to the 'hardly separable' layers of blue and how he read Creation into it, along with the troubled undersong of female violence. As early as "Loomings" he had confessed an identification with Narcissus. In "The Mast Head" he comically acknowledged the threatening power of that identification. Ruminating "Pantheists," aloft in the mast feel how the 'identity comes back in horror' when they let a foot slip and plunge to death. In fact, much later, in "The Life-Buoy," an anonymous crew member falls from his watch post, his body unrecovered. The description of this 'falling phantom' echoes 'the ungraspable phantom of life' that all Narcissuses seek, according to the philosopher of "Loomings." Finally, the only vestiges of the fallen watchman were 'white bubbles in the blue of the sea.'

Restoring Ishmael to his role as Narcissistic gazer at the beginning of "The Symphony" does not necessitate displacing Ahab. Ishmael reminds us that he is there only *after* the scene has been visualized. This is a ploy in paragraph arrangement that repeats the strategy of withholding the grammatical subject in two successive paragraph-long sentences. Ishmael had been forgotten at the beginning of the chapter. Contextual clues point us to read the opening description as if it mimed Ahab's perceptions. Only retrospectively do we learn that those perceptions were Ishmael's. The effect is a fusion of Ahab and Ishmael. Here the narrator disposes of the accustomed antithesis of I and Ahab.

Not only does he transfer the Narcissus-type from himself to the captain by portraying him as he 'watched how his shadow in the water sank and sank to his gaze,' he adds two other images as well, which had been used previously to define Ishmael's mentality. They are orphanhood and live burial. The very first mention of sleep in the novel, and the earliest menacing woman, were evoked when the narrator found himself in Queequeg's embrace. He recalled a punishment inflicted by his stepmother on the summer solstice. In an intermediate state between dreaming and waking, cruelly confined to his bed, he had the uncanny sense of a 'supernatural hand' in his. When Ahab drops a tear into the ocean, experiencing the Panic epiphany that Ishmael knew twenty-one chapters before, he is embraced by 'the stepmother world,' another female image for the mild air. The word 'stepmother' reminds us that the mad mother, who named Ahab, died when he was an infant. Yet, the only 'stepmother' in the book is Ishmael's. This term smuggles a sinister note into the superficially benign moment and brings Ahab another step closer to Ishmael.

The third image transferred from Ishmael's psychic history to Ahab is that of Adam buried under time. In the Whaleman's Chapel, the markers for men lost at sea re-inspired the narrator's reverie of paralysis. Here that paralysis moves from Ishmael to the captain: '…in what eternal, unstirring paralysis, and deadly, hopeless trance yet lies antique Adam who died sixty round centuries ago…' Ahab, in turn, confesses to Starbuck, who saw him drop his tear into the sea, that he feels 'as though I were Adam, staggering beneath the piled centuries since Paradise.' Then he breaks into a Lear-like cry to be annihilated.

The transference of Ishmael's 'hypos' to Ahab prepares the

way for the complete divestment of the narrating persona in the book. The three final chapters, the only ones in which Moby-Dick appears, have no traces of Ishmael. In fact, when he resurfaces on Queequeg's coffin in the "Epilogue," Ishmael provides the astonishing news that 'I was he… who, when on the last day three men were tossed from out of the rocking boat, was dropped stern.' This is astonishing simply because he had written, in the neutral third-person, of an unnamed 'third man' falling overboard. This is the most blatant of the retrospective admissions of the narrator. When he does, at last, plunge to his predicted fate as a modem Narcissus, we do not see him, nor does he really drown.

We know that Melville wrote the end of the novel in a feverish rush; the "Epilogue" and two paragraphs of "The Symphony" were among the passages that do not appear in the British edition, which preceded the American. However, haste and sloppiness do not account for the disguise of Ishmael in the finale. Something more is at stake. There is a deliberate gesture of calling our attention to the loss of the first-person voice by the end of the book. Even the phrase 'I was he…' reflects, on the level of grammar, the fated substitution of Ishmael from the otherwise unknown bowsman, who, replacing the dead Fedallah, left a position to be filled. In a sense Ishmael does die: 'I' becomes 'he.' He does not, like Pip, lose the capability of saying both 'I' and his own name, after falling into the sea. He has already lost his name and his auto-narrating authority in the final chapters. The epilogue restores both to him. But before that he was buried as the 'third' person – Melville wrote 'third man' – when he was lost.

IS AHAB FEDALLAH?

The two blue fields, air and water, are projections of sexual difference on what Ahab called 'the pasteboard mask' of the visible world. Its imminent blankness generated Ishmael's horror and Ahab's violent, Oedipal quest. Starbuck, who lacks the Emersonian absolutism of either Ishmael or Ahab, attempts to divert the tragic conclusion by promoting the differences emerging in the seascape. He humanizes and idealizes the female figures, otherwise virtually expelled from the novel.

Earlier Starbuck had failed as an imitator of Ahab. His monologue in the chapter called "The Musket" brings his own wife's name – Mary – into the text for the first time. But even the thought of her and of his son cannot bring him to murder the captain. Thinking back to the oath on the Quarter-Deck, he realizes that his mutiny would earn him the name of Ahab. He rejects that option: 'Aye, and say'st the men have vowed thy vow; say'st all of us are Ahabs. Great God forbid!'

When 'the step-mother world' coaxed a tear from Ahab, breaking his Narcissus-like trance, Starbuck approached him. In the ensuing dialogue, he vainly attempted to convince the captain to abort his quest and sail for Nantucket. For a moment, the mate seemed to penetrate Ahab's solipsism. The captain was attracted by the mirroring of his first mate's eyes: 'Let me look into a human eye; it is better than to gaze into sea or sky; better than to gaze upon God.' Sea and sky stand for sexualized nature here; coming face to face with God has the Mosaic consequence of death, as a careful reader of chapter eighty-six would know. In facing Starbuck, Ahab turns from the primal scene of nature and from his Oedipal rage at the apotheosized whale toward a domestic humanism that cannot satisfy him.

In Starbuck's eyes Ahab sees his own shunned family. Rather than divert his course, he urges the mate to remain on board when the boats are lowered to chase Moby-Dick. The dialogue they share does not effect the drama. The narrator compares that dialogue to an apple of Sodom, drawing his allusion from *Paradise Lost,* according to all the annotators. This vegetative image of delusive nourishment actually completes the very first portrait of Ahab the narrator drew at the end of the twenty-eighth chapter. There an allegorical figure pictures April and May as tripping 'dancing girls' (like elfin Martha and Miriam later) returning to 'the wintry, misanthropic woods,' where even strongest 'thunder-cloven oak' would respond to them by sending 'forth some few green sprouts, to welcome such gladhearted visitants; so Ahab did, in the end, a little respond to the playful alluring of the girlish air.'

In *Moby-Dick* dialogue itself leaves cinders in the mouth of advocates of reason. No characters are more fit for verbal exchange than Starbuck and Ahab, yet this is the only moment in which meaningful discussion even seems possible. Nor can Ahab speak fruitfully to the captain of the Samuel Enderby, who lost his arm to the white whale. The intimate companions, Ishmael and Queequeg, are constrained by the latter's 'broken phraseology' and many incomprehensible words. Fedallah speaks oracularly to Ahab; he, in turn, misconstrues the sense of Fedallah's words as fatally as Macbeth the rhymes of the witches. Stubb sadistically forces the old Black cook, Fleece, to preach to sharks or 'diddles' the French-speaking captain of the *Rosebud* (itself a ribald joke about female sexual anatomy) out of ambergris through an interpreter. Neither the carpenter nor the blacksmith truly converses with Ahab; they respond to his monologues. Of course, Ahab prefers monologue. He keeps Pip by his side after the cabinboy had seen 'God's foot upon the treadle of the loom, and spoke it' in a schizophrenic idiolect without control over his name or the first-person pronoun. Pip's eyes, as well, suit Ahab because he does not see his 'reflection in the vacant pupils.'

The voices of *Moby-Dick* are heard in sermons, formal tales of the adventures of ships encountered at sea, pandemonian rallies in the cult of white-whale hatred, and, above all, in monologues, which increase in frequency in the final section of the book, once

Ishmael has completed his inventory of the ship and his whale lore.

At the end of "The Symphony" the reader feels the predominance of monologue over dialogue when he learns, again after the fact, that Starbuck had 'stolen away' during Ahab's climactic rumination on fate. This delayed revelation necessarily identifies us with the monomaniacal Ahab; we are bound by his speech even when no one else is listening; like Ahab, we do not realize we are alone. In this manner, the shift of emphasis, from a language controlled by Ishmael to one articulated by Ahab, finds a dramatic form.

The speech itself contains a drift of tone. From the high rhetoric of the opening questions that try to displace responsibility for the deadly quest from Ahab to a god of fate, the monologue comes to speak of the naturalization of predatory instincts. God and man become consubstantial through murder. Finally, it beautifully tails off with a pastoral image that reinterprets the softening force of the weather. Eliminating the sexuality of the opening paragraphs, unless a faint trace of Samson can be detected in the picture of the mowers sleeping in hay, Ahab tortures himself with a parable about the destructive power of time. The sleeping mowers have not been given enough time to complete their appointed task. In their deathly sleep there is also an echo of his own castrative scar: 'Sleep, Aye, and rust amid greenness; as last year's scythes flung down, and left in half cut swaths.'

Ultimately the erotic softening engendered by the imagined intercourse of sea and air brings home to Ahab his fateful crippling. He fancies the reapers are asleep 'somewhere under the slopes of the Andes.' The mild wind then blows from the symbolic world of the doubloon, nailed to the mast for the man who first sights Moby-Dick. Of course, that will be Ahab himself. The coin, as he interpreted it, showed 'Ahab... Ahab... Ahab... Ahab.' His attempt to penetrate the profundity of his Biblical name in his next to last address to Starbuck turns out to be the captain's final soliloquy, bringing him to a depth somewhere under the epizeuxis of 'Ahab.'

Throughout the novel, the depths of Ahab's mind are associated with the ghostly Fedallah. Before Fedallah made his first appearance, Ishmael had compared 'the larger, darker, deeper part' of Ahab's mind to the Roman baths under the Hotel de Cluny where a 'captive king' upholds 'on his frozen brow the piled entablatures of ages.' Fedallah gives him what he most needs, the assurance that he will not be undone by time. Rather, Ahab takes that assurance by reading Fedallah's prophecy to his own advantage. When he completes his speech and notices that Starbuck has departed, he goes back to studying his image in the sea-mirror:

> Ahab crossed the deck to gaze over on the other side; but he started at two reflected, fixed eyes in the water there. Fedallah was motionlessly leaning over the same rail.

At the end of the chapter, as again and again within it, we have to read backwards. The eyes Ahab sees reflected are his shadowy harpooner's. But here the final sentence is poised ambiguously. We can read the conclusion as Ahab startled by his own fixed eyes with Fedallah monitoring him. Then again, if both sets of eyes are superimposed on the same reflecting surface, we find ourselves in the now familiar but still disturbing realm of what is 'hardly separable.' They are eyes without a name.

Herman Melville by Joseph Eaton, 1870

2

Called Ishmael

Jay Leyda published his monumental book, *Kino: A History of the Russian and Soviet Film* in 1960, just as I began to cultivate a passionate interest in cinema. I quickly realized he had been the translator of *The Film Sense* and *Film Form*. I owned a copy of those two collections of Sergei Eisenstein's theoretical writing that had been united in a paperback edition in 1957. Together these three books constituted my primary education in film. Leyda ascended to heroic stature in my adolescent pantheon when I discovered that he had also compiled a meticulous documentary biography of my favorite author, *The Melville Log* (1951), in two boxed volumes, much too expensive for me to buy at that time. The same year he edited *The Portable Melville* (New York: Viking Press), a chronological compendium of short stories, poems, and scenes from the novels, as well as the whole *Typee*.

But it wasn't until I met Leyda in 1967 – the start of a twenty-one-year friendship – that I learned he had begun his Melville research at the behest of Eisenstein, who asked him to collect and send him whatever he could find about the then neglected American author when Leyda was departing from his lengthy stay in the Soviet Union to assume a curatorial position in the

Film Department of the Museum of Modern Art.

One of the central tenets of Eisenstein's essays had been that the cinematic imagination functioned in literature long before cinema, and especially, montage, was invented. He analyzed Milton, Pushkin, El Greco, Flaubert and others as proto-cinematic artists. Leyda, his student, shared that conviction. For him, as presumably it was for Eisenstein, *Moby-Dick* was a masterpiece of *cinematic* construction.

In this we differed. *Moby-Dick* was *il mio libro*, but by the time I met Leyda I no longer thought of montage as the cornerstone of cinema, nor did I respond favorably to the notion of 'cinematic' literature. Yet Leyda often spoke to me of the great films that might have been. One example was John Huston's *Moby-Dick* (1956), a movie I deplored. Leyda described it as Huston's most ambitious project – one had he had meditated for decades and for which he had hoped to cast his father as Ahab. But Walter Huston had been dead for four years by the time the film entered production, with an inadequate script (according to Leyda) and with Gregory Peck foisted on Huston by the producers to play Ahab.

The habit of adapting or translating books into films simply struck me as a failure of imagination. Admittedly, the very greatest filmmakers – Dreyer, Bresson, Visconti, Kurosawa, Oliveira – have made great films from good books and plays, and even succeeded in utterly transforming literary masterpieces into great films, such as *Pickpocket* (1959) from *Crime and Punishment*, *La terra trema* (1948) from *I Malavoglia*, *A Carta* (1999) from *La Princesse de Clèves*, *Throne of Blood* (1957) from *Macbeth*. These were very unusual exceptions. John Huston was never a filmmaker of their order.

I still find the most fascinating qualities of *Moby-Dick* to be verbal and irrelevant to any cinematic mise-en-scène, real or conceptual. I attempted to analyze some of those linguistic elements thirty years ago in "Ahab's Name: A Reading of 'The

Symphony'".¹ In that essay I touched upon the issue of the narrating voice of *Moby-Dick*, but the puzzle it poses continues to obsess me. Here I shall make another attempt to come to terms with it.

In 1960, when I could afford neither the clothbound *Kino*, still less the pricey *Melville Log*, I was able to muster $1.25 for the Evergreen paperback reprint of Charles Olson's *Call Me Ishmael* (New York: Reynal & Hitchcock, 1947) by Grove Press (New York, 1958). In my repeated failures to imitate its extraordinary style, I began to teach myself how to write. I had never heard of Olson before buying the book, although his writings were to become a preoccupation for me and the subject (with Maurice Blanchot) of my 1980 dissertation. In his extraordinary prose-poem on Melville, Olson seems to have been the first to propose that *Moby-Dick* was written twice:[2]

> Moby-Dick was two books written between February 1850 and August 1851.
> The first book did not contain Ahab. It may not, except incidentally, have contained Moby-Dick. (p.35)

I assumed Olson divided the two books at chapter 23; for there, Melville had dismissed Bulkington, the character he so carefully threaded into the early chapters. To this day I do not fully understand why Olson surmised the first draft had no Ahab. His mysterious absence, or phantom presence, looms through chapters 16 to 21, even though he does not make an entrance until Chapter 28 ("Ahab"). Of course, if we take "The Lee Shore" (Chapter 23) as a revision written to whisk Bulkington out of sight for the remainder of the novel, those early intimations of Ahab's

---

[1] *Herman Melville (Modern Critical Views)*, ed. Harold Bloom (New York: Chelsea House, 1986); reprinted in *Herman Melville's Moby-Dick*, ed. Harold Bloom (New York: Chelsea House, 1986).
[2] In their magisterial Northwestern-Newberry Edition of *Moby-Dick* (pp. 649-53), Harrison Hayford, Hershel Parker, and G. Thomas Tanselle take Olson to task for cavalierly capitalizing on the scholarship of Leon Howard and Harrison Hayward (without acknowledging them), although both authors had already made their own, more scrupulous, use of Olson's earlier academic essays for Wesleyan and Harvard Universities.

tragedy might have been, more meticulously, revisionary afterthoughts as well.

In any case, the man who calls himself Ishmael is a conventional first-person narrator, recounting what he saw and heard for the first twenty-eight chapters. Then there follow conversations the narrator might have overheard without acknowledging it. An unlikely scenario. But by Chapter 38 ("Dusk") he freely enters the minds of crew members – first, with Starbuck's soliloquy. Not only that. No sooner does the narrator bid adieu to Bulkington than he tacitly separates from Queequeg; after that he remains no closer to him than any of the other crew members.[3]

When I was preparing to teach *Moby-Dick*, decades after first encountering *Call Me Ishmael*, I read George Stewart's academically rigorous essay "The Two *Moby-Dicks*".[4] It followed up on Olson's intuition and expanded it in a more scholarly fashion. Later James Barbour proposed an even more elaborate three-part schemata,[5] consisting of (1) an *ur-Moby-Dick*, (2) a subsequent version including all the cetological chapters, and (3) a major revision which he, following Olson, attributes to Melville's encounters with Hawthorne and his reading through all the plays of Shakespeare. That third part corresponded closely Olson's second, to which Barbour added the major influence of Thomas Carlyle's prose and affixed a chronology of revised chapters.

We know that Melville's financial difficulties and his publishing contract obliged him to complete *Moby-Dick* in a rush. The British edition, which preceded the American, was botched. Even the revised title arrived too late; so, it was published as *The*

---

[3] Harrison Hayward postulated that Bulkington was originally to be the companion of Ishmael, but when Melville transferred many of his qualities to Ahab, he revised the earlier chapters to make Queequeg the companion only to let him revert to his minor role as one of the harpooners once the voyage of the Pequod began. See Harrison Hayward, "Unnecessary Duplicates: a Key to the Writing of *Moby-Dick*" in *New Perspectives on Melville*, ed. Faith Pullin (Edinburgh: Edinburgh University Press, 1978), pp. 128-62; summarized in the Northwestern-Newberry *Moby-Dick*, pp. 646-47.
[4] *American Literature* 25, (Jan. 1954), pp. 417-448.
[5] "The Composition of *Moby-Dick*" in *American Literature*, vol. 47, no. 3 (Nov. 1975), pp. 343-360.

Whale, reflecting the preliminary drafts. Nevertheless, Olson had been quick to find poetry in the hybrid American text:

> In the Lee Shore chapter of the book Bulkington is explicitly excluded from the action, but not before Melville has, in ambiguities, divulged his significance as symbol. Bulkington is Man who by 'deep earnest thinking' puts out to sea, scorning the land, convinced that 'in landlessness alone resides the highest truth, shoreless, infinite as God.'
> ...Bulkington remains a 'sleeping partner' to the action. He is the secret member of the crew, below deck always, like the music under the earth in *Antony and Cleopatra*, strange. He is the crew's heart, the sign of their paternity, the human thing...Ishmael is fictive, imagined as are Ahab, Pip, and Bulkington, not so completely perhaps, for the very reason that he is so like his creator. But he is not his creator only: he is a chorus through whom Ahab's tragedy is seen, by whom what is white and what is black magic is made clear. Like the Catskill eagle Ishmael is able to dive down into the blackest gorges and soar out to the light again. (p. 57)

Since Olson asserted that *Moby-Dick* was the fusion of two books and implied that the very fusion enriched its meaning, every subsequent time I read the novel, I clung to those tenets, noting each occasion when the narrator 'is able to dive down' and if I noticed a change in his strategy of authorship, I discerned too that he is able to 'soar out...again.'

Unlike Leyda whose *Moby-Dick* was a masterpiece of vivid scenes and major characters, mine was a great prose epic of *words*, or even of the letters that make up words. Taking a cue from the "Etymology" that one first encounters on opening the volume (after the dedication and the "Contents"), I am persuaded that Melville wanted us to consider that 'whale' is, first of all, a *word*, a noun, a *syllable*. However, he was so slack in compiling the etymology that the Northwestern-Newbury edition has corrective notes or emendations for more than half of the thirteen etymological instances. From the start, Melville focusses on the H, placed ambiguously after or before the W. Out of ignorance, misreading a strange orthography, or perhaps deliberately, he gives HE NUN as the Hebrew for the creature. If the error is intentional, it not only reproduces the emphasis on H, but theologizes it. God's unutterable name in Hebrew scriptures is represented by four letters: Yod He Waw He or YHWH. (Ancient Hebrew writing always omitted vowels.) H is doubled in the sacred, all-powerful divine Name, often called the Tetragrammaton. That crossover from Yahweh to *whale* is later refracted in Chapter 86 ("The Tail") where the 'faceless' whale reminds the narrator of the impossibility of surviving the sight of God's face in Exodus 33.

So, from the very start, even before the start of the narrative proper, this will be a book about words, letters, and names, where words might be enclosed within words: such as Bull, Kin, King, Bulking, and Ton in Bulkington. The caricature of the 'pale Usher' who supplied the etymologies, like that of the 'Sub-Sub Librarian' who follows the Usher with his chronological accumulation of nearly eighty "Extracts" or cited references to whales, initially might be taken as a fictional associate of the (real) author, whose dedication of the book to Nathaniel Hawthorne is the first text we see upon opening the volume. But once we have read, and considered, the opening chapter, ("Loomings") we might retrospectively surmise that the usher and the librarian were rather the associates of the narrator who asks us to call him Ishmael. When we soon learn that he had been a schoolmaster before throwing over the job to opt for whaling, they would appear to be fitting associates:

> …if just previous to putting your hand into the tar-pot, you have been lording it as a country schoolmaster, making the tallest boys stand in awe of you. The transition is a keen one, I assure you, from a schoolmaster to a sailor, and requires a strong decoction of Seneca and the Stoics to enable you to grin and bear it. But even this wears off in time.

Retrospectively, the usher – a term for a schoolmaster's assistant in the Nineteenth Century – and the librarian were his likely colleagues in a grammar school and a local library. While the authorial status of the "Etymology" and the "Extracts" hovers between the fictive associates of Herman Melville and 'one Ishmael," imagining them as assisting the narrator in his task characterizes Ishmael himself as a 'scholarly' theologizer of the Whale, obsessed by word origins and literary precedents.

Let us take the latter option and, furthermore, call Ishmael's linguistic and literary obsessions examples of his 'hypos.' That is what he affably calls his neuroses in "Loomings" and again in "The Whiteness of the Whale." His hypos are plural: they include an obsession with death, suicidal thoughts, fear of isolation, narcissism, a tendency to press for deep meanings in phenomena (such as whiteness or blackness) and a passion to comprehend other minds. I assume he coined it by truncating *hypochondria*, a term for melancholy in the mid-Nineteenth Century. It stood for a predominately male disorder in contradistinction to *hysteria* for women; the former supposed to be located in the upper abdomen, the latter in the womb.

In the 1830s *hypochondria* (from the Greek for 'under-cartilage,' where the liver, spleen and gall bladder were said to be located) could also have the more familiar meaning of an unjustified apprehension of ill health. But the only times Ishmael uses *hypochondriac* in *Moby-Dick* he wittily applies it to a 'dispirited' whale (Chapter 74: "The Sperm Whale's Head").

The narrator of *Moby-Dick*, at first, reflects the biography of Herman Melville, who taught briefly in two grammar schools before shipping on the whaler Acushnet. Both the real and the fictional authors had previously served on merchant ships; Melville as a cabin boy. Ishmael also admits that poverty, – a perpetual problem for the young Melville – as well as his anxiety over the impulse to suicide or random violence, drove him to sea. Thus, the first paragraph introduces both the fiscal and philosophical themes of the novel, while succinctly foregrounding the narrator's psychology:

> Some years ago – never mind how long precisely – having little or no

money in my purse, and nothing particular to interest me on shore, I thought I would sail about a little and see the watery part of the world. It is a way I have of driving off the spleen and regulating the circulation. Whenever I find myself growing grim about the mouth; whenever it is a damp, drizzly November in my soul; whenever I find myself involuntarily pausing before coffin warehouses, and bringing up the rear of every funeral I meet; and especially whenever my hypos get such an upper hand of me, that it requires a strong moral principle to prevent me from deliberately stepping into the street, and methodically knocking people's hats off – then, I account it high time to get to sea as soon as I can. This is my substitute for pistol and ball. With a philosophical flourish Cato throws himself upon his sword; I quietly take to the ship.

Whaling was big business in the early Nineteenth Century. The United States nearly held an international monopoly on the source of high-quality night-light because of it. Each whale represented an enormous financial gain. So, this is also a book about capitalism at its height. Before the Civil War the United States Constitution did not authorize issuing paper currency. Individual banks issued paper notes, but they were notoriously unstable and subject to forgery. Therefore, 'the little money' Ishmael had in his purse was in coins. Coinage requires symbolism, usually political symbolism; or, more exactly, political symbolism tinged with theological references. In the course of his voyage for personal profit Ishmael finds himself simultaneously in quest of a key to the symbolism of money. He comes to realize, nearly at the loss of his life, that it represents another 'ungraspable phantom.' But that is not before the culminating meditation on coined money in "The Doubloon" (Chapter 99), where Ahab, Stubb, Flask, the old Manxman, Queequeg, Fedallah, and even the cabin boy, Pip, turned mad after nearly drowning, offer their interpretations of the embossings on the Peruvian gold piece Ahab has nailed to the mast as a reward for the first crewman to spot Moby-Dick.

Cato, in that same opening paragraph, is the first of many philosophers this former schoolmaster will invoke: in the course of his account he shows off his familiarity with Pythagoras, Plato,

Aristotle, Seneca, Stoics, Descartes, Pascal, Spinoza, Hobbes, Locke, Rousseau and Kant. He is even more adept at alluding to figures from the Old and New Testaments. In fact, he is so bookish that he presents his readers with a taxonomy of whales as if they might be classified by the relative sizes of bound volumes: Folio, Quarto, Octavo, and Dodecimo species.

To write this book at all the narrator had to survive the sinking ship. Except in diaries, fictional or real, narrated events are over before the book begins. Ishmael even alludes to the fictive date of writing this very account of his encounters with Ahab and the white whale; for he gives the reader a precise acknowledgment of the moment of penning Chapter 85 ("The Fountain"):

> That for six thousand years – and no one knows how many millions of ages before – the great whales should have been spouting all over the sea, and sprinkling and mistifying the gardens of the deep, as with so many sprinkling or mistifying pots; and that for some centuries back, thousands of hunters should have been close by the fountain of the whale, watching these sprinklings and spoutings – that all this should be, and yet, that down to this blessed minute (fifteen and a quarter minutes past one o'clock P.M. of this sixteenth day of December, A.D. 1851), it should still remain a problem, whether these spoutings are, after all, really water, or nothing but vapor – this is surely a noteworthy thing.

And in "The Dart" (Chapter 62) he even offers the one surprising allusion to his (again fictive) life between the destruction of the Pequod and the writing of *Moby-Dick*:

> ...long experience in various whalemen of more than one nation has convinced me that in the vast majority of failures in the fishery, it has not by any means been so much the speed of the whale as the before described exhaustion of the harpooner that has caused them.

For here I take 'in...whalemen' to mean in various whaling ships.

One of the novel's key words, *phantom*, emerges snow-covered in the final sentence of "Loomings," before we have yet to realize that this will be a book about noumenal energies and ghosts *looming* under and through phenomena; in fact, they loom under the minds of men and behind the most massive living creature in the history of the planet. The drolly learned narrator presents his neuroses as alternatives to the philosophical tradition. Thus, he meditates with a touch of parody on the profound meanings of the fascination with water; for, the whole first chapter constitutes his good-humored, self-deprecatory essay on narcissism as a neurosis:

> Surely all this is not without meaning. And still deeper the meaning of that story of Narcissus, who because he could not grasp the tormenting, mild image he saw in the fountain, plunged into it and was drowned. But that same image, we ourselves see in all rivers and oceans. It is the image of the ungraspable phantom of life; and this is the key to it all.

The blackness that prevails in the opening chapters is merely the first of the phenomenal keys to the Noumenal. The parable about poor Lazarus and Dives (the wealthy man) in Chapter 2 ("The Carpet-Bag") marks the earliest index to the noumenal meaning of money. In the next chapter, proprietor Coffin of the Spouter-Inn favorably judges the 'cannibal' harpooneer by the fact that he pays on time. By referring to the yet unseen Queequeg with whom Ishmael must share a room (with just one double bed) in purely financial terms, Coffin initiates an elaborate joke on the gullible Ishmael for the amusement of his other lodgers.

The delayed introduction of Queequeg (Chapter 4: "The Counterpane") is the first of several such theatrical suspensions. Ahab's will be even more prolonged and dramatic (Chapter 28: "Ahab"); then, after issuing mysterious ghostly sights and strange sounds, Fedallah (Chapter 50: "Ahab's Boat and Crew – Fedallah") emerges from the hold of the ship; finally at the end of the novel, we encounter Moby-Dick (Chapter 103: "The Chase – First Day") the most anticipated of them all.

The narrator's sense of humor first manifests itself in the way he depicts Coffin's joke on him and its consequences. By not acknowledging his own naiveté here, Ishmael makes the gag funnier. Nor does he spell out the prophetic and ironic significance of the proprietor's name. The reader only comes to realize it in the "Epilogue," where Ishmael alone of the Pequod's crew survives because he floats on the coffin Queequeg commissioned from the ship's carpenter when he had intimations of death. *Moby-Dick* is a vast epic of intricate internal echoes, of which the verbal link between Coffin and Queequeg is typical.

'Sailors sleep together' is one of Coffin's witticisms, when they drown and sleep in the sea; but Ishmael does not get his joke either. Nor does he ultimately share the sea-bed with his companion in death, but sharing the bed with him in the Spouter-Inn dramatically illustrates the epistemological and psychological framework of the novel. In the same good-humored vein, the narrator illustrates how the good cop/bad cop routine of the ship owners, Captains Bildad and Peleg, dupe him into accepting a very meager share of the ship's profit for his wages (Chapter 16: "The Ship").

The ironic language of Ishmael's initial fear of Queequeg registers a relationship between his neuroses and classical epistemological problems. As he wakes beside him, the optical 'blending' of his bedfellow's tattooed arm with the quilt, and his unexpected embrace, evoke the only memory of the narrator's childhood in the book: a scene in which his stepmother (!) punished him by sending him to bed in the afternoon, and kept him there supperless, becomes an intimation of noumenal presences. Ishmael realizes that there is a profound psychological connection between his strange or queer feelings at that moment of waking beside Queequeg and his traumatic childhood:

> My sensations were strange. Let me try to explain them. When I was a child, I well remember a somewhat similar circumstance that befell me; whether it was a reality or a dream, I never could entirely settle. The circumstance was this. I had been cutting up some caper or other

– I think it was trying to crawl up the chimney, as I had seen a little sweep do a few days previous; and my stepmother who, somehow or other, was all the time whipping me, or sending me to bed supperless, – my mother dragged me by the legs out of the chimney and packed me off to bed, though it was only two o'clock in the afternoon of the 21st June, the longest day in the year in our hemisphere. I felt dreadfully...

I lay there dismally calculating that sixteen entire hours must elapse before I could hope for a resurrection... At last I must have fallen into a troubled nightmare of a doze; and slowly waking from it – half steeped in dreams – I opened my eyes, and the before sun-lit room was now wrapped in outer darkness. Instantly I felt a shock running through all my frame; nothing was to be seen, and nothing was to be heard; but a supernatural hand seemed placed in mine... Now, take away the awful fear, and my sensations at feeling the supernatural hand in mine were very similar, in their strangeness, to those which I experienced on waking up and seeing Queequeg's pagan arm thrown round me. (Chapter 4 "The Counterpane")

Then in Chapter 7 ("The Chapel"), reflecting on the memorials to sailors lost at sea, he offers a hypo to rhyme with it – that eternal rest is nothing more than a forced sleep, without any promise of resurrection:

In what census of living creatures, the dead of mankind are included; why it is that a universal proverb says of them, that they tell no tales, though containing more secrets than the Goodwin Sands;... in what eternal, unstirring paralysis, and deadly, hopeless trance, yet lies antique Adam who died sixty round centuries ago; how it is that we still refuse to be comforted for those who we nevertheless maintain are dwelling in unspeakable bliss; why all the living so strive to hush all the dead; wherefore but the rumor of a knocking in a tomb will terrify a whole city. All these things are not without their meanings.

The philosophical Ishmael suggests that we perceive phenomena but we must reason or have faith in the noumenal world beyond what we perceive. *Moby-Dick* is poised on that problem. Later, the narrator will actually name both Kant and Locke as he meditates on the conundrum of intrinsic knowledge while observing two whale heads balanced on either side of the ship (Chapter 74: "Stubb and Flask Kill a Right Whale; and Then

Have a Talk over Him").

His skepticism about the existence of Heaven exacerbates his death-hypo. He tacitly accepts an afterlife, while fearing it may be the nothing but the frozen, silent stillness of a vengeful god. His observation that the ladder by which Father Mapple ascends to his pulpit (Chapter 8: "The Pulpit") 'must symbolize something unseen' forecasts dozens of chapters about whaling paraphernalia that turn on attempts to capture the noumenal meaning of those practical, phenomenal objects as symbols, or 'ungraspable phantoms.' In the subsequent chapter (Chapter 9: "The Sermon") the unstated point of the Book of Jonah may be that God uses his prophets against their will; He has no obligation to fulfill the prophecy He forces them to utter. But Mapple does not acknowledge that; he omits the end of the Biblical book – what happens after the fish spits out Jonah. Instead, his anaphoric ode to *delight* extolls suffering from 'God's quick wrath.' (Near the end of *Moby-Dick* the Pequod meets a ship misnamed The Delight (Chapter 131).) Mapple's insistence on *delight* seems a grimly positive twist on Ishmael's hypo that he will be eternally doomed to Adam's 'unstirring paralysis.'

"The Chapel" (Chapter 7) had terminated with a Shakespearean soliloquy in which Ishmael temporarily coaxes himself out of this persistent hypo into a Transcendentalist optimism:

> Yes, Ishmael, the same fate [death at sea] may be thine. But somehow I grew merry again. Delightful inducements to embark, fine chance for promotion, it seems... Yes, there is death in this business of whaling – a speechlessly quick chaotic bundling of a man into Eternity. But what then?... Methinks that what they call my shadow here on earth is my true substance. Methinks that in looking at things spiritual, we are too much like oysters observing the sun through the water, and thinking that thick water the thinnest air. Methinks my body is but the lees of my better being. In fact take my body who will, take it I say, it is not me.

Because Quequeg could not read, he alone notices Ishmael in

the whalemen's chapel where he and others are engrossed reading the monuments inscribed to lost sailors. There, to read is to be blind to all but absence. Yet the bookish Ishmael even attempts to read his bedfellow's mysterious tattooed body as a symbolic text. Conversely, Queequeg, who worships Yojo, a wooden idol, assumes that Ishmael's Bible is another such sacred *thing*, merely an object to mediate divinity. So, when his narrator wryly proclaims: the Presbyterian Church 'infallible,' by transferring the romish adjective to the antipopish Presbyterians, Ishmael is suggesting that he had come to share the fusion of American Protestants and Roman Catholics in Queequeg's mind, insofar as they both made an idol of a Book (in translation). Recognizing that their views of each other's religions were complementary, brings Ishmael to his first intimations of an exchange or conjunction between the mind of another and his own:

> I was a good Christian; born and bred in the bosom of the infallible Presbyterian Church. How then could I unite with this wild idolator in worshipping his piece of wood? But what is worship? thought I. Do you suppose now, Ishmael, that the magnanimous God of heaven and earth – pagans and all included – can possibly be jealous of an insignificant bit of black wood? Impossible! But what is worship? –to do the will of God – *that* is worship. And what is the will of God? – to do to my fellow man what I would have my fellow man to do to me – *that* is the will of God. Now, Queequeg is my fellow man. And what do I wish that this Queequeg would do to me? Why, unite with me in my particular Presbyterian form of worship. Consequently, I must then unite with him in his; ergo, I must turn idolator. (Chapter 10: "A Bosom Friend")

That imaginary fusion was at stake even before Ishmael actually saw Queequeg, when he had tried on his prospective bedfellow's exotic poncho. The mirror image of his inverted narcissism terrified him:

> I put it on, to try it… I went up in it to a bit of glass stuck against the wall, and I never saw such a sight in my life. I tore myself out of it in

such a hurry that I gave myself a kink in the neck. (Chapter 3: "The Spouter-Inn")

The subsequent homoerotic language of Ishmael's 'marriage' to the cannibal and their 'honeymoon" marks the explicit dimension of the narrator's sexualized interpretation of his own behavior. The title of Chapter 31, "Queen Mab," in which second mate Stubb recounts a dream, represents the clever narrator's most oblique sexual allusion, by way of the witty interpretation Mercutio offers of Romeo's dream in *Romeo and Juliet*. He twisted Romeo's words into sexual jokes; for example, in their exchange around the word 'prick.' The nature of this playfulness is serious for Melville (and for Ishmael) who intuit the unconscious or underlying levels in dreams and in words. By transforming Romeo's pathetic, unrequited passion for Rosalind (he has yet to encounter Juliet) into the orgasmic mechanics of fornication, Mercutio was offering Romeo a verbal therapy.

In Stubb's dream, Ahab's ivory leg is a double indication of (primarily) castration and (secondarily) a permanently stiff erection – typical of the antithetical aspects of dream images – turning Stubb's nightmare into his fear of, and failed vengeance against, phallic and paternal aggression. If to be kicked by Ahab means to be the subject of anal-erotic rape, the dreamer tries and fails to pass that aggression onto a victim he wants and expects to overpower in turn – the merman – only to discover his victim has a defensive protection of a multiplicity of hard pricks.

Thomas Beale's *The Natural History of the Sperm Whale* (London, 1839) was a major source of whale facts and lore for Melville as he was writing *Moby-Dick*. If he did not already know that the viscous substance in the spermaceti whale's cranium was not semen, he would have learned it in Beale:

> That it was not the spawn of the whale, according to vulger [sic] conceit or nominal appellation, philosophers have always doubted, not easily conceding the seminal humor of animals should be inflammable, or of a floating nature. (Chapter ix, p. 127)

Yet Melville never disabused his narrator of this myth. It was too rich a source of humor and fantasy for Ishmael to abandon. Almost all the gams – meetings of other ships at sea – have sexual overtones – blatantly in The Bachelor, a ship so bursting with spermaceti it seems about to ejaculate, and in The Virgin, a ship without one drop of the viscous substance, so deprived she has to beg sufficient oil to light her lamps from the Pequod. The Town-Ho's sailors (Chapter 54) recount an extensive tale of phallic violence, and symbolic homosexual aggression (Chapter 54), the Jerobaum is plagued by a mad prophet of the Shakers – a sect who renounce all sexual activity (Chapter 71) – while Stubb 'diddles' the French ship Rose-Bud (Chapter 91) (whose name puns on a vulgar term for the clitoris) out of his foul smelling but very lucrative ambergris. In "A Squeeze of the Hand" (Chapter 94), sailors kneading a vat of what they take to be sperm make manual contact in a barely-suppressed parody of mutual masturbation. To this Aristophanic erotic theater, Ishmael adds that the mincer in "The Cassock" (Chapter 95) wears a hieratic coat made from a whale's penis; while in "The Grand Armada" (Chapter 87) he is among the sailors watching whales copulate.

Furthermore, the massive, destructive creature at the heart of his tale, Moby-Dick himself, thus became a phallic hyperbole. At the conclusion of his comic taxonomy of whales (Chapter 32: "Cetology"), having earlier compared himself as an 'architect, not the builder' of his system, the narrator puns on *erections*:

> But I now leave my cetological System standing thus unfinished, even as the great Cathedral of Cologne was left, with the crane still standing upon the top of the uncompleted tower. For small erections may be finished by their first architects; grand ones, true ones, ever leave the copestone to posterity. God keep me from ever completing anything. This whole book is but a draught – nay, but the draught of a draught. Oh, Time, Strength, Cash, and Patience!

Robert Shulman explicated it thus:

> ... like Sterne, for whom sexuality and artistic creativity are insepar-

able, Melville uses his phallic joke to convey a precise sense of what creating books means to him…

Ishmael's daring imagery is appropriate in still other ways. He has been satirizing systems and systematizers, particularly those who, like the critics of *Tristram Shandy*, want a book to proceed in a regular, classical order. His dislike of conventional aesthetic systems is closely related to his rejection of the respectable social order, including its economic, political, and religious systems. Primal, sexual energy is intrinsically subversive of conventional order and of respectable systems. Such energy can be horribly destructive; but it is also essentially creative, since in the natural world it is the source of all life. Ishmael's gigantic sexual pun is thus a perfect vehicle for conveying his radical rejection of conventional systems and their makers. His enormous phallic imagery also embodies Melville's belief that the sources of artistic and sexual creation are closely related. Similarly, the very irreverence of his language renders his view of the artist as an independent man in touch with some of the sources of his creativity and at odds with forces which would restrict it.

("The Serious Functions of Melville's Phallic Jokes" in *American Literature*, Vol. 33, No. 2 [May, 1961, pp. 186-87])

To Shulman's cogent analysis, I would add that if the speculators on the two or several *Moby-Dicks* are right, this passage may obliquely refer to transformation of the original plan of the novel – the sea story of Ishmael, Bulkington, Peleg, and Queequeg – waggishly alluded to as if it were a minor onanastic story. In its place the amateur cetologist now prays for "Time, Strength, Cash, and Patience" to allow his new, *unconventional* Shakespearean and encyclopedic epic to rise like a massive erection. For the Shandean architect of this tale, his expanded narrative is the copestone, the ithyphallic draught of a draught, once the conventional first-person account gives way, to make Ahab and Ishmael specular epicenters of the novel in which the very nature of storytelling keeps rising to the surface.

That nature must now be tragic, in the highest sense. It even requires that the narrational prose gives way to the explicit use of stage directions, formal dialogues, and extended soliloquies. Yet, as he shifts the manner of his storytelling, the narrator recognizes that American democracy had radically altered the context for tragedy. In Chapter 33 ("The Specksnyder"), not long after he had begun to introduce soliloquies and scenes beyond the range of his seeing or hearing, Ishmael acknowledges that in shifting his role closer to that of a tragic dramatist, he had to take account of the paradox of erecting tragedy with the utterly inadequate 'trappings' of democracy:

> Nor, will the tragic dramatist who would depict mortal indomitableness in its fullest sweep and direct swing, ever forget a hint, incidentally so important in his art, as the one now alluded to [that the trappings of royal hierarchy are essential].
> But Ahab, my Captain, still moves before me in all his Nantucket grimness and shagginess; and in this episode touching Emperors and Kings, I must not conceal that I have only to do with a poor old whale-hunter like him; and, therefore, all outward majestical trappings and housings are denied me. Oh, Ahab! what shall be grand in thee, it must needs be plucked at from the skies, and dived for in the deep, and featured in the unbodied air!

The shift that occurs here has several manifestations. Ishmael no longer portrays himself in the character of the gullible tyro he had so carefully constructed in the early chapters. It might even be said he no longer *portrays* himself at all, or only barely and intermittently. The good-natured jocularity of his deliberately high-flown rhetoric also wanes very quickly; for his humor too has changed; it now only peeks through his whale lore and his frequent sexual puns and allusions. At once, the playful epistemological studies of a fearful or bewildered observer disappear. They are replaced by longer metaphysical speculations on the noumenal meaning of the paraphernalia of the whaleship. Above all, a dialectical movement drives his narrative consciousness. The alternations of dramatized scenes in the Shakespearean manner with essays by the changed and still changing narrator hint at a mind at times carried off in a Dionysian frenzy of identification with Ahab and the mad quest he has inculcated in his crew, and at other times struggling to recover its equilibrium. The frequent, tangential allusions to acts of rebirth are the closest Ishmael comes to openly acknowledging this rhythm.

The Biblical Jonah, Tashtego's 'deliverance' by Queequeg's daring 'obstetrics' from his nearly fatal fall into the decapitated head of a Right Whale (Chapter 78, "Cistern and Buckets") and the rescue of Pip, all forecast Ishmael's virtual rebirth in the "Epilogue" where, like Job's servants, he 'only...escaped to tell' the story, after his near-death encounter with the sublime, having seen 'God's foot upon the treadle' (as Pip experienced in Chapter 93: "The Castaway.").

✦

At this point in my argument, just as Ishmael introduces his reader to the crew of the Pequod in two chapters (26 and 27) both entitled "Knights and Squires," I believe an abstract, reductive recapitulation and summary of *his* construction of his story is in order: He is a bookish narrator who tells us he tries whaling to escape his depression (hypos) and poverty. First, he encounters Queequeg, a 'noble savage,' the paradigm of human virtue, with whom he joins forces. At the same time, he is intrigued by Bulkington, a charismatic, compulsive sailor, but dismisses him on Xmas day with intimations of 'the Infinite.'

The shock of seeing Captain Ahab (Chapter 28: "Ahab") requires this schoolmaster, steeped in Shakespeare, Milton, and philosophy, to attempt a different mode of narration in order to reflect his shift of consciousness. The straightforward first-person narrative that Herman Melville (whose first five novels were conventional first-person narratives), and so many others, had previously employed in conjuring the exotic aspects of sea life would be inadequate. In its place, Ishmael adapts elements from Shakespearean tragedy to the fictional mode of *Tristram Shandy* (or Diderot's *Rameau's Nephew*), occasionally offering us clues to his method. Thus "The Crotch" (Chapter 63) begins with an organic metaphor for the structure of *Moby-Dick*:

Out of the trunk, the branches grow; out of them, the twigs. So, in productive subjects, grow the chapters

And it ends with Ishmael's *ut pictura poesis*:

> All these particulars are faithfully narrated here, as they will not fail to elucidate several most important, however intricate passages, in scenes hereafter to be painted.

The narrator finds that even whales need Shakespearean 'science.' His literary Cetology (Chapter 32) is a first, but inadequate, defense against the fatality of the quest to which Ahab requires complete submission. Right after the reverie (Chapter 35: "The Mast-Head"), in which he imagines that any ruminative sailor aloft in the watch – an amateur Platonist – must recognize his proximity to death, Ishmael confesses that Ahab's declaration of their mission and his grand proclamation of the metaphysics of phenomena as 'pasteboard masks' has effected his own Dionysian seduction into choral impersonality in the crew (Chapter 36: "The Quarter-Deck"). When even the gesture of contrasting Ahab's diabolical whale (Chapter 41: "Moby-Dick") to his own extended meditation on noumenal whiteness (Chapter 42: "The Whiteness of the Whale") cannot wholly shrive him of that intermittent loss of identity, he resorts to a battery of tropes from Shakespearean tragedy to express the cadences of his identification with, and separation from, Ahab (and with others of the crew).

Ishmael knows he is almost out of control but he cannot stop himself. He is in the thrall of the numinous. Near the end of "The Whiteness of the Whale" he states boldly:

> Though neither [buffalo nor colt] knows where lie the nameless things of which the mystic sign [whiteness] gives forth such hints; yet with me, as with the colt, somewhere those things must exist. Though in many of its aspects this visible world seems formed in love, the invisible spheres were formed in fright.

The aspects of his mind take on autonomy to the degree that

Ahab's presence approaches the narrator's sense of the whale as 'a vacated thing... light without an object to color... a blankness in itself.' In the extraordinary final paragraph of that chapter he intimates that if Ahab sees malice in the noumenal, divine sphere, he fears there may be nothing beyond. White, for him, is the 'colorless, all-color of atheism'.

The narrator is so profoundly threatened by the loss of self on the Quarter-Deck that he has to ventriloquize the thoughts of Ahab in soliloquies to underline his separation, and the Captain's autonomy. Concordantly, he attempts to recover his ironic selfhood by composing the essay on the whiteness of Moby-Dick. In the ensuing chapters he affirms the activity of his own mind as he struggles to understand the issues of bodies and souls (Chapter 44: "The Chart"), agency, chance, necessity, free will (Chapter 47: "The Mat Maker"), and fate (Chapter 61: "The Line') that were at stake in his cetological autodidacticism.

Glauco Cambon, acknowledging the earlier efforts of interpretation by Richard Sewall and Merlin Bowen, succinctly addressed the problem of the narrative shifts:

> ... Ishmael is the artist in the act of telling us, and struggling to understand, his crucial experience. When his autobiography becomes the history of the *Pequod* and Ahab, he is liberated from his 'hypos' for the second time, and in a deeper sense: he attains the liberation of imaginative objectivity. Thus his vanishing from the stage after a certain point does not constitute a breach of poetical continuity, but a dialectical movement that reproduces and expands the repeated transition from narrative to drama, from memory to visionary actuality, from *conjuring subjectivity to conjured objectivity*. It will help to recall that Chapter 32 ("Cetology") humorously describes the sizes of the various species of whales in terms of book-formats, an obvious literary metaphor, and that the allusions to the story as a book in the making (often attuned to self-mockery) abound significantly.
>
> If so, it should be possible to accept Ishmael as a *persona* of Melville, invisibly present *through* his narration when he ceases to be directly present *in* it; and that this persona, even as he ceases to have objective existence, has dramatic existence as actor-spectator of a half-remembered, half-conjured action. Ishmael is the self-ironizing

> writer seeking, and finally achieving, realization through self-effacement in the work of art; following him in the process, we see the poetry arise from its (cetological) materials, and the discontinuities acquire the meaning of imaginative gesture within the context of a work in progress. They are indeed the structural equivalents of the copious hyperboles which animate Melville's baroque prose.
> ("Ishmael and the Problem of Formal Discontinuities in Moby Dick," *Modern Language Notes* Vol. 76, No. 6 [Jun., 1961], p. 523.)

Despite the admirable elegance of the conjuring and conjured opposition of 'half remembered, half-conjured action,' the brilliant suggestion that the transition to theatrical omniscience marks a liberation from the narrator's hypos is too optimistic to be convincing. If we are to ignore the serious philological and characterological problems of Melville's unexplained shift of style and project them into the psychodynamics of Ishmael's narrative problematic as Cambon did, and I am doing now, we might alternatively posit the recourse to Shakespearean dramaturgy as the most obsessive of Ishmael's hypos, wherein he struggles to transcend his epistemological limitations in his need to comprehend and realize what he can neither observe nor otherwise explain.

One of Ishmael's defenses against those hypos and against the intoxication of Ahab's monomania is quantification. He even jokes that he had tattooed the whale skeleton's dimensions on his arm (Chapter 102: "A Bower in the Arcasides"). In that respect he also follows Pythagoras, half-ironically in affirming metempsychosis; that is to say, he faces his potential doom by seeing nature endlessly repeated in cycles.

Eventually Ishmael issues an affidavit because he finds it necessary to persuade the reader that he is writing of real, plausible events, that his story corresponds to facts; that malicious monster whales really exist. The opening sentence of "The Affidavit" (Chapter 45) stresses that behind the 'narrative' we are reading there are important realities; one of them would be the validity of charting whale paths:

> So far as what there may be of a narrative in this book... I care not to perform this part of my task methodically; but shall be content to produce the desired impression by separate citations of items, practically or reliably known to me as a whaleman...
>
> I do not know where I can find a better place than just here, to make mention of one or two other things, which to me seem important, as in printed form establishing in all respects the reasonableness of the whole story of the White Whale, more especially the catastrophe. For this is one of those disheartening instances where truth requires full as much bolstering as error. So ignorant are most landsmen of some of the plainest and most palpable wonders of the world, that without some hints touching the plain facts, historical and otherwise, of the fishery, they might scout at Moby Dick as a monstrous fable, or still worse and more detestable, a hideous and intolerable allegory.

The narrator's 'here' yet again locates us in front of the page of the book we are reading. He is about to refer to other 'printed' books; for Ishmael has 'swam through libraries' as he claims in "Cetology." He insists this is not a 'fable' like Aesop's – an animal tale with a moral. Nor is it 'a hideous and intolerable allegory.' This last phrase has encouraged much controversy. Unquestionably, *Moby-Dick* is allegorical. Melville seems to mean that it is not the intolerable sort of allegory in which there are equations of meaning; i.e. Ishmael stands for perception; Ahab for vengeance; Moby-Dick for God, *ad nauseam*.

The terrifying presence of a real (nameless) whale and, thus, the sublime physicality of natural phenomena (Chapter 49: "The Hyena") forces him to suspend his idealist musings. He even wrote his Will after his fright at his first lowering. After writing it, he described his 'rebirth' with an ironic allusion to the Gospel of John, 11:38-41:

> It may seem strange that of all men sailors should be tinkering at their last wills and testaments, but there are no people in the world more fond of that diversion. This was the fourth time in my nautical life that I had done the same thing. After the ceremony was concluded upon the present occasion, I felt all the easier; a stone was rolled away from my heart. Besides, all the days I should now live would be as good as the days that Lazarus lived after his resurrection; a supplementary clean gain of so many months or weeks as the case might be.

> I survived myself; my death and burial were locked up in my chest. I looked round me tranquilly and contentedly, like a quiet ghost with a clean conscience sitting inside the bars of a snug family vault.

However, the certainties he had known on land were no longer available to him, as he admits in yet another variation on Narcissus in Chapter 85: "The Fountain":

> While composing a little treatise on Eternity, I had the curiosity to place a mirror before me; and ere long saw reflected there, a curious involved worming and undulation in the atmosphere over my head… And so, through all the thick mists of the dim doubts in my mind, divine intuitions now and then shoot, enkindling my fog with a heavenly ray. And for this I thank God; for all have doubts; many deny; but doubts or denials, few along with them, have intuitions. Doubts of all things earthly, and intuitions of some things heavenly; this combination makes neither believer nor infidel, but makes a man who regards them both with equal eye.

In his numerous digressions into philosophical and historical essays on the tools and processes of whaling (and on picturing whales in the three chapters (55-57) that follow the long interpolated tale of the violence aboard the Town-Ho), the schoolmaster-whaler is doing at least two things at once: he is putting a brake on the action by slowly reintroducing his comic pedantry, and stressing the *visible* (that is, phenomenal) world; at the same time he is informing us that the sperm whale, being far more massive than any dinosaurs were, cannot ever be 'seen' alive. They are too big to haul out of the water. Whalers get to see only the portions of them that surface, or the parts that they dissect. Thus "Of the Monstrous Pictures of Whales" (Chapter 55) concludes:

> … any way you may look at it, you must needs conclude that the great Leviathan is that one creature in the world which must remain unpainted to the last. True, one portrait may hit the mark much nearer than another, but none can hit it with any very considerable degree of exactness. So there is no earthly way of finding out precisely what the whale really looks like. And the only mode in which you can derive

even a tolerable idea of his living contour, is by going a whaling yourself; but by so doing, you run no small risk of being eternally stove and sunk by him.

In "The Age of the Fossil Whale", he excuses his grandiose prose as fitting to his immense subject, the size and time span of the whale: from prehuman to posthuman. This epic declaration will terminate his cetological lore.

Ishmael fades out of the narrative insofar as he ceases to use the first-person for many chapters, after addressing himself three times in the Shakespearean fashion in "A Bower in the Arsacides." Subsequently, bits of whale lore imply his didactic presence; he barely inserts himself into "Queequeg in His Coffin" (Chapter 110) with a couple of uses of 'us', one 'I', and a 'my.' Similar minimal intrusions of the first-person show up in "The Pacific" and "Candles" (Chapters 111 and 119). Then he disappears entirely from the British edition (which omitted the "Epilogue" and eliminated the single problematic 'I' of "The Symphony" (Chapter 132)).

As the narrator moves toward the Shakespearean fifth act of *Moby-Dick*, language comes to the foreground (as I discussed in "Ahab's Name"); it has become the very fragile life-line that holds Pip after he saw God's foot on the treadle. He has become insane, repeatedly declining unanchored pronouns. He even lost the connection to his name, although as the shortest possible palindrome – just three letters with 'i' as the pivot – no name could be easier.

In the "Epilogue" Ishmael wrote out the magic formula upon which fiction turns, the theoretical postulate that invents personae, and puts a mask on the persona of a narrator 'I was he…' Maurice Blanchot made that the 'secret center' of "The Essential Solitude," the essay focused on Kafka that he selected to open his volume, *The Space of Literature*:

> The writer, it is said, gives up saying 'I.' Kafka remarks, with surprise, with enchantment, that he has entered into literature as soon

as he can substitute 'He' for 'I.' This is true, but the transformation is much more profound. The writer belongs to a language which no one speaks, which is addressed to no one, which has no center, and which reveals nothing.... The notion of characters, as the traditional form of the novel, is only one of the compromises by which the writer, drawn out of himself by literature in search of its essence, tries to salvage his relations with the world and himself... The third person is myself become no one, my interlocutor turned alien; it is my no longer being able, where I am, to address myself and the inability of whoever addresses me to say 'I': it is his not being himself.
(*The Space of Literature*, trans. Ann Smock [Lincoln: University of Nebraska Press, 1982], pp. 26,27,28)

Fedallah had to be replaced in Ahab's boat after he was killed the second day of chasing of Moby-Dick. But it is not until the "Epilogue" that Ishmael, returning to the center of the narrative when everyone else is dead, tells us: 'It so chanced, that after the Parsee's disappearance, I was he whom the Fates ordained to take the place of Ahab's boatsman.'

'*I was he.*' This chapter comes down to a gloss on those three words. Maurice Blanchot never even mentioned Ishmael the two times he wrote on *Moby-Dick.* Both in "Le secret de Melville" (*Journal des débats*, 1-2 septembre 1941), in *Faux Pas* (1943) and "Le Chant du Sirène" (*La Nouvelle Revue française*, no. 19, juilliet 1954) in *Le livre à venir* (1955), he identified Melville himself as the narrator of the book, which he advised his readers to read, in Jean Giono's 1941 French translation 'with no expectation beyond pleasure.'

In an otherwise astute and exacting interview John Huston made with Eduoard Laurot in *Film Culture* in 1956, he too spoke as if the narrator were Melville, not Ishmael:

> He seems to have written the book with several parts of his nature. It isn't just one man and one point of view – It's half a dozen men and different points of view. It is the writer, the moralist, the philosopher, the scientist, the cetologist, the dramatist. I didn't attempt consciously to correlate all his facets in my film, but let them exist in their original richness and spontaneity.
> ("An Encounter with John Huston: Excerpts from a Conversation

between John Huston and Edouard Laurot", *Film Culture*, vol. 2, no. 2 [8, 1956, p.2].)

The one purely *cinematic* trope to which Huston refers in the interview – the desaturation of color throughout the film – has no relevance to the articulation of point of view.

By the time Blanchot came to write *L'Entretien infini* (1969), where he elaborated the function of pronouns in fiction, *Moby-Dick* was no longer in his sights. Ann Banfield worked out the epistemological parameters of Blanchot's insights in reference to Descartes' *Cogito* in "The Name of the Subject: The 'Il'?' There she proposed that literary theory might be called upon to illuminate some of the problems Russell, Meinong, and Kripke discovered in the ambiguity of the first-person pronoun in Descartes 'proof':

> The grammar of subjectivity in the novel... distinguishes between three kinds of referring expressions, the relations among which have preoccupied all the major philosophical theories of reference...We can speculate that the notion of character specific to the novel crucially involves the relation between the pronoun referring to the self, the proper name conceived of in the Kripkean fashion as a rigid designator, and the description. ("The Name of the Subject: The 'Il'?," in *Yale French Studies* No. 93, *The Place of Maurice Blanchot* [1998], p. 166.)

What she might make of 'one Ishmael' whose proper name is anything but a rigid designator, and whose only 'description' in the technical sense in which she uses that term, might be 'I was he,' is opaque.

I like to fancy that six years after the author of *Faux Pas* revealed "Le secret de Melville," Charles Olson (who knew nothing of Blanchot) was responding to him, by writing, '... but [Ishmael] is not his creator only: he is a chorus through whom Ahab's tragedy is seen, by whom what is black and what is white magic is made clear.'

'I was he.' Olson's compacted prose suggests that only under the spell of Ahab, in the necessity to invent an American mode of tragedy, the pseudonymous narrator becomes a 'chorus.' The captain's black or goetic magic nearly erases his capability of asserting 'I', but not completely, since with the restorative power of white, or theurgic magic, Ishmael's 'apotheosis… leaps up from the spray of thy ocean-perishing – straight up' as he had written of Bulkington in "The Lee Shore."[6]

---

[6] I am grateful to Daniel Heller-Roazen for urging me to return to Banfield's brilliant essay – which I had read much too hastily twenty years ago – and to consider the implied pronoun as a chorus. Reading Banfield again brought me face to face with my own 'hypo,' a compulsion to domesticate Melville's openness to the eruptions of narrative and dramatic language in terms of the psychology of the character he projected as a narrator.

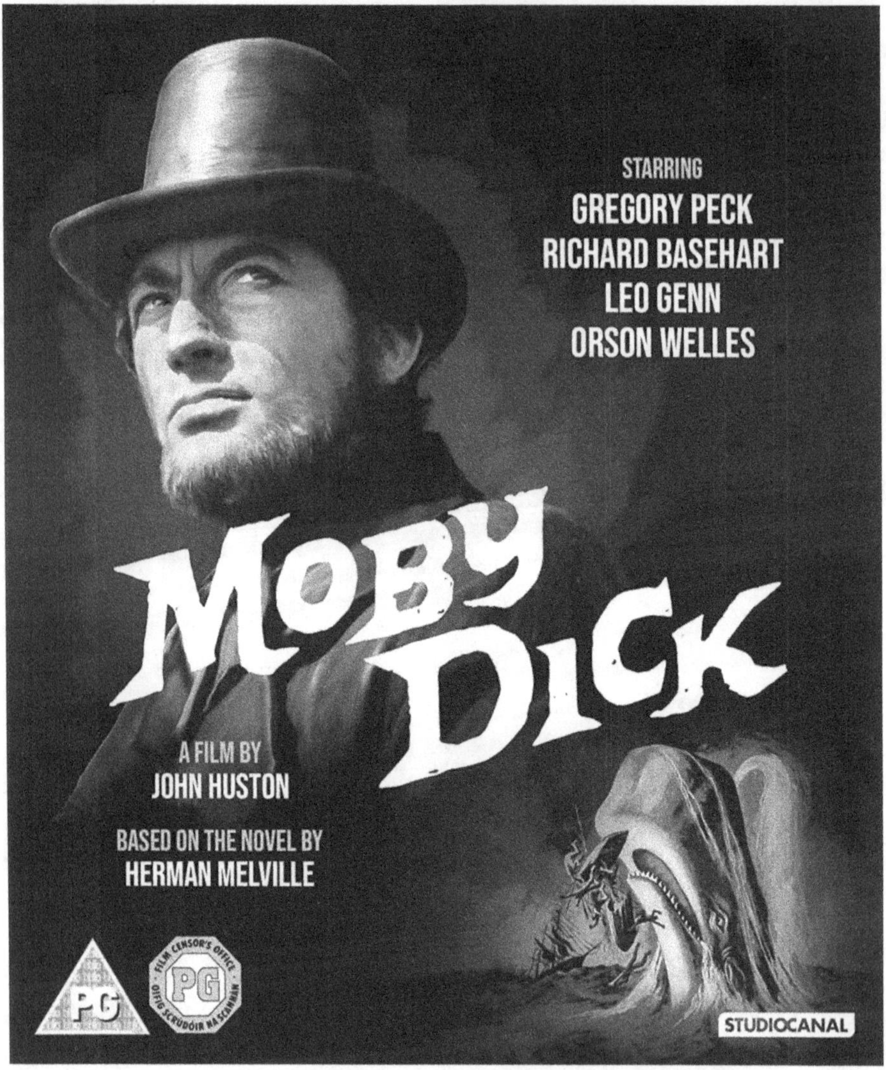

Moby Dick (John Huston, 1956).

3

The Sonnet That Names Itself

Le mot n'a de sens que s'il nous débarasse de l'objet qu'il nomme; it doit nous en épargner la présance ou le 'concret rappel'… Mallarmé a été frappe par le caractère du langage qui est d'être significative et abstrait. Tout mot, même un nom proper, même le nom de Mallarmé, désigne, non pas un événment individual, mais la forme generale de cet événment qu'il soit, il reste une abstraction.

(The word has meaning only if it rids us of the object it names; it must spare us its presence or 'concrete reminder.'… Mallarmé was struck by the characteristic of language to be both meaningful and abstract. Every word, even a proper noun, even Mallarmé's name, designates not an individual event but the general form of this event: whatever it may be, it remains an abstraction.)

(Maurice Blanchot, "The Myth of Mallarmé" in *The Work of Fire*, trans. Charlotte Mandrell, p. 30)

In his elegy for the poet Théophile Gautier, "Toast funebre," (1873), Mallarmé wrote:

Le Maître, par un oeil profond, a, sur ses pas,
Apaisé de l'éden l'inquiète merveille
Dont le frisson final, dans sa voix seule, éveille
Pour la Rose et le Lys le mystère d'un nom.

(The Master, with a profound eye, has, in his steps,
Calmed the anxious miracle of Eden,
Whose last frisson in his lone voice, awoke,
For the Rose and the Lily the mystery of a name.)

In French *nom* means both *name* and *noun* (and a homonym for the negative adverb *non*). Mallarmé's poetry is haunted by the lost or 'abolished' Adamic language that bestows real names. Yet, even as the Master Poet steps into Eden, he does not step at all; for the word *pas*, both denotes *step* and connotes negation; for *pas* is also the particle that usually completes the negative adverb *ne...pas*.

For decades I have been pondering Stèphane Mallarmé's two versions of his 'sonnet en yx,' where the act of naming and its ineluctable abolition is fundamental. I published a brief interpretation of it in the "Introduction" to *Modernist Montage*. Over the subsequent three decades I have gleaned some additional minor insights from my reading. But the most striking revelations about the poems came from an essay by Jean-Claude Milner given to me by Daniel Heller-Roazen. Previously, Heller-Roazen acquainted me with Milner's genius with a gift of his *Constats* (2002). The book includes the text of his *Mallarmé au Tombeau* (1999), a brilliant linguistic and critical analysis of the sonnet 'Le vierge, le vivace, et le bel aujourd'hui' and its relation to Baudelaire's 'Le Cygne' over six chapters. Although the critical literature on Mallarmé is vast (and I am far from familiar with all of it), Milner's work stands out as exceptional.

The essay on the 'sonnets en yx' – "Mallarmé selon Saussure" – was equally dazzling. It was enormously gratifying to read his confirmation of a few of the observations I had made in *Modernist Montage* (which Milner surely never saw). Yet, much more profound was his utterly persuasive hypothesis about why the poet made crucial changes between the initial completion of the sonnet – as "Sonnet allégorique de lui-même" (1868) – and its untitled publication as "Ses purs ongles dédiant leur onyx" (1887). Milner attributes the revisions to the death of the poet's young son, Anatole.

    Here are the two versions:

    La Nuit approbatrice allume les onyx
    De ses ongles au pur Crime, lampadophore,
    Du Soir aboli par le vespéral Phoenix
    De qui la cendre n'a de cinéraire amphore

    Sur des consoles, en le noir Salon: nul ptyx,
    Insolite vaisseau d'inanité sonore,
    Car le Maître est allé puiser de l'eau du Styx
    Avec tous ses objets dont le Rêve s'honore.

    Et selon la croisée au Nord vacante, un or
    Néfaste incite pour son beau cadre une rixe
    Faite d'un dieu que croit emporter une nixe

    En l'obscurcissement de la glace, décor
    De l'absence, sinon que sur la glace encor
    De scintillations le septuor se fixe.

. . .

    Ses purs ongles très haut dédiant leur onyx,
    L'Angoisse, ce minuit, soutient, lampadophore,
    Maint rêve vespéral brûlé par le Phénix
    Que ne recueille pas de cinéraire amphore

    Sur les crédences, au salon vide: nul ptyx
    Aboli bibelot d'inanité sonore,
    (Car le Maître est allé puiser des pleurs au Styx
    Avec ce seul objet dont le Néant s'honore.)

    Mais proche la croisée au nord vacante, un or
    Agonise selon peut-être le décor
    Des licornes ruant du feu contre une nixe,

    Elle, défunte nue en le miroir, encor
    Que, dans l'oubli fermé par le cadre, se fixe
    De scintillations sitôt le septuor.

    (Approving Night lights up the onyx
    Of its nails in the pure lampbearing Crime
    Of the Evening abolished by the vesperal Phoenix

For whose ash there is no ash urn

On the console, in the black Salon: no ptyx
Unusual vessel of sonorous inanity,
For the Master has gone to gather the water of the Styx
With all the objects that the Dream respects.

And according to the passage in the vacant North, a fatal gold
Incites for its beautiful frame a brawl
Made by a god who believes he carries a nixie

Within the obscurity of the mirror, décor
Of absence, save that on the mirror even
The flickerings of the seven [stars] fix themselves

* * *

Its pure nails very high up dedicating their onyx,
Anguish, this midnight, keeps up, lampbearing.
Many a vesperal Dream burned by the Phoenix
That is not gathered in an funereal ash jar,

On the Credences in the empty salon: no ptyx,
Abolished trinket of sonorous inanity,
(For the Master has gone to gather tears in the Styx
With the only object for which the Nothingness takes pride)

But near the passage at the vacant north, a gold
Agonizes perhaps depending on the stage set
of unicorns running from fire up against a mermaid

She, dead, naked [or a cloud] in the mirror, although
In the forgetfulness closed by the frame, instantly
From flickerings the seven stars would fix themselves)

Whereas Milner predicated his work on "Le vierge..." with a subtle exposition of the syntactical ambiguities of the sentences in the sonnet, he marshals his vast knowledge of the theories of Indo-European phonology available to linguists at the time of the sonnet's composition to reveal hidden structures within the sound of the word *ptyx* around which "Ses purs ongles..." revolves.

It had been my contention, in *Modernist Montage*, that the

mysterious 'ptyx' referred to the sonnet form itself (Milner comes to the same point), and that the sonnet form was an 'aboli bibelot d'inanité sonore' because of its archaic rhyme schemes, as well as the vestiges of Biblical, mythological, and poetic allusions that cling to the sonnet convention. As such, the sonnet was 'allegorical of itself' as well as allegorical of the French pronoun 'Lui-même.' Although I can add nothing to the dazzling phonemic display of Milner's article, I still want to return to the sonnet in both its versions to spell out their allusions and differences in greater detail.

The tour-de-force rhyme scheme had only the slightest changes between 1868 (ABAB ABAB baa bba) and 1887 (ABAB ABAB bba bab): in the final line Mallarmé replaced *se fixe* with *septuor*; *rixe* disappeared from the eleventh line of the 1868 version to make room for the displacement of *se fixe*, as part of the general transposition of rhymes in the two final tercets in 1887. Of course, it was Mallarmé's quixotic search for rhymes in 'yx' that generated the neologism/ archaism *ptyx*. In a frequently quoted letter to Eugène Lefébure (May 3, 1868) he sought more information about the curious Greek noun:

> I made a sonnet and have only three rhymes in yx. Try to send me the real meaning of the word *ptyx*: I have been assured that it has none in any language, which I would greatly prefer, for this would give me the charm of having created it by the magic of rhyme.

Presumably he would have had the confirmation that the noun 'ptux' (*ptyx*) is not to be found anywhere in Classical Greek. It seems to be related to the verb *ptusso*, meaning 'to fold' (*pli* ['a fold'] is a key term in Mallarmé's oeuvre). Its dictionary entry presumes an imaginary nominative *ptux* to account for the oblique cases of *ptuchis*... *et al.* where the letter *xi* [ksi] becomes *chi* [chi]. Later he wrote to Dr. Henri Cazalis (July 18, 1868):

> I have extracted this sonnet which I dreamed up one day this summer from a projected study of *the Word*: it is inverse, I have to say that the

meaning if it has one (but I am consoled on the other hand by the dose of poetry it contains, in my opinion) is evoked by the internal mirage of the words themselves… I took the subject of an empty sonnet [*sonnet nul*] which reflects itself in every way because my work is so well prepared and stratified, representing as it can, the Universe, that I would not have known, without damaging any of my graded impressions, how to take anything out – and no sonnet would have occurred.

'Mirage interne' would describe primarily the creation of 'ptyx' from the contagion of the rare rhyme scheme. But just as well, the metaphor of 'onyx' for the 'ongles' derives from that contagion, and the insertion of the adverb 'sitôt' in the revision of the final line from the letters of 'septuor' with one of the three 'i's within 'scintillations.' Finally, when the poet moved 'aboli' from the third to the fifth line, he anagrammatized it to create 'bibelot' as a perfect substitute for 'vaisseau'; for it not only reflects the etonym 'biblos' (book), but reduces the allegorized sonnet form to a knick-knack or a preserved curiosity of auditory inanity.

The following resumé precedes Milner's essay – (I presume the author himself wrote it):

The word ptyx appears in a Mallarmé poem published in 1887. To establish its meaning, one must closely reexamine the Sausurian distinction between *signifié* and *significant*. The *significant* depends on Indo-European linguistics, in the version formulated by Franz Bopp. Mallarmé used it; the proof comes from his *Les Mots anglais*.

The article attempts to demonstrate that the sequence /ptyks/ allows in its permutations and modifications the entre framework of possible consonants found in all Indo-European words.

Mallarmé would have held no illusions about Proto-Indo-European as the Adamic language. He knew it was merely the *terminus ad quem* to which his French might be retraced. The failure of the Greek noun **ptuch* (*ptyx*) to survive in the fragmentary literature preserved from Pre-classical and Classical times is further evidence of the discontinuities in the chains of linguistic transmission of even the best documented tree of languages.

The *ptyx* lacks the vowel /a/ which Bopp considered fundamental to Indo-European. Milner contends that that /a/ is what the poet goes searching for in the river Styx. Starting from there, one can illuminate both the poetic function of the *ptyx* at the heart of the poem and the poem itself. The hypothesis of anagrams becomes a rich clue, in this regard.

Between the composition of the two versions of the sonnet, Anatole Mallarmé, the poet's eight-year-old son, died. Milner successfully accounts for the changed tone and several terms by pointing to the elegiac aspects of "Ses purs ongles...", especially 'ce seul objet' that the Master seeks in the Styx. The *seul objet* would be the vowel 'A' – found twice in 'Anatole' – missing from the concatenation of phonemes in *ptyx*. The Hellenic cast of the sonnet might be construed to support this quest for the missing name. Not only is Anatole a French version of *anatole*, the Classical Greek word for 'sunrise,' the Maître himself went by the Greek version of his baptismal name, Étienne Mallarmé: he Hellenized the first name to Stéphane, from Greek *stephanos*, meaning 'crowned'.

Octavio Paz took the *ptyx* to be a conch shell, following Gardner Davies in his otherwise splendid reading of the early version of the sonnet.[1] But the *ptyx* is *not* an object in the phenomenal world; it isn't even a copy of Bopp's *Vergleichende Grammatik des Sanskrit, Zend, Griechischen, Lateinischen, Litthauischen, Altslawischen, Gotischen und Deutschen* (1833-1852), resting on the credence, even though it was already in process of being 'aboli' by Karl Brugmann's 5-volume *Grundriss* (outline of Indo-European languages), published from 1886–1893. As most of the numerous commentators agree, the poem annuls phenomenal references. I would go further still: the annulment is itself one of the chief subjects of the poem. The *ptyx* is the only object that Nothingness honors – because it is *nothing* or the icon of

---

[1] See Octavio Paz, "Stéphane Mallarmé: Sonnet in 'ix'," trans. Agnes Moncy, in *Delos* 4 [1970], pp. 14-28; on p. 19 Paz refers of Garder Davies's *Mallarmé et Le Drame Solaire* [Paris, 1959].

annulment itself. All of its connotations are negated, erased. Thus, it is NOT the folds or any folded object such as a conch shell conjured by the surviving oblique cases of *ptuch*. If the Greek word connotes 'pnyx,' it is only to deny that the Hill of Justice in Athens has any metonymic force here. More cogently, any contagion to the 'pyx' of Catholic ritual is negated. The word itself comes from the Greek for the 'boxwood' from which the vessel that holds the viaticum communion wafer is carried. (It is traditionally housed to the north of the altar.) There is no pyx – nor any Real Presence of the sacrificed Master within the *ptyx*. The change of 'consoles' to 'crédances' doubles the religious allusion only to undermine it. There is nothing to believe. The credence is not an altar, but merely an item of bourgeois furniture. But not even that: all these 'things' are merely words, letters, phonemes. Nothing else emanates from the scene – just inane sounds forming the derived Indo-European words of a sonnet with no more substance than that of a pronoun reflecting a noun in a dying reverberation of echoes.

There is even an annulment of the momentarily vivid connotation of Holy Saturday – when the consecrated hosts are removed from the altar, and the tabernacle where it is usually kept is left open to emphasize its emptiness. On that day, the Church celebrates the descent of Christ to Harrow Hell. But in both versions of the sonnet the Master has gone to scoop water (later tears) from the Styx with a framework Casserole or Dipper – like the sieves of the Danaids – that can hold nothing. If the Catholic ritual is conjured, the sonnet emphatically negates that liturgical drama.

Over and over the language repeats the void, in dream, forgetting, death, and Nothingness: *rêve... cinéraire amphore... vide... nul ptyx... Néant... nord vacante... défunte... l'oubli...* The only phenomena here are astronomical – the rotation of the earth creating the illusion of day and night, a gradual (*vespéral*) change of light that hides and then reveals the stars that are always there anyway. But the seven stars forming an asterism shaped like a pan that the French call Casserole and Anglophones a Dipper, is in truth merely an illusion of perspective, flattening out an array of stars millions of light years apart from each other, in different depths of space. Yet we figure them, constellate them, into terrestrial creatures, animals (Ursa Major), mythic heroes and household objects.

Milner aptly begins his book with the bold declaration: 'The constellations do not exist; only the stars that compose them exist.' Just so, we artificially posit 'minuit', the indeterminate point when 'aujourd'hui' becomes 'hier' and 'demain' becomes 'aujourd'hui.' To resolve the temporal contradiction between midnight and dusk in the poem, Milner reads 'ce minuit' as a metaphor for 'Angoisse'. He writes: 'le démonstratif *ce* n'est pas un déictique, mais il recatégorise: Angoisse *comme* un minuit, precipitant le sujet dans le noire reverie.' (p. 61) As a metaphor for Angoisse, rather than as a designation for the time of the poetic event, it allows Milner to read the quatrains in opposition to the tercets – a interpretation he grounds on the word 'mais' that begins the tercets; for both 'minuit' and 'mais' appear only in the sonnet of 1889. This reading encourages us to understand 'Angoisse' as an ephemeral and perspectival illusion, as artificial and insubstantial as the arbitrary invention of Midnight.

In a metonymic orgy of Pathetic Fallacies, the diminution of a ray of sunlight, occasioned by nothing more than the planet's rotation, becomes gold (*or*) and dies a slow death (*agonise*). The process mythologizes itself as the conflagration of the Phoenix (naturally, under Mallarmé's obsessive negative sign), and even the pseudo-baroque framework of a mirror suggests unreal beings: unicorns fleeing a fire and kicking with their hind legs (*ruant*) a dead mermaid (*nixe…défunte*) into the cloudy depths of a mirror: for 'nue' puns human nudity into a cloud. As the mythic connotations unravel the tales of Hercules and Deinara, or Ixion and Hera – of course negated – the seven stars, turned musical as a Septet, may be reflected in the fourteen mirroring lines of every sonnet.

'Le septuor' appears in both versions of the sonnet. It is another keystone in the connotations of the poetic tradition Mallarmé inherited. At the start of Canto 30 of the *Purgatorio,* Dante invokes the seven stars of the dipper (*Quando il settentrïon del primo cielo*) echoing the seven oxen (*septem triones*) of Virgil's *Georgics* and Boethius's *Consolation of Philosophy*. The complex analogy of the 'settentrïon' to the seven gifts of the Holy Spirit sets the scene for the *disappearance* of Virgil and the meeting of Dante and Beatrice, and thus, for the only utterance of the Pilgrim's name in all of the *Commedia*. Milner, without reference to Dante, argues that the Septuor refers to the seven letters in Anatole's name. Although the nomenistic flurry of *Purgatorio 30* might support this, Milner makes no attempt to account for the Septuor in the version Mallarmé composed long before Anatole Mallarmé was born.

Of course, the seven letters of 'septuor' reflect the seven of 'nul ptyx,' taken together to allegorize the fourteen lines of every sonnet. As the afternoon light wanes, obscuring the *nul ptyx*, its visual echo, the ghostly *septuor*, casts its reflection. Mallarmé thus acknowledges that the vestiges of representation are ineluctable even in the erasure of conventional diction, even in the most self-referential of sonnets.

Scholars argue whether or not Dante's settentrïon designates the Big Bear (Dipper) or the Little Bear. We know from Mallarmé's letter to Cazalis, about the first version of the poem, that he had 'le grand Ourse' in mind. But, of course, he knew that the asterism of its stars was mirrored by the seven of the lesser Bear, just as it is doubled by the mirror image in the poem, to make up the fourteen points corresponding to a sonnet's lines. He would also have known the passage in the Book of Amos (5:8) where the seven stars of the Pleiades (so designated in French translations of the Bible) are linked to the passage of day and night and to God's name. As a teacher of English, he might even have been familiar with the wonderful translation of that line in the King James Version:

> Seek him that maketh the seven stars and Orion, and turneth the shadow of death into the morning, and maketh the day dark with night: that calleth for the waters of the sea, and poureth them out upon the face of the earth: The Lord is his name.

By calling the asterism 'le Septuor' the Maître aligns the stars with music. There is also a subtle association with language. Ever since Johann Bayer assigned Greek letters to stars based on magnitude in *Uranometria* (1603), astronomers followed his lead, labelling the brightest star Alpha, the next Beta, etc. Furthermore, Psalm 147:4 praises God for his infinite naming of the stars: 'He numbers the multitudes of stars; and calls them all by names.' (in the Septuagint Psalm 146:4 [sic] is *ho arithmon plethe ástron kaì pâsin autoîs onómata kalon*.

William Blake, who knew the Bible better than Mallarmé, and surely gave it more credence, explicitly saw the starry sky as a text. In Plate 91 of *Jerusalem*, we find:

> Los reads the Stars of Albion! the Spectre reads the Voids
> Between the Stars; among the arches of Albions Tomb sublime

Blake was not widely known or read in the Nineteenth Century, but Swinburne wrote to the French poet about him in February, 1876. Mallarmé replied that Swinburne's *William Blake: A Critical Essay* was 'one of the best aesthetical readings made by a poet.' Furthermore, W. B. Yeats attended some of Mallarmé's Tuesday salons when he visited Paris. He was largely responsible for initiating the serious attention to Blake's long prophetic poems through *The Symbolical System of William Blake* (1893), which he co-authored with Edwin John Ellis. It is possible Mallarmé, who shared Yeats's fascination with the revival of hermeticism in his time, saw the three-volume tome. Blake's hermetic astronomy may even account for the change from 'water' to the 'tears' (l'eau/pleurs) the Maître tries to scoop from the Styx with the sieve-like dipper, if Mallarmé heeded the famous couplet from 'The Tyger:'

> When the stars threw down their spears

And water'd heaven with their tears[2]

The opposition of the natural order of astronomy (night and day) and the imaginary order of language, poetry and myth occurs both instantly (*sitôt*) and over time. In this respect the change of 'encore' (still, yet, even) to 'encore que' is significant: the temporal designation changes into a contrary-to-fact conjunction (although) to do the work previously assigned to *sinon que* (except, save that) in the earlier sonnet, while the reflexive verb 'se fixe' need not change at all to shift from the present active to the subjunctive voice in the contrary-to-fact clause.

By removing the title "Sonnet allégorique de lui-même" the poet erased the ambiguity whereby the sonnet allegorized at once both the sonnet form and the reflexive pronoun. Yet he consoled the poem by adding a new pronoun, 'Elle,' to start the last tercet. Grammatically, it seems unambiguous, if it refers back to the 'nixe.' But that mermaid is itself a lexical and mythological oddity. A *nixe* is a German mermaid. Mallarmé not only chose the feminize form of the loan word – attested in the poetry of Heinrich Heine – he underlined it by juxtaposing the pronoun, 'elle.' Yet 'elle' – naked, dead, and cloudy – is no sooner conjured than she instantly disappears into the imaginary space of the mirror. Mallarmé invented and annihilated its reference in one spontaneous poetic gesture.

Pronouns are slippery. They are capable of standing in for all the nouns of their number and gender. So, according to Ellen Burt, 'croisée' is a viable candidate for *elle*'s reference; or even, if proleptic, it could take either 'défunte' or 'nue' as its reference,

---

[2] See Robert Essick, *Blake and the Language of Adam* (New York: Oxford University Press, 1989) and R. Paul Yoder, "Unlocking Language: Self-Similarity in Blake's Jerusalem," in *Romantic Circles*, (March 2001) and Nelson Hilton, *Literal Imagination: Blake's Vision of Words* (Berkeley: University of California Press, 1983), especially chapter 9 "Stars and other Bright Words". In the essay that Mallarmé extolled, Swinburne called "The Tyger" 'that most famous of Blake's lyrics,... a poem beyond praise for its fervent beauty and vigour of music.' He did not quote the couplet but paraphrased it thus: 'Or, when the very stars, and all the armed children of heaven, the 'helmed cherubim' that guide and the 'sworded seraphim' that guard their several planets, wept for pity and fear at sight of this new force of monstrous matter seen in the deepest night as a fire of menace to man...'

since both are simultaneously feminine nouns and matching adjectives ('naked corpse', or 'dead cloud').³

In recasting "Sonnet allégorique de lui-même" as "Se spurs ongles…", the poet introduced a new feminine noun as the subject of the opening sentence: 'L'angoisse.' Poetically, but not syntactically, it replaces 'Crime'. The latter, etymologically derived from Latin *crimen* via Old French *crimne*, carries the connotation of a mortal sin. In the course of the earlier sonnet the crime or sin turns out to be the human propensity to constellate, mythologize, and project its temporal and spatial limitations on the phenomenal universe. Whereas 'Crime' is objective *sub specie aeternitatis*, 'L'Angoisse' is radically subjective. Derived from /angh/ through Latin *angustus*, it evokes the physical 'tightness' of psychic and moral pain. Its pronoun would be 'elle' as well; perhaps the very same 'Elle' of line twelve.

The close proximity of the words 'pur' and 'lampadophore' floating through both versions may point to yet another literary and philosophical allusion and its ineluctable denial.

The dying Socrates of *Phaedo* tells his coterie of followers of the purer and brighter realm beyond phenomena into which he happily dies. In *Phaedo* 110c, the Greek comparative 'lamprotéron' means brighter: ek lamprotéron kaì katharotéron he toúton.

I have italicized the phrase in David Gallop's translation:

> Well then, my friend, first of all the true earth, if one views it from above, is said to look like those twelve-piece leather balls, variegated, a patchwork of colours, of which our colours here are, as it were, samples that painters use. There the whole earth is of such colours, indeed of colours *far brighter still and purer than these*: one portion is purple, marvellous for its beauty, another is golden, and all that is white is whiter than chalk or snow; and the earth is composed of the other colours likewise, indeed of colours more numerous and beautiful than any we have seen.⁴

---

3 See Ellen Burt, "Mallarmé's 'Sonnet en yx': The Ambiguities", in *Modern Crtiicial Views: Stéphane Mallarmé*, ed. Harold Bloom, (Chelsea House, 1987).
4 Plato, *Phaedo*, trans. with notes by David Gallop (Oxford: Clarendon Press, 1975), p. 64.

The purity of which Socrates speaks here and in *Phaedo*: *katheràn en kathere keîsthai toi ouranoi* [109b] describes a cosmic mythos of the purer sky beyond the deceptive atmosphere of the earth:

> and the earth itself is *set in the heaven, a pure thing in pure surroundings*, in which the stars are situated, and which most of those who usually describe such things name 'aether.'

Yet, for our poet, there is no sky. The blue canopy – celebrated and decried in 'L'Azur' (1846) with many of the same terms – is merely an illusionary veil blocking out the depths of the void on those parts of the planet flooded with blinding sunlight – a 'pure Crime.' Socrates, like Mallarmé's favorite avatar of Anguish at midnight, Hamlet, is yet another dead Maître, gone to scoop tears from the Styx with a sieve.

The Maître is also the poet himself. Both sonnets describe the divestiture of subjectivity, leaving a space or room desolated, where phonemes alone constellate themselves into an inane septet and its reflection. But there isn't even a true septet in the structure of a sonnet: its fourteen lines break into two quatrains and two triads. The ferocious negation abolishes every noun once it is proposed. Both incarnations of the sonnet use two sentences interrupted by a parenthetical observation that the master has gone to the land of the dead. In the early sonnet the 'la nuit' takes the verb 'allume' to light up the onyx nails of the torch-bearer. The oxymoron, that night might be a source of illumination, reflects the poet's famous declaration in "Crise de verse" (1886/92/96) that the word 'nuit' is bright while 'jour' emits dark sounds. And then 'un or' uses 'incite' to set the brawl going between unicorns and mermaids.

In "Ses purs ongles…", L'Angoisse uses 'soutient' to hold up the Platonic torch, and again 'or' serves as the subject of the final sentence, but its verb, 'Agonise' is the mirror image of the initial noun. The subject of the latter sentence in both poems is a curious word: *or*. 'Or' is really two incompatible words, a noun and an adverb or a conjunction, claiming two different derivations; the noun from *aurum* and the adverb from *hora*. The army of commentators agree in taking 'or' to be the noun meaning 'gold.' Noting that it stands as a metonymy for a ray of light, probably refracted off of the gilded 'cadre' of the unicorns and mermaids. The image of dying light fits neatly with this inevitable reading of 'un or... agonise' and even allows for the more oblique inciting of mythic action in its last flickering pulse.

The article 'un' might give the conjunction 'or' a substantive force, but it would be difficult to accept its personification as dying or inciting without a radical shift of context. The indexical word, 'or,' is an ambiguous, even flexible adverbial conjunction, meaning 'now', 'yet', or 'but.' Nevertheless, both versions, and the latter especially, are spectacular condensations of syntactical fireworks, from an ablative absolute to a concessive clause, amid a flurry of appositions and locative prepositional phrases. In a purely linguistic context an adverbial conjunction of time or of qualification might be said either to get started or to bring to a close a fragile visual image, subjunctively stabilized for an instant.

Intimidated by the brilliance of Milner's phonemic discoveries, I have concentrated so far on the lexical and etymological ramifications of the poems. There is yet another dimension to its range of allusions, and perhaps even to the origins of its composition. It is grounded in echoes of Greek, Latin and French poetry. The very rhyme schemes – ABAB ABAB baa bba and ABAB ABAB bba bab – alternate words derived from Greek (Aa) with those derived from Latin (Bb, excepting *nixe*, a German word from Greek *nizo* (according to the Grimm Brothers' great *Deutsches Wörterbuch* of 1856)).

In the evocation of ancient poetry, the oblique case instances of **ptuch* are highly significant. An instance of the word appears in a puzzling moment in the sixth book of the *Iliad*. Scholars presume Homer's epic dated from a preliterate era. Certainly, the action of the poem precedes the use of writing; there is only one instance of it: *Iliad*, 6. 169 – Glaucus tells the story of his father, Bellerophon, who was exiled for killing his brother. He was sent away with a note to have him killed. Of course, he was unlettered, but the Iliadic version presumes both the sender and the receiver of the note could read. The crucial line is:

grâpsas en nínaki ptuktôi thumophthóra pollá
(written many terrible things in a folded tablet)

Ptuko would be the dative singular of *ptuch*, the unrecorded nominative.

An even more important use of the term can be found in Pindar's "First Olympian Ode," the initial work in all standard collections of the greatest Greek lyric poet. His epinician odes are complex, labyrinthian poems, honouring an athlete and/or his patron, while weaving mythological references with gnomic reflections on the sublimity of poetry. In *Olympian l*.105 we find:

…emè dè stephanôsai
keînon hippíoi nómoi
Aíoleïdi molpaî
chré: pépoitha dè xénon
mé tin' amphótera kalón te hídrin amaî kai dúnamin kuriôteron
tôn ge nûn Kutaîsi daidalosémen húmnon ptuchaîs
(I must crown that man with the horse-song in the Aeolian strain. I am convinced that there is no host in the world today who is both knowledgeable about fine things and more sovereign in power, *whom we shall adorn with the glorious folds of song*.)

According to Basil Gildersleeve (whose commentary was published long after Mallarmé first issued "Sonnet allégorique de lui-même" and two years before the revision, in his *Pindar: The Olympian and Pythian Odes* [New York. Harper and Brothers, 1885]), the dative plural *ptuchaîs* refers to ''sinuous songs', this in and out of choral song and music and dance.' We don't know how Mallarmé would have interpreted *ptuchaîs*, or even if Lefébure actually sent him the reference. I like to think that he did, because

"Olympian 1" begins with a couplet possibly bearing on the 'or' of sonnets:

> Áriston mèn húdor, ho dè chrusòs aithómenon pûr
> háte diaprépei nuktì megánoros éxocha ploûtou
> (Water is best, and *gold*, a blazing fire that stands out in the night supreme of all lordly wealth.)

There they are: gold, the blazing (torch) fire at night, and water... at the start of the opening poem of arguably the greatest lyric poet of the ancient world. But *hudor* does not *sound* like *l'eau*, nor does *chrusos* resemble *or*; even though the Greek word for fire, *pur*, is a homophone to *purs*. To *hear* the reverberations of ancient sonorous inanities in the great poetic tradition, Mallarmé had to turn to Latin. For instance, if he wanted to look up the *locus classicus* for the Phoenix, he would have turned to Ovid's *Metamorphosis,* book XV, lines 391ff:

> Haec tamen ex aliis generis primordia ducunt,
> una est, quae reparet seque ipsa reseminet, ales:
> Assyrii phoenica vocant; non fruge neque herbis,
> sed turis lacrimis et suco vivit amomi.
> Haec ubi quinque suae conplevit saecula vitae,
> ilicis in ramis tremulaeque cacumine palmae
> unguibus et puro nidum sibi construit ore.
> Quo simul ac casias et nardi lenis aristas
> quassaque cum fulva substravit cinnama murra,
> se super inponit finitque in odoribus aevum.
> Inde ferunt, totidem qui vivere debeat annos,
> corpore de patrio parvum phoenica renasci;
> cum dedit huic aetas vires, onerique ferendo est,
> ponderibus nidi ramos levat arboris altae
> fertque pius cunasque suas patriumque sepulcrum
> perque leves auras Hyperionis urbe potitus
> ante fores sacras Hyperionis aede reponit.
> (At length, these creatures receive the basics of life from others: there is one, a bird, which renews itself, and reinseminates itself. The Assyrians name it 'phoenix.' It does not eat herbs, but tears of incense, and cardamom sap. When it has completed five centuries, it then builds a nest in the branches of a swaying palm tree, using only its claws and its pure mouth. As soon as it has lined it with cassia bark,

and smooth spikes of nard, cinnamon and golden myrrh, it settles on top, and ends its life among the perfumes. Out of the body of its father, a little phoenix is reborn, from which, they claim, it ought to live the same number of years. When age has given it manly strength, and it can bear the burden, it lightens the branches of the tall tree of its nest, and piously carries its own cradle, that was its father's tomb, and, reaching Hyperion's city through the light air, lays it down before the sacred doors of Hyperion's temple.)

'Unguibus et puro' in line 397 might well have triggered 'ongles au pur' and later 'purs ongles' in our Poet's ear.

Ignoring the classical poets, Milner cites two French authors central to the Maître's heart; for Victor Hugo and Charles Baudelaire were le Maître's maîtres. Milner mentions Hugo only in passing here. Like most of the previous commentators he notes that the word 'ptyx' could be found in Hugo's philosophical poem 'Le Satyre' from his epic *La Légende des siècles* (1859). In fact, he very slightly misses the point when he calls Hugo's Ptyx 'le nom proper d'une colline de Rome, le Janicule' (p. 45). Here is the passage from 'Le Satyr' with the line in my italics:

> Un satyre habitait l'Olympe, retiré
> Dans le grand bois sauvage au pied du mont sacré;
> Il vivait là, chassant, rêvant, parmi les branches;
> Nuit et jour, poursuivant les vagues formes blanches.
> Il tenait à l'affût les douze ou quinze sens
> Qu'un faune peut braquer sur les plaisirs passants.
> Qu'était-ce que ce faune ? On l'ignorait ; et Flore
> Ne le connaissait point, ni Vesper, ni l'Aurore
>
> Qui sait tout, surprenant le regard du réveil;
> On avait beau parler à l'églantier vermeil,
> Interroger le nid, questionner le souffle,
> Personne ne savait le nom de ce maroufle.
> Les sorciers dénombraient presque tous les sylvains;
> Les aegipans étant fameux comme les vins,
> En voyant la colline on nommait le satyre;
> On connaissait Stulcas, faune de Pallantyre,
> Gès, qui, le soir, riait sur le Ménale assis,
> Bos, l'aegipan de Crète; on entendait Chrysis,
> *Sylvain du Ptyx que l'homme appelle Janicule,*

Qui jouait de la flûte au fond du crépuscule;
Anthrops, faune du Pinde, était cité partout;
Celui-ci, nulle part; les uns le disaient loup;
D'autres le disaient dieu, prétendant s'y connaître;
Mais, en tout cas, qu'il fût tout ce qu'il pouvait être,
C'était un garnement de dieu fort mal famé.
(A satyr lived at Olympus
in a great wild forest at the foot of the holy mountain
he lived there, hunting, dreaming amid the branches
night and day, following vague white forms
on the lookout for what passing pleasures a faun's
twelves or fifteen senses might catch.
Who was this faun? One did not know. Even Flore
knew nothing of him, nor Vesper, nor Aurora
who knows everything, surprising [even] the wakeup glance.
Ask the birdnest, ask the wind,
nobody knew the name of this maroufle.
The magicians had counted nearly all the forest creatures;
the capricorns were as well known as wines.
Surveying the hill called the Satyr,
one would know Stulcas, the faun of Pallantyre;
Guess who, sitting on Maenalon, laughs in the evening,
Bos, the capricorn of Crete; one heard Chrysis,
the forest creature of the Ptyx one calls Janiculum,
who plays the flute in the depths of twilight;
Anthrops, the faun of Pindus, was cited everywhere;
this one here, never. Some said he was a wolf,
others called him a god, pretending to know it,
but in any case that was all he might be:
he was a rough brat of a god.)

'Ptyx' is not so much the proper noun for what humans call the Janiculum, but the hill's name in an ur-language of satyrs and faunes. The commentators generally suggest that Mallarmé might have read the Hugo's poem and lodged the word in his unconscious. None of them, including Milner, observed the obvious point that in composing 'L'Après-midi d'un faune' (*circa* 1865), the Maître would probably have looked again at Hugo's poem, even though the comparison *post facto* is a recurring topic of Mallarmé criticism. Apparently, Hugo knew enough Greek to realize that the geological 'fold' of a hill would fall within the range of *ptuch*'s meanings. Consequently, his reader, Mallarmé, would have gathered that 'Ptyx' was a place-name from a time preceding human languages. Even the poet Yves Bonnefoy, in his evocative essay "La hantise du ptyx", ignores the uniqueness of Hugo's satyr-language when he mentions Ptyx only as 'un autre nom de Janicule'. That is all the more remarkable because Bonnefoy reads *ptyx* as a vestige of an 'outre-langage' beyond human words. Furthermore, he wholly accepts the dubious thesis of Anne-Marie France that Mallarmé depended solely upon the definitions for *ptyx* provided by Joseph Planche's *Dictionnaire grec-françois* (1809).[5]

Milner makes more of the allusions to Baudelaire than to Hugo. Commenting on the final tercets of "Ses purs ongles…," he proposes a series of deflationary substitutions from Baudelaire's 'La Beauté': 'Elle' for 'Je suis belle, ô mortels! comme un rêve de pierre'; a dark nocturnal sky for 'Je trône dans l'azur comme un sphinx incompris;' for the 'sphinx incompris' a 'nixe' (needing no special comprehension); a dying cloud for 'un rêve de pierre.' He takes Baudelaire's 'Recueillement' (published in 1868 after "Sonnet allégorique de lui-même" appeared) to inflect only "Ses purs ongles…", insofar as he believed Mallarmé reworked the earlier sonnet in the *angoisse* of grief for Anatole. 'Just as Baudelaire had prophesized the sinking of the sun of Romanticism, Mallarmé prophesized the sinking of the Baudelairean sun.' (p.62). To this I would merely add that Hugo and Baudelaire were such powerful predecessors of the Maître that he might have drawn the penumbra of Pindar and Ovid into his sonnets to deflect the shadows they cast over him.

Perhaps Baudelaire's prose poem 'La Chambre double' encroaches upon the imaginary vision of an interior room even more dramatically. The first-person narrator begins in ecstasy describing the 'crépusculaire' chamber where 'les meubles ont l'air de rêver.' The 'langue muette' of the furniture and décor is a positive mutism, favorably compared to 'soleils couchants'

---

5 See Yves Bonnefoy, *L'imaginarie métaphysique,* (Paris: Seuil, 2006).

because a woman, 'l'Idole', is sleeping in his bed, until an intruder destroys the narrator's timeless pleasure, turning the space into a depressing hovel where nothing matters but 'un seul objet connu me sourit: la fiole de laudanum.' In the end 'Le Temps règne en souverain maintenant; et avec le hideux vieillard est revenu tout son démoniaque cortége de Souvenirs, de Regrets, de Spasmes, de Peurs, d'Angoisses.' The publication date of Baudelaire's *Petits poèmes en prose* – 1869 – after the writing of the first version of the Mallarmé's sonnet – may have thrown exegetes off the scent. Yet our poet would have been able to see its publication in *La Presse* in 1862. In his earlier book, *Mallarmé au tombeau*, Milner elaborately showed how Mallarmé's sonnet, 'Le vierge, le vivace et le bel aujourd'hui' responded to and reversed Baudelaire's great homage to Victor Hugo, 'Le Cygne.' In the same way, Mallarmé divested the interior scene of 'la Chambre double' of its narrator, of its Ideal woman – there isn't even a bed in the room unless, as Jacques Derrida speculated, there is one every time a poet would write 'abo*lit*' – and the crucial 'seul object' is emphatically missing, its consoling opium transformed into the ungraspable tears of Styx water. Mallarmé's interiors are bourgeois salons, not sordid, Baudelairean dumps. Rather than places to bring an ideal woman for sex, they are family rooms, or after 1872 perhaps the locale for Mallarmé celebrated Tuesday evening gatherings of poets and artists.

At times, Milner will relegate some of his most enlightening observations to footnotes. In the final chapter ("Le sociologue cruel") of *Profils perdus de Stéphane Mallarmé* he returns to the notion of *nul* in his analysis of the key word, *pénultième*, of the prose poem "Le Démon d'analogie." I shall translate all of his note 5 to that chapter:

> The reader won't fail to spot the preview of the word *nul*, that one rediscovers in the two versions of the poem in – x, as *nul ptyx*. The older of them is practically contemporary with *Le Démon d'analogie*. One will note that the phonemes buried in *pénultième* and *nul ptyx* intersect: /p/, /n/, /u/, /l/, /t/; even the /i/ semi-vowel in *ptyx* and

semi-consonant in – *ième* reflect each other. The sole divergence occurs in the name of the letter *m* and the presence of the letter *x*, two symbols used in algebra, often to indicate the unknown. (p. 132)

In the main text, Milner offered a phonological reading of the sentence obsessing the narrator of *Le Démon d'analogie*: 'la pénultième est morte.' Pointing out that in the late Nineteenth Century the letter *k* was omitted from the twenty-five letter French alphabet as a foreign (i.e. Germanic) element (and adding that Mallarmé would have similarly excluded *x* from Greek), the phonemic repetition of em/ em from *–ième est m*(orte) – stresses the name ('em') of the middle letter of the alphabetic sequence.

Yet there are still more reasons to consider "Le Démon d'analogie" in a discussion of the two poems in -yx. Yves Bonnefoy implies a connection by couching his analysis of the word *ptyx* in the language of "Le Démon d'analogie" without ever citing the prose-poem explicitly. However, aside from the suggestions of Milner and Bonnefoy, the prose-poem calls for our attention because it is a text about a primarily linguistic phenomenon. This time Mallarmé employs a Baudelairean first person narrator, who is shocked by the uncanny materialization of a verbal tic in the domain of visual objects. But unlike Baudelaire's passionate confessors, the protagonist of "Le Démon d'analogie" is the purely passive vessel besieged by the secular Visitation of odd sensations, verbal sounds and corresponding sights. He steps out of his apartment with the sensation of a wing gliding over a stringed instrument and a voice chanting the words 'La pénultième est morte' in a lowering tone ('sur un ton descendant').

'The penult' is a linguistic term commonly used in prosody, referring to the accent on the next to last syllable of a word. Here the predicate turns the paroxytone into an allegory of itself, insofar as the penultimate syllable of *pénultième* is *nul*, proving that even linguistic terminology is susceptible to poetic connotations; for an autonomous word hidden within an unrelated word is the very paradigm of connotation. In its original publication in 1874, the prose poem was entitled 'La Pénultième.' It might as aptly have been retitled 'The Demon of Connotation.'

The prose poem throws some light on the more obscure, or controversial, aspects of the two sonnets in -yx. If the term, *la pénultième*, can be the agent of poetic action, why not the adverb *or* and the pronoun *lui-même*? In 'Le Démon d'analogie' the human agent hears the recurring sentence as if it were a verse; the descending oxytone of *pénultième* indicates a line break, after which the 'est morte' is 'vide de signification' presumably because it is a redundancy following musical chord of *nul*, sounding as if a wing or a palm caressed a lute.

The voice repeating the phrase detaches itself from the agent until, with a shock, he sees reflected in the glass of a musical instrument shop window the image of his hand caressing the feathers and palm leaves below the hanging instruments. The metalepsis of proceeding from abstract, linguistic and musical terms and sensations to the concrete visual correlatives of those sensations constituted an 'intervention du surnaturel' triggering 'l'angoisse sous laquelle agonise mon esprit...' Thus, in revising the sonnet nul as "Ses purs ongles...," the Maître imported the pleonastic noun/verb sequence 'l'Angoisse... agonise...' to serve as the master sentence of his revision.

In *Mallarmé au tombeau* and more extensively in *Profils perdus*, Milner reads 'la penultième est morte' as the poet's declaration of the end to the revolutionary aspirations that repeatedly convulsed France since the end of the Eighteenth Century. He identified *la penultième* as the politically significant day before the last which has 'already been devalued in advance,' 'always completely forgotten.' Noting the pun on 'lutte' (struggle) implicit in the shop of the 'luthier' (lute maker), he saw the old instruments as signs of the passé lyricism of the French Romantic poets, and the bird wings and palm fronts decoratively scattered on the floor of the window display as taxidermic leftovers from Baudelaire's Cygne; for the word *palme* applied, in the Nineteenth Century, to 'palmipèdes' fowl.

But "Le Démon d'analogie" owes as much to Baudelaire's prose poem 'Le mauvais vitrier' as "Sonnet allégorique de lui-même" does to 'La Chambre double.' In its turn, 'Le mauvais vitrier' closely follows Edgar Allen Poe's 'The Imp of the Perverse."' The descent from Poe to Mallarmé charts a progressive de-dramatization and transposition from the objective realm of 'crime' to the interiority of poetics. Mallarmé even uses Poe's term when he speaks of the 'perversité' of the contradictory luminosity of certain words in "Crise de vers": 'A côté d'*ombre*, opaque, *ténèbres* se fonce peu; quelle déception, devant la perversité conférant à *jour* comme à *nuit*, contradictoirement, des timbres obscur ici, là clair.' (Next to *ombre*, opaque, *ténèbres* darkens a bit; what deception, in the face of the perversity of conferring upon *jour* as if it were *nuit*, contradictorily, dark tones here, there light.) Poe's narrator awaits his execution for giving into the imp of the perverse by impulsively confessing a murder from which he had escaped punishment; Baudelaire's abuses a glazier for failing to adhere to his self-deceptive but consoling aesthetics; but Mallarmé's narrator – little more than the pronoun 'je' – has decidedly less 'personality' than the voice that continually repeats a phrase within his mind.

In 'Le mauvais vitrier', Baudelaire describes the perverse impulse that possesses him to harass a glazier descrying his wares on the street before his apartment. First, he calls him up, hoping he might break the panes of glass he carries on his back as he negotiates the seven flights of stairs; then he insults and dismisses him because he has no rose-tinted glass. All his panes are transparent, and thereby incapable of lending aesthetic coloring to the exterior world; and finally, he drops a flower pot on him when he regains the street, shattering 'toute sa pauvre fortune,' while repeatedly shouting 'la vie en beau!' In the weaponized 'petit pot de fleurs' there may even by a sly allusion to *Les Fleurs du Mal*.

In rejecting the glazier's transparent glass, Baudelaire connoted the failure of direct, unfiltered denotation to evoke beauty: '...des vitres de paradis? Impudent que vous êtes! vous osez vous promener dans des quartiers pauvres, et vous n'avez pas même de vitres qui fassent voir la vie en beau!' (... some windows of Paradise? How rude you are! You dare to walk through poor neighborhoods and you don't even have windows that make one see life as beautiful!). Baudelaire's fictive subjects respond directly to the material world; the sexualized presence of the Ideal woman sensualizes the entire environment in 'La chambre double;' her absence depresses it, driving the subject to the artificial paradise of drugs. The transparency of uncolored glass symbolizes denotative language, while connotative tints are needed to sensualize the world it simultaneously exhibits and separates from the perverse/ poetic subject.

Mallarmé reversed and radically depersonalized Baudelaire's aesthetic epistemology: the panes of his allegorical windows are never the transparent media separating the subject from whatever phenomena can be seen through them. They always reflect his ghostly gestures and reveal expiring reminders of the inescapable, but bizarre, referentiality of language (even the technical language of prosody). Language comes first, folded upon itself. It can generate a subject, sometimes a mere pronoun, in order to haunt the poem (rather than the absent poet or his abolished narrator) with intoxicating sounds and teasing sights, just as it forecasts the symbols that might be taken for real objects. In "Crise de vers" Mallarmé offered a theoretical justification for this process:

> L'œuvre pure implique la disparition élocutoire du poëte, qui cède l'initiative aux mots, par le heurt de leur inégalité mobilisés; ils s'allument de reflets réciproques comme une virtuelle traînée de feux sur des pierreries, remplaçant la respiration perceptible en l'ancien souffle lyrique ou la direction personnelle enthousiaste de la phrase.
> (The pure work implies the elocutionary disappearance of the poet, who hands over the initiative to the words, animated by the clash of their different strengths; they light up their mutual reflections like virtual fireworks on gemstones, replacing perceptible breathing with the ancient lyrical inspiration or the phrase exercising its enthusiastic

personal direction.)

"La Démon d'analogie" dramatizes the 'disparition élocutoire du poëte' by transferring 'direction personnelle enthousiaste' to the phrase 'la pénultième est morte.' Mallarmé's ultimate nullity is the *ptyx,* the black hole through which poets and sonnets disappear.

Stéphane Mallarmé by Félix Nadar

4

The Autobiography of a Metonomy

In his novel *Si gira* (1915) (*Shoot!*), Pirandello focused upon the film industry as both an example and an allegory of the alienation and dehumanization of modern life. His detailed examination of all aspects of film production is not merely the first and most rigorous representation of filmmaking in modern fiction, it is a brilliant compendium of speculations on the implications of the apparatus and the syntax of cinema. No previous essay in film theory can match its depth and range.

Si gira was first serialized in 1915 in six consecutive issues of the distinguished literary and cultural journal *Nuova antologia*, where Pirandello had published since 1902. At that time the Italian film industry commanded international prominence. Italians had pioneered the production of feature length films with the historical epics *The Last Days of Pompeii* (1913) and *Quo Vadis?* (1913). The imaginary reconstruction of Carthage in *Cabiria* (1914) preceded and likely influenced the vision of Babylon in D. W. Griffith's *Intolerance* (1916). Coincident with the emergence of the long spectacular film, the *diva* had just become the central presence in Italian melodramas. Every studio – in Torino, Milano, Rome, Naples – had a female star, an idealized beauty, around whose gestures and bodily presence a drama of eros and thanatos was constructed in film after film with minor variations. In 1916, the year Treves (the publisher of the most distinguished Italian authors in the early Twentieth Century) issued *Si gira* in book form, Antonio Gramsci wrote of Lydia Borelli, the most famous of these divas: 'This woman is a primordial relic of prehistoric humanity. They say they admire her for her art. That's not true. No one can explain the art of la Borelli because it doesn't exist. La Borelli doesn't know how to play anyone but herself.... La Borelli is the artist par excellence of the cinema whose language is the human body in its perpetually renewed plasticity.'[1] In Pirandello's novel, the *femme fatale* La Nesteroff is the diva of the Kosmograph studio. Her incomprehension of the modes of cinematic representation, fused to her instinctive destructiveness, becomes the principal object of Gubbio's obsessive 'study.' Her extreme alienation in her work mirrors his.

Every studio had its own clowns as well. Many of them were French actors: Marcel Fabre was Robinet at L'Ambrosio studios; Ferdinand Guillaume was Tontolini at Cines, and later Polidor at Pasquali; André Deed played Cretinetti at L'Italia. The fictional Kosmograph's Fantappiè represents the native Italian version of this figure. At the Cines studio in Rome, which Pirandello frequently visited, he would have encountered Fernando Guillaume ("Tontolini"), Lea Giunchi ("Lea"), Giuseppe Gambardella ("Kri Kri"), and Eusebio Cavalloni ("Coco"). The Italian short farces remain among the chief glories of the pre-World War I cinema. In addition to their exuberance and genius, they provide us with a guide to the social and cultural commonplaces of the period through the objects of their fun. The clowns often satirize the excesses of the film industry itself. Deed assumed drag to play a diva in *Cretinetti e gli stivali del brasiliano* (*Cretinetti and the Brazilian's Riding Boots*, 1914). Furthermore, several farces included encounters with wild beasts once they became stock elements of the historical epics and melodramas. Since *Quo Vadis?* (for which Cines kept a menagerie of twenty

---

[1] Antonio Gramsci, "In principio era il sesso", *Cronache Torinese* (16 febbraio 1917).

lions), large cats were frequently used in the spectacles. A year earlier for *In pasto ai leoni,* Cines dramatized the lover's revenge of a lion tamer who fed his rival to his fierce cats. The comedians spoofed this flirtation with disaster. At least once the disaster was actual. Guido Aristarco pointed to the mauling of an actress by a leopard (reported in the Torinese journal *Il Maggese Cinematografico* October 25, 1913) as a probable source for the climax of *Si gira*: the attack of the tiger.[2]

This was also the period of the first avant-garde cinema when Italian Futurists made a few films and published film projects. The Futurist manifesto on the cinema appeared in 1916; that is, after the serialization of *Si gira*, but the Futurists began making films in 1912 (none of them survive, although Anton Guilia Bragalia's *Thais* (1916) sets its melodrama before Futurist sets). Some of their projects, for both cinema and the stage, limited all action to the synecdoche of feet.[3] Perhaps the clown of L'Ambrosio studios took advantage of the reputation of this avant-gardist project; for Fabre made *Amor pedestre* (1914) shooting only the feet of his cast in an elliptical narrative in which a dandy slips a note into the shoe of a married woman which her husband finds. A duel follows, after which the wife consoles her wounded lover with sex; the metonymy of her dress falling to her ankles in the final shot apparently did not disturb the censors. For the Futurists the cinema was a prime factor in the mechanical revolution that they hoped would create a cultural revolution in Italy, to drive the nation into parity with the industrial powers of Europe. *Si gira* gauges the spiritual cost of such an enthusiasm.

The Futurists were not alone in their speculations on the potential of cinema to become more than what Gubbio bitterly describes as the 'illogical and extravagant… grotesquely heroic and contradictory… stupid work' that feeds his camera. In 1909

---

[2] See Guido Aristarco, "Il leopardo, l'orso e la tigre," in *La musa inquietante di Pirandello: il Cinema,* eds. Nino Genovese and Sebastiano Gesù (Acicatera: Bonanno editore, 1990), pp. 105-07.

[3] Tom Gunning wrote to me (June 26, 2003) that the 'feet-only film is a long-term genre of early cinema with at least one Italian example from 1908: *The Tale of Lulu as Told by her Feet* (Ambrosio).'

Edmondo De Amicis entitled a short story of the fantasies and impressions of a bored man "Cinematografo cerebrale," equating for perhaps the first time in Italy, the flow of thought with a cinematic sequence. Even earlier Giovanni Papini had urged his fellow philosophers to pay close attention to the cinema. I quote at length from the conclusion of his short essay "The Philosophy of the Cinematograph" (*La Stampa* May 18, 1907), because this very early and important attempt at a film theory, which has never been available to English readers, presents sympathetically some of the principles that alienate Serafino Gubbio.

> So even the cinemas are objects worthy of reflection, and I would strongly advise serious and wise men to attend them more often. They can begin by asking why this luminous spectacle so quickly captured the favor of the crowd. Whoever thought a little about the characteristics of modern civilization will have little difficulty connecting the cinematograph with other facts that reveal the same tendencies. In respect of the theater – which it partially attempts to replace – the cinematograph has the advantage of being a shorter, less tiring, and cheaper spectacle, therefore requiring less time, less energy, less money…. The cinematograph satisfies in one blow all these tendencies toward economy. It is a short phantasmagoria of twenty minutes, which one can attend for thirty or twenty cents. It doesn't demand a great deal of culture, or attention, or energy to follow. It has the advantage of demanding *only one sense*, sight – since no one pays attention to the mediocre and monotonous music that accompanies the unrolling of the film – and this one sense is artificially subtracted from the distractions by means of the Wagnerian darkness of the room which impedes any wandering of the attention, those nods and those glances that are to be observed so frequently in over-lit theaters.
>
> But the current success of the cinematograph not only reflects these rather stingy economic causes. It is also due in great part to other advantages of the cinematograph over the theater, to which it is certainly in so many other ways inferior. The most important of these advantages consists in the *representation in time of vast and complicated events*, which could not be reproduced on the stage despite the most advanced machinery. A hunt with all of its locations, a rescue operation, the launching of a ship, a voyage to the polar regions are spectacles that would require incessant changes of scenes and the most expansive space to give the illusion of verisimilitude. However, in front of the white screen of the cinematograph we have

the sensation that these events are *true events* seen as we might see them in a mirror that could follow their vertiginous path through space – but which give an impression of reality more than from the wings and the painted scenery of the most sophisticated theater.

The cinematograph has the advantage over the theater of offering the spectacle of important real events just a few days after they happen, and not only as a description in words or photographs in an illustrated magazine, but as a succession of movements shot from reality and full of life. In this instance the cinematograph unites the domain of daily journalism with the illustrated magazines: the newspapers describe the fact in time, but without providing images; the magazines give the images, but they are motionless, fixed in space, while the cinematograph gives us visible figures performing in time. It can offer our curiosity what nothing else can give: scenes of transformation.

Thanks to the secrets and tricks of photography that have already produced unreal photographs (a man with his own head in his hands, etc.) and false ghostly photographs (cloudy or transparent human beings), they can obtain from the film the most unreal and extraordinary things: men who suddenly dissolve on the pavement; ...miraculous divisions of bodies; processions of heads without bodies or bodies without heads; statues that come to life... or animals that change into men; men that walk through walls, and everything else a person can imagine in his wildest... dreams. On account of this the cinematograph is an aid to the development of the imagination, a kind of opium without adverse consequences; a visible realization of the most unreal fantasies. Thanks to its photographic deployments, it allows us to think up a world in two dimensions more marvelous than our own.

But if these observations reflect, if only partially, the unforeseen success of the ingenious invention of Lumière, that still does not justify my advice to philosophers. Nevertheless, both moralists and metaphysicians can come for inspiration in these dark halls instead of wandering in the markets or the town squares like Socrates, or among the graves like Hamlet, or on the mountains like Nietzsche. The world the cinematograph presents is full of a great lesson in humility. It is made up merely of *little images of light*, little images in two dimensions that nonetheless give the impression of motion and of life. It is a spiritualized world reduced to its minimum, composed of the most ethereal and angelic material, without depth, without solidity, silent, like a dream, quick, fantastic, unreal. See how human life can reduce itself without giving up verisimilitude!

Contemplating such ephemeral and luminous images of ourselves we feel like gods contemplating their creations, made in their image and likeness. Unwittingly, we are led to think that there is *someone* who looks at us as we look at the cinematographic figures and before whom we – who deem ourselves concrete, real, eternal – would only be colored images that rush quickly to death to give pleasure to their eyes. Might the universe not be a huge cinematographic spectacle, with a few program changes, made to pass the time of a crowd of unknown powers? And just as we discover, thanks to photography, the imperfection of certain movements, the ridiculousness of certain mechanical gestures, the grotesque vanity of human affectations, so these divine spectators guffaw at us as we scurry about this world, running furiously in every way, anxious, stupid, driven, comic until our role ends and we descend one by one into the silent darkness of death. (ellipses mine)

In 1916 Gabrielle D'Annunzio essentially reiterated Papini's enthusiasm for the trick film to an interviewer:

I spent a few hours in a film studio to study the techniques and particularly to take account of the role played by what the professionals call 'tricks.' I think there may emerge from the cinema a charming art, the essence of which would be 'the marvelous.' *The Metamorphoses* of Ovid! There's a true cinematic subject. Technically, there are no limits to the representation of prodigies and dreams.

If, as Francesco Callari has argued in his *Pirandello e il cinema*, (Venice: Marsalio, 1991) Pirandello first conceived of his novel in 1904, abandoned it and then revived it in 1913 under the provisional title, *La tigre* (*The Tiger*), there is good reason to believe that during that crucial decade he was aware of the evolution of filmmaking and film criticism that was making Italy one of the most vital centers for emerging ideas about cinema and cinema one of the most vital artistic phenomena in Italy. The most remarkable artifact of that vitality is the novel, *Si gira*, itself.

Si gira is the autobiography of a metonymy, as if a rhetorical trope could tell its own story. Insofar as six characters could go searching for an author (as they do in Pirandello's best-known play), a trope can generate a fictive autobiography. The remarkable opening sentence poses the epistemological problem that shapes the novel: 'I study people in their most ordinary occupations, to see if I can succeed in discovering in others what I feel I myself lack in everything that I do: the certainty that they understand what they are doing.' The first of many italicized words – *'oltre'* in the Italian text – on the next page, reformulates the lack: 'There is *something more* in everything.'

Metonymies reverse cause and effect, whole and part, container and contained; they leave things out. Only a scrap wood collector or an ironmonger would respond to the enticements of a Bar and Grill, if those metonymies did not indicate the indispensable commodities of the establishment: alcoholic drinks and cooked meals. Metonymy indicates 'there is *something more.*'

The fictive premise of *Si gira* represents the novel as seven consecutively written notebooks kept by Serafino Gubbio, a cameraman for the (fictional) Kosmograph film studio in Rome, perhaps in 1914. The notebook pretense allows Pirandello to narrate his novel from the perspective of a writer who does not know the outcome of his story as he is telling it. In fact, in the second section of the first notebook, he offers his excuse for writing at all:

> I satisfy, by writing, a need to let off steam which is overpowering. I get rid of my professional impassivity, and avenge myself [mi vendico] as well; and with myself avenge ever so many others, condemned like myself to be nothing more than *a hand that turns a handle* [*una mano che gira una manovella*].

Girare is the Italian 'to turn.' The reflexive imperative of the verb, 'si gira!', is the command the director gave to his cameraman – shoot! –, in that period when films were hand cranked. The coming of sound at the end of the Twenties required a mechanical regularity to maintain an even pitch on the soundtrack. Hand-cranking was then replaced by electrical motors. Gone too were the noisy sets of silent filmmaking in which the director could command both the actors and the cameraman all through the scene.

When I claimed *Si gira* is the autobiography of a metonymy, as if a rhetorical trope could tell its own story, I might as well have reframed the final clause: as if an autobiography could be anything other than the narration of a metonymy. Our proper names are conventionally the more or less arbitrary coupling of a saint's name (often shared with an ancestor) and a family name, itself metonymically derived from a trade, a place, or merely the sound of prestige. In western societies these two names are endlessly recycled. The infant is not so often named, as born into his name: he is Luigi to differentiate him from his brothers; they are all Pirandello. The attempt to turn such metonymies into metaphors is one of the allegorical giveaways of fiction, e.g. Stephen Dedalus for 'Martyr Artificer'.

The character who calls himself 'I' writing the notebooks does not reveal a proper name until his friend, Simone Pau, introduces him to an alcoholic violinist in the fifth section of the first notebook: "Serafino,' he said, 'let me introduce to you a great artist.' But he doesn't disclose his surname, Gubbio, before the second section of the second notebook. At the Kosmograph film studio he is denominated by a more radical metonymy – retaining the initial letters of his Christian name and his surname, they nicknamed him 'si gira':

> They greet me:
>   'Hallo, Gubbio.'
>   'Hallo, *Shoot!* [*Si gira*]...'
>   *Shoot*, you understand is my nickname.
>   [Suppose a peaceful tortoise was lurking just in the spot where an ignorant scamp squats to do his business. A little later, the poor unsuspecting beast continues peacefully its slow march with the business of the scamp on its shell, an unanticipated tower.]
>   The difficulties of life!
>   You have lost an eye in it, and your case has been serious. But we are all of us more or less marked, and we never notice it. Life marks us; and fastens a beauty-spot on one, a grimace on another.
>   (Luigi Pirandello, *Shoot*, trans. C.F. Scott Moncrieff, [Chicago: University of Chicago Press, 2005], p. 53] in brackets I have restored in my own translation as the paragraph probably censored in the original 1926 publication of Scott Moncrieff's translation.)

Marked by metonymy: Fantappiè, the studio's comic star and stamper of nicknames, gave it to the cameraman. S/G: 'Si gira'/ Serafino Gubbio. The metonymy reflects a homogram. By writing, that is by inscribing letters in his notebooks, *Si gira* avenges the trope by which he has been stamped, as if shat upon, and at the same time studies the lack inscribed in his nickname.

It should be no surprise, then, that the very first character he encounters, and the last he sees, would be Simone Pau, the figure of metonymy as metaphor, who declares upon their accidental encounter after many years on the very first night of Gubbio's arrival in Rome: ''I am the mountain.' What are we? We are whatever, at any given moment, occupies our attention.' Pau's elective poverty inspires Gubbio's reflections on *superfluidity*, the anguishing hunger for meaning and value that infects consciousness. If Pau tropes the superfluidity as metaphor, Gubbio insists it can only be metonymy.

Gubbio confesses that he writes to avenge himself and others. If the first vendetta drives the extraordinary epistemology of tropes, the revenge for others motivates a more conventional narrative that begins to unfold in the second notebook. For seven pages Pirandello toys with us readers; for we have no reason to know that the nostalgic enthusiasm of the notebook writer for the home and characters of the 'grandparents' is not focused on his own family, until he informs us that he was brought into that house as the Greek and Latin tutor of the grandson, Giorgio Mirelli. Consequently, that ellipsis signals the intensity of identification of tutor with pupil.

The formal irony of the novel is the articulation of how Gubbio's very passivity avenges the suicide of that young man, who had found himself in an unbearable erotic triangle with la Nesteroff (who ends up as the diva of the Kosmograph studio). The banal story of betrayed love and revenge, compounded by the cameraman's affection for a young actress in love with Mirelli's former rival, Aldo Nuti, lurks within the dazzling series of reflections on the epistemology of tropes. Many such melodramas were the ostensible object of the extraordinary tropology of cinematic representation during this remarkable phase of the Italian silent cinema.

With the decline of the centrality of theater in our culture, Luigi Pirandello's reputation has waned. As the preeminent dramatist of the generation following Ibsen and Strindberg he had been the Nobel Laureate of 1934. His fiction, however, always shared the unfortunate fate of all modern Italian writers, eclipsed by the literature of more powerful states – British, French, German, Russian. Yet *Si gira* is an extraordinary novel. It is perhaps the least known of the major European novels of the period just before the First World War; it certainly deserves more attention than it has received, even if it is overshadowed by the very strongest fiction of its time: Proust published *Swann's Way* two years before Pirandello's novel appeared in 1915, which was the year of Joyce's *A Portrait of the Artist as a Young Man* and of Franz Kafka's *The Trial* (which was not published until the author's death a decade later).

However, when *Si gira* is read today, it is largely for its evocation of the ambience of the film studio in the period just prior to the First World War. Although Pirandello was not an enthusiast of the new art, he was such an astute observer and he grasped the aesthetic and moral implications of the elements of cinematographic representation so uncannily that his novel can be seen as the most sophisticated work of film theory of its time. Fortunately for its readers, it is also a brilliant novel.

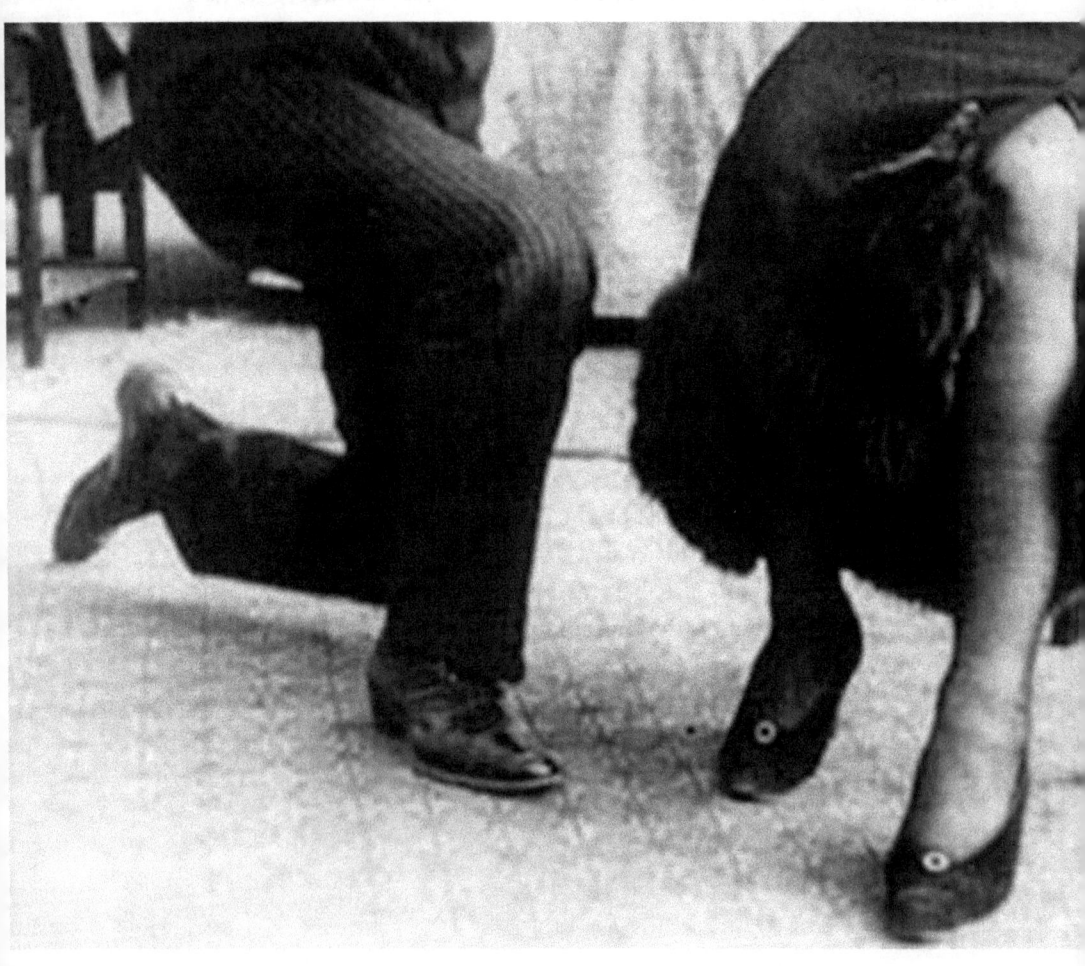

Amor Pedestre (Marcel Fabre, 1914).

5

Naming the Evasive Heart

> I can't blame you for not seeing as much in 'Chaplinesque' as myself because I realize that the technique of the thing is virtuousic and open to all kinds of misinterpretation.
>
> Hart Crane to Gorham Munson, November 3, 1921

The birth of the avant-garde film (ca. 1913), with its premium on originality and on the visible 'signature' of the filmmaker as an artist, was simultaneous with the emergence of several avant-garde movements in literature and the plastic arts – Dada, Suprematism, Futurism. It also coincided with the development of the feature length film and with the international recognition of the first popularly acknowledged film personality, Charlie Chaplin. Yet it was not until 1921 that Chaplin made his own first feature, *The Kid*.

Hart Crane saw *The Kid* in September of 1921, the year the film was released. On the first of October, he wrote to his friend Gorham Munson about it:

> Comedy, I may say, has never reached a higher level before.
> We have (I cannot be too sure of this for my own satisfaction) in

Chaplin a dramatic genius that truly approaches the fabulous sort. I could write pages on the overtones and brilliant subtleties of this picture, for which nobody but Chaplin can be responsible, as he wrote it, directed it, – and I am quite sure had much to do with the settings which are unusually fine. If you have not seen it in New York, it may now be in Paris. It was a year late in arriving in Cleveland, I understand, on account of the state board of censors!!!! What they could have possibly objected to, I cannot imagine. It must have been some superstition aroused against good acting! But they will always release any sickening and false melodrama of high life and sex, lost virginities, etc. Well, I am thankful to get even what their paws have mauled of the Caligari sort. My poem is a sympathetic attempt to put in words some of the Chaplin pantomime, so beautiful and so full of eloquence, and so modern.

The poet must have been composing "Chaplinesque" at the time he wrote that letter, for on October 6 he wrote again, forwarding the rest of the poem:

Here you are with the rest of the Chaplin poem. I know not if you will like it, – but to me it has real appeal, I have made that 'infinitely gentle, infinitely suffering thing' of Eliot's into the symbol of the kitten. I feel that, from my standpoint, the pantomime of Chaplin represents fairly well the futile gesture of the poet in the U.S.A. today, perhaps elsewhere too. And yet the heart lives on.

Apparently, Crane saw in 'the pantomime of Chaplin' a free play of metaphoric images roughly equivalent to the ambiguity of names in poetic language.

In the film, the mistress of an impoverished painter deposits her newborn infant in a limousine. The car is promptly stolen by thugs who leave the baby in a slum alley. Into this alley strolls Chaplin, the discriminating collector of cigar butts, a would-be gentleman whose white gloves have no fingertips. Once he discovers the baby, Chaplin cannot get rid of it without seeming to be a criminal in the eyes of a poor mother and a policeman passing by.

The central episodes of the film describe the affection between the ragamuffin boy and his adopted father as they pursue their picaresque adventures at the fringe of the law. Eventually, the moral authorities take the boy from Chaplin, but at the last moment the mother shows up and she and Chaplin are reunited with the boy.

In despair when he thinks he has lost the boy, Chaplin dreams of an improved world, a heaven erected in the alleys of his slum neighborhood where the characters of the film fly with angel wings. The naïve and touching dream fantasy may have spurred Crane's identification of Chaplin with modern poets who imaginatively redeem their spiritual poverty through language.

A somewhat peeved letter to William Wright (October 17, 1921) makes the poet's intentions explicit:

> I am moved to put Chaplin with the poets (of today); hence the 'we.' In other words, he, especially in *The Kid*, made me feel myself, as poet, as being 'in the same boat' with him. Poetry, the human feelings, 'the kitten,' is so crowded out of the humdrum, rushing, mechanical scramble of today that the man who would preserve them must duck and camouflage for dear life to keep himself from annihilation.

"Chaplinesque" appears as the ninth poem in *White Buildings* (1926):

> We make our meek adjustments,
> Contented with such random consolations
> As the wind deposits
> In slithered and too ample pockets.
>
> For we can still love the world, who find
> A famished kitten on the step, and know
> Recesses for it from the fury of the street,
> Or warm torn elbow coverts.
>
> We will sidestep, and to the final smirk
> Dally the doom of that inevitable thumb
> That slowly chafes its puckered index toward us,
> Facing the dull squint with what innocence
> And what surprise!
>
> And yet these fine collapses are not lies

More than the pirouettes of any pliant cane;
Our obsequies are, in a way, no enterprise.
We can evade you, and all else but the heart:
What blame to us if the heart lives on.

The game enforces smirks; but we have seen
The moon in lonely alleys make
A grail of laughter of an empty ash can,
And through all sound of gaiety and quest
Have heard a kitten in the wilderness.

Crane's dense puns are the linguistic equivalent of Chaplin's wonderful acrobatic duckings (which are especially moving in the fight with a monstrous bully in *The Kid*) and his camouflage. In the opening stanza, the words *deposits* and *pockets* suggest the advantages of money, which neither the Chaplin hero nor the poet possess. Instead the *wind* as the poetic spirit, both the *afflatus* of Apollo and the religious *Spiritus Sanctus* inflate the economically depleted poets. Chaplin portrays the gentleman of 'meek adjustments' when we first see him in the film 'contented with [the] random consolations' of what he can salvage from trash cans. His imaginative power as a *bricoleur* appeared in the first scene within his squalid apartment where we see the Rube Goldbergesque contraption he erected to transform his kettle into a baby feeder for his foundling. Crane's vision of his own art is that of 'meek adjustments' of common words to allow the inspired 'content' of a language that is vestigially poetic and religious to fill squalid and overextended vehicles.

Sometime before seeing the film he had adopted a stray kitten, an act which obviously reinforced his identification with the film. Just as the boy became the ally and companion in mischievous survival with his step-father, breaking windows to provide him with work as a part-time window repairman, so the kitten follows the poet in finding 'random consolations' by making an ideal home out of a ruined easy chair or a jacket, torn at the elbows.

Yet another letter to Munson (November 3, 1921) adds

something to Crane's idea of the poetic mimesis of the film: 'It is because I feel that I have captured the arrested climaxes and evasive victories of his gestures in words somehow. I like the poem as much as anything I have done.'

In the third stanza, the imitation of Chaplin's manoeuvres is most developed. In the film's introductory scene, with perfect timing, Chaplin sidesteps a cascade of garbage thrown from an upper floor into the alley he is exploring for treasures. Of course, that ability to move suddenly to the side insures his later success in the boxing match with the big bully. The complex of forces that oppose, and eventually overwhelm, both the movie hero and the poet are conjoined in the curiously ambiguous synecdoche of the thumb and the almost unpicturable index finger that follows it. The difficulty and the brilliance of representation here stem from the fusion of a series of incompatible gestures that characterise the police, censors, bankers, and finally Death itself. 'The doom of the inevitable thumb' must first evoke the imperial judgment of death to an heroic gladiator. Yet it is also the jerking gesture of the policeman, thrusting his thumb toward his shoulder to indicate expulsions. Chaplin's early films are crammed with that gesture throwing out the unwanted Tramp.

The third line of the third stanza cancels out, without completely removing, the images of those two related gestures. Unless we see the index chafing the air as a premonitory anticipation of the 'inevitable thumb' – the humiliating warning of authority that must be disobeyed so that the 'inevitable' punishment follows – the gesture shows contact of index and thumb in a demand for money. The gesture is familiar to Chaplin's viewers from his encounter with the brutal waiter in *The Immigrant* who demands payment for the meal the Tramp has eaten but cannot afford. Furthermore, the first letter to Munson which I have quoted in part brings into play the issue of censorship, suggesting that between the thumb and index is the sheet paper – the poetic text – subjected to inevitable rejection.

The film and the poem both obstruct the machinery of doom

by a temporal ploy: the play for time, 'dally' (Crane may have read 'Like dallying of doom' in Melville's poem "Aurora Borealis" whose 'retreatings and advancings' complement "Chaplinesque"). In this context, the 'recesses' of the third line of the second stanza must sacrifice a measure of their spatial security when read as a temporal breaks in the subtext of Crane's extrapolations from the film.

He may be interpreting Chaplin's feigned innocence when caught outside the law, as a poetic strategy. In May, 1922, he wrote Charmion Wiegand, 'You know I worship Chaplin's work. Think he is the greatest living actor I've seen, and the prime interpreter of the soul imposed upon modern civilization.' The modernity, then, of Chaplin's pantomime that he extolled in the first letter to Munson turns out to be a negation, or at least a retardation of the instantaneous transmission of meaning. It stands in opposition to the exchange of money, the prime instance of the mechanical response to a sign 'imposed by modern civilization.' The brutal pantomimic demands, so complexly dissected and reassembled in the third and fourth lines of the third stanza, represent the reduction of language to an exchange system that poetry resists by interposing a feigned, childlike ignorance of its mechanism. The verb *dally* indicates that the temporal prolongation takes a coquettish form of gestures, as in Chaplin's familiar assumption of a feminine attitude when confronted by either harsh authority or female attractiveness, while its verbal equivalent would be *to trifle*, or talk mockingly or beguilingly. The substitution of *enterprise* for *undertaking* in the fourth stanza is the evasion of a trifling pun on the language of the mortuary: *our obsequies are, in a way, no undertaking*. Here 'enterprise' displaces the cruder joke on *undertaking* by repeating the economic theme of the poem (our funeral rites are no business matter), and at the same time foreshadowing the idea of the quest-romance which climaxes the final stanza (our adventure is not *post-mortem*).

Crane acknowledges that the artist's identification with the pose of the child ('with what innocence/ and what surprise!') is a mask, a sidestepping that points to the proleptic message of the final stanza, or at least buys the time for it to assume the role of another meek adjustment or an obsequiousness that does not touch the heart of the poetic enterprise. The mask, he qualifies, is not a falsehood. The 'fine collapses' are not just the clown's finely executed, and painless, pratfalls but are 'these' collapses of the allegory of poetic vocation upon the action of the film; and more than that, they are the 'fine collapses' or *puns that are the words of the poem*. Like Chaplin's thin cane, which can afford him no practical support, they extend and magnify the dance of his evasions. The self-referential demonstrative adjective prepares us for the two central puns in the poem; his verbal equivalents to the 'arrested climaxes and evasive victories,' of the film: *obsequies* and *heart*. The first collapses burial rites upon obsequious adjustments, declaring neither to be part of the commercial exchange characteristic of 'modern civilization.'

There are two crucial names hidden at the heart of "Chaplinesque." In Biblical narrative the first artificer of feigned innocence and surprise was not the guilty Adam or Eve, but pliant Cain whose verbal pirouettes – 'Am I my brother's keeper?' – failed to evade the judgment of God. The pun on *heart* (which makes the middle name that Harold Hart Crane preferred identical with the organ of 'human feelings') following so closely on Cain/cane, brings the poet to the verge of blasphemy (which is the root meaning of *blame*). The *we* in the poem are poets, pliant Cains, who 'live on' yet apart from the automatons of modern civilization whose language, even in burial rites, speaks of business.

In this very early poem, Hart declares his vocation and his anticipation of continued poetic powers. He is also defending himself against the reproach of sentimentality which had made him anxious about his response to *The Kid*. In the November 3, 1921 letter to Munson he had written: 'Chaplin may be a sentimentalist, after all, but he carries the theme with such power and universal portent that sentimentality is made to transcend itself into a new kind of tragedy, eccentric, homely yet brilliant.' The poet cannot evade the self-transcending power of Chaplin's sentimentality: he lives on it, by refashioning it to his poem.

The religious hints in the first four stanzas become explicit in the fifth and final one. The kitten, of course, is Chaplin, the tragedian, 'the prime interpreter of the soul in modern civilization.' Like Galahad, his possession of the Grail is temporally circumscribed, a fleeting glimpse disguised as a final explosion of laughter. The Biblical allusions of the final phrase ground the future temporality of the entire poem. 'The voice of one crying in the wilderness' (Mark 1:3) as the typological completion of the same phrase in Isaiah 40:3, and as a more remote echo of the 'still small voice' of Kings 19:12, is that of the precursor John, preparing the way for the Christ event. Thus, Crane smuggles the Baptist into the company of poets buying and marking time.

"Chaplinesque" provides us with a brilliant, if obscure, reading of *The Kid*, including its comic vision, while it looks forward prophetically to the religious exfoliation of Crane's more mature poetry, especially *The Bridge* and "The Broken Tower." It implies that the structure of a poem, like that of the best films, arises from a rhythmic gesture that prolongs itself and delays its ineluctable termination. The modern poem keeps itself open to the 'random consolations' of ancient promises embodied in the synecdoche of 'the heart', yet it can sustain no false optimism about its temporal destiny: it *lives on* and *hears through*, thankful of finding company in films 'of the Chaplin and *Caligari* sort.'

The later poems, "O Carib Isle!" and "A Name for All," protest the denotative function of names. The former uses the anagrammatic play of 'crab' and 'Carib' to generate the pyrotechnic display of metaphoric language as a stand against the 'death' of fixing a name:

> The tarantula rattling at the lily's foot
> Across the feet of the dead, laid in white sand
> Near the coral beach – nor zigzag fiddle crabs

> Side-stilting from the path (that shift, subvert
> And anagrammatize your name) – No, nothing here
> Below the palsy that one eucalyptus lifts
> In wrinkled shadows – mourns.
>
>   And yet suppose
> I count these nacreous frames of tropic death,
> Brutal necklaces of shells around each grave
> Squared off so carefully. Then
>
> To the white sand I may speak a name, fertile
> Albeit in a stranger tongue. Tree names, flower names
>
> Deliberate, gainsay death's brittle crypt. Meanwhile
> The wind that knots itself in one great death –
> Coils and withdraws. So syllables want breath.

The leftover 'i' of the anagram emerges as the first-person pronoun in the final stanza:

> Slagged of the hurricane – I, cast within its flow,
> Congeal by afternoons here, satin and vacant.
> You have given me the shell, Satan, – carbonic amulet
> Sere of the sun exploded in the sea.

By now the poetic wind of "Chaplinesque" has become a hurricane, and the convulsive voice of the poet names the figure of death, 'Satan.'

The three stanzas of "A Name for All" return to the mortifying denotations of living creatures. Such ineluctable naming offers at least the usurpation by metaphor – moon-moth and grass-hopper – of the poetic afflatus that endures ['still wing on'] when the substantive 'wing' becomes a verb:

> Moonmoth and grasshopper that flee our page
> And still wing on, untarnished of the name
> We pinion to your bodies to assuage
> Our envy of your freedom – we must maim
>
> Because we are usurpers, and chagrined –
> And take the wing and scar it in the hand.

> Names we have, even, to clap on the wind;
> But we must die, as you, to understand.
>
> I dreamed that all men dropped their names, and sang
> As only they can praise, who build their days
> With fin and hoof, with wing and sweetened fang
> Struck free and holy in one Name always.

In his violent repudiation of conventional names, the poet invents the metaphor comparing the bestowing of names on persons and objects to a collector killing and pinning insects.

• • •

The "-esque" in "Chaplinesque" comes from the late Latin suffix -iscus (itself derived from Proto-IndoEuropean *-skos) meaning "like" or "pertaining to". Adding the suffix creates a metaphor from the name "Chaplin." Yet the name itself designates the genius for whom all physical things were metaphoric. The insight to see in the spout of a kettle the nipple of a baby's bottle corresponded, for Crane, to the connotative power of pliant words. In "General Aims and Theories" he wrote:

> …the motivation of the poem must be derived from the implicit
> emotional dynamics of the materials used, and the terms of
> expression employed are often selected less for their logical (literal)
> significance than for their associational meanings. Via this and their
> metaphorical inter-relationships, the entire construction of the poem
> is raised on the organic principle of a 'logic of metaphor,' which
> antedates our so-called pure logic, and which is the genetic basis of
> all speech, hence consciousness and thought-extension.

According to 'the logic of metaphor' Hart has a heart like Chaplin's. Their individuality is dissolved in the first-person plural as poets.

The Kid (Charlie Chaplin, 1921).

6

Calling Judy Madeline

I Confess (1953) may be the most thoroughly Roman Catholic of all of Hitchcock's films insofar as it dramatizes the dilemma of a priest, Father William Logan, falsely accused of a murder for which he might exculpate himself only by breaking the sacred bond of the confessional. Nevertheless, the most startling Catholic moment in Hitchcock's oeuvre would have to be the turning point of *The Wrong Man* (1957): Manny Balestrero, helpless and in despair because he too has been falsely accused – of armed robbery – finally falls to prayer before a kitsch representation of the Sacred Heart of Jesus. Superimposed over his face as he prays we see his lookalike about to commit another robbery and, this time, be caught in the act.

Many of Hitchcock's other American films introduce Roman Catholic or Biblical elements, but usually they are smuggled into the films in ways to attract little attention to themselves. Yet they often seem to suggest that the protagonists err in blindness to the sacraments or by turning a deaf ear to the citations of scripture around them, sometimes out of their own mouths. In a sense, Hitchcock puts his viewers in a position parallel to his criminal heroes and heroines, sneaking the scriptural or liturgical danger sign past them. Some of these same films even imply that film-going, and filmmaking, arises from a propensity to sin: to see and identify with acts of sex and violence, at the price of moral blindness.

The Birds (1963) offers an interesting example of this. Few viewers could be expected to realize that the etymology of the heroine's name, Melanie (in Greek) Daniels (in Hebrew), means 'the blackness of God's judgement,' but everyone hears the Irish drunk in the Tides Restaurant when he proclaims 'This is the end of the world.' He cites the Bible in support of his vision, naming book and chapter: 'Behold I, even I, shall bring a sword upon you and I will devastate your high places (Ezekiel, chapter 6)', but the waitress wryly counters with 'Woe unto them that rise early in the morning that they may follow strong drink.' He himself identifies the passage as 'Isaiah, chapter 5,' but she gets the better of this exchange. We can identify with her comic authority (even though the sensible ornithologist in the very same scene is proven woefully wrong). Her rejoinder effectively neutralizes the apocalyptic citation, suggesting that one can quote the Bible to any opportune purpose. We are left with the conclusion that man at the end of the bar is a drunk, not a prophet, as if those two roles were incompatible. In this way Hitchcock manages to introduce the apocalyptic vision into his film and immediately deflect attention from it.

There are other Biblical quotations so deviously inserted into the films they have escaped critical attention, as far as I can determine. For instance, in *Shadow of a Doubt* (1943) Uncle Charlie, who has murdered widows for their money, still retains his seductive charm when he impishly quotes St. Paul – 'Take a little wine for thy stomach's sake' – in presenting an unaccustomed bottle of sparkling burgundy to his sister's family table. It could not be an accident that this sympathetic moment of mildly blasphemical wit tacitly cites the very chapter (1 Timothy 6) in which Paul prescribes the proper care of widows in the Church.

When Lisa Freemont, in *Rear Window* (1954), demands L.B. Jeffries's full attention, taking his mind off the brutal murder he thinks he has uncovered in the apartment across the courtyard, she threatens 'to move into the apartment across the way and do the dance of the seven veils every hour,' if that is what is needed to engage him. Her sassy identification with a clockwork Salome, casting Jeffries as Herod Antipas, gives a religious register to the film's dominant themes of sexual voyeurism and castration-anxiety too fleeting to have attracted the attention of the numerous psychoanalytical exegetes of the film. Yet critics have noted the reference to the film experience in her gesture at that moment, closing the blinds as if bringing down a curtain before she says, 'Show's over. Preview of coming attractions,' referring to the negligee she is about to don. However, to understand Hitchcock's invocation of religion requires that we see the cinema as our modern version of Herod's grizzly entertainment.

On some level, Hitchcock seems to have considered sinful the fundamental voyeurism driving both the desire to see films and to make them. While his films often provide occasions to indulge violent fantasies and imagine erotic scenarios, they question the moral consequences of such indulgence. This is never so apparent as in the opening of *Psycho* (1960) when the camera descends from an overview of Phoenix, Arizona to inch under the shade of a nearly blocked window for a glimpse of the heroine, Marion Crane, just as she ends a lunch-hour tryst with her lover. In the very same film, we will recognize the perverseness of Norman Bates when he pushes aside a painting in his motel office to peep at Marion taking a shower. The violent consequence of this act of voyeurism is one of the best-known sequences in film history: her murder in the shower. Few viewers would have been able to notice, or recognize, that the picture Bates moved depicted the Biblical scene of peeping – Susanna seen bathing by the elders, rejected from the Hebrew Bible and Protestant editions, but retained in the Roman Catholic and Greek Orthodox versions of the Book of Daniel.

Melanie Daniels is far from the only ominous name in Hitchcock's oeuvre. The redemption of Balestrero in *The Wrong*

Man might have been anticipated by his Christian name – Emmanuel. Hitchcock, of course, would have known that an Englishman too young to be addressed as 'Mister' can be called 'Master'. So, the name of *Psycho*'s perverted and infantilized Norman Bates would suggest the play on 'self-abuse.' The titular thief of *To Catch a Thief* (1945) turns out to be John Robie. Above all, there is a cascade of symbolic names as allegories in *North by Northwest* (1959) where the villain is Van*damm*, the seductress *Eve* Kendall, and the divorced protagonist, Roger O. Thornhill, has the initials *ROT*.

Hitchcock was born into a British Catholic family. They gave him a Jesuit education. He continued to attend Mass – for his mother's sake, according to Donald Spoto, until her death in 1942. However, John Russell Taylor claims Hitchcock continued to practice his religion all his life. He required his wife's conversion before they married, and they raised and educated their only daughter in the Church. He was buried with Catholic rites.

To be sure his position on the Church was intensely ambivalent. Spoto tells us he had an order to keep priests off his set: 'they all hate me.' Taylor nearly concludes his biography with the following anecdote:

> When he was in Rome in the early 1970s, his hosts arranged, thinking it would please him, for Hitch to have an audience with the Pope. But Hitch bowed gracefully out. 'What would I do,' he said, 'if the Holy Father said that in this world, with so much sex and violence, I ought to lay off?' Just a gag, possibly – but most likely not. What *would* a dutiful son of the Church do? Best not to run the risk.
> (John Russell Taylor, *The Life and Times of Alfred Hitchcock* [New York: Pantheon Books, 1978], p. 310.)

The Pope was Paul VI, but Hitchcock would remember Pius XII's Encyclical "Miranda prorsus" (September 8, 1957, while *Vertigo* was in production) in which he wrote:

> It has been Our pleasure to receive in audience those professionally engaged in motion pictures, radio, and television. After expressing to

them Our wonder at the marvelous progress made by specialists in these fields. We have pointed out the duties incumbent upon each of them, the high praise they already deserve, the pitfalls in which they can easily fall, and the high ideals which should enlighten their minds and direct their wills.[1]

The Encyclical called for ecclesiastical agencies throughout the world to evaluate all films released and to publish which films met the Church's standards of 'truth and virtue' and which were to be condemned as injurious to souls, including the works of 'those who adhere to incorrect philosophies of art.' In America the Legion of Decency had long been doing just that.

Hitchcock had no interest in making the kind of films the Holy Office favored. His favorite ploy of allowing, or enticing, the viewer to identify with a protagonist despite a serious moral flaw, risked construction as an 'incorrect philosophy of art' and censure from the Legion of Decency. In fact, he shot an alternative ending to *Vertigo*, for use only if the Legion objected that he violated one of its strictures – that no criminal should go unpunished. It turned out to be unnecessary; the film was released as Hitchcock wanted it initially. In the alternative conclusion, John 'Scotty' Ferguson and his friend Midge would hear over radio news that Gavin Elster, the villain who had murdered his wife and manipulated Scotty as an unsuspecting witness on his behalf, was apprehended in Europe.

In the film, Ferguson, a lawyer turned police detective, suffers from disabling acrophobia after a fellow officer dies falling from a roof in the act of saving him. The surname Ferguson underlines the vectors of his character with an oxymoron: 'Fergus' or 'Feargus' is a fusion of 'fear' and 'force.' At his weakest moment, reduced to a catatonic state, Midge treats him as if he were *her* son: visiting him in a sanatorium, she says, 'You're not lost. Mother is here.'

Near the start of the film, Elster, a forgotten college acquaintance, lures him into a job of private detection. He is to

---
[1] http://www.vatican.va/content/pius-xii/en/encyclicals/documents/hf_p-xii_enc_08091957_miranda-prorsus.html.

follow Elster's wealthy wife, Madeline, who seems to be the reincarnation, unbeknownst to her, of great-grandmother, Carlotta Valdez, who committed suicide. Scotty not only follows her, fishing her out of San Francisco Bay during what appears to be an attempted suicide; he falls in love with her. When she ascends a mission tower to jump, he cannot follow her. Brutally reproved at the inquest by all but Elster, he falls into a catatonic state for which he is hospitalized.

This is only half of the story but it occupies nearly three-quarters of the film; it is as long, in fact, as most feature films of the period, an hour and a half. As such it would be the masterpiece of the romantic ghost film genre in America. Throughout this part we watch Madeline through Scotty's eyes, first as he trails her, later as they 'wander' together, in continual shot/countershot exchanges. In those exchanges we are induced to identify with the benign, good humored detective: we learn about Madeline as he does and (except for one moment when Midge, who seems to have been briefly his college girlfriend and who apparently still loves him, spies Madeline leaving his apartment late at night), we see nothing that he does not see. The mystery and glamour of Madeline attracts all the attention to shots of her in these exchanges, so much so that *Vertigo* became the principal example of 'the male gaze' in the most influential text of feminist film theory, Laura Mulvey's "Narrative and Visual Pleasure."

The reincarnation plot capitalizes on the enormous success of Morey Bernstein's *The Search for Bridey Murphy* (1956). In 1952 Bernstein had hypnotized a woman he called Ruth Simmons in Pueblo, Colorado. She reportedly regressed into memories of her former incarnation and death at sixty-six as 'Friday' or 'Bridey' Murphy, an upperclass Irish woman of the turn of the Nineteenth Century. Bernstein's findings were serialized, then published as a book which became an instant best seller. The same year a film was made of it. Edith Head, costumier for most of Hitchcock's American films did the wardrobes; like *Vertigo* it was shot in VistaVision.

The book was denounced in Roman Catholic pulpits for encouraging the theological error of reincarnation. *Life* magazine sent a reporter to Ireland to corroborate the details of Murphy's life. The result was negative. More damagingly, *The Chicago American* discovered that a Bridie Murphy Corkell had lived across the street from Virginia Tighe (the real Ruth Simmons) during her childhood. Her family stories were the source, it claimed, for what Bernstein insisted was a reincarnation.

If the first part of *Vertigo* seduces an audience that wants to believe in reincarnation and repetition of the Bridey Murphy kind, it also offers much to literary intellectuals of the period dominated by the study of mythological archetypes. Joseph Campbell's *The Hero with a Thousand Faces* had appeared as early as 1949. But the mid-1950s was the crest point for that mode of literary analysis. Mircea Eliade published *The Myth of the Eternal Return* in 1954. The most sophisticated theory of literary myths, Northrop Frye's *Anatomy of Criticism*, was published in 1957, the year *Vertigo* was made.

Seen in the light of such archetypes, the film retells a version of the myth of Persephone, the daughter of the grain goddess, Demeter, seized by Hades of the Underworld to become his wife. When Demeter refuses to let the earth bear fruit until her daughter is found, a compromise is reached. Persephone returns to life for half a year and spends half in Hades.

The color scheme of the film underlies the Persephone analogy. After the prologue in which he witnesses the policeman's fall, we see Scotty in Midge's apartment. She is a graphic artist working in advertising and an amateur painter. The colors are uniformly autumnal. He wears brown; the shades are yellow straw; he mounts a yellow kitchen stool. This is in direct contrast to the red interior of Ernie's Restaurant where he first sees the vernal Madeline, in a vivid green dress. Later she shows an intense identification with vegetable life: when Scotty trails her through a dark alleyway, Hitchcock suggests a pagan mystery rite by capping the sequence with a shot of her in a brightly lit florist shop. She leads her pursuer to Carlotta's grave in a richly flowered churchyard, where she places the flowers, and then to a museum where she sits in front of a portrait of Carlotta holding a bouquet of flowers. When they wander together, she brings him to a redwood forest where she points to the cross-section of a giant sequoia tree: 'There I was born and there I died,' she intones. The 'Homeric Hymn to Demeter' describes Persephone:

> [Persephone] was playing with the full-breasted daughters of Oceanus
> Plucking flowers from the soft meadow...and as a decoy for
> The flower-like girl that
> Earth made to bloom by Zeus's will to the pleasure of [Hades]...
> Forcing her, unwilling, into his golden chariot...
> He carried her away crying....
> An acute pain struck the heart of [Demeter, her mother] and from her ambrosial
> Hair she ripped the covering
> Then tossing a blue clothe around both her shoulders,
> She rushed like a bird over rich land and water,
> Insane [in her search of Persephone]. No one would tell her truly what she wanted to know,
> Neither gods nor mortal men...

The ancient description of Demeter's despair anticipates the story of Carlotta, as told by Pop Liebl, the bookseller and amateur historian:

> He [a rich and powerful man] kept the child and threw [Carlotta] away. You know, men could do that in those days. And she became the sad Carlotta, alone in the great house, walking the streets alone, her clothes becoming old and patched and dirty; and the mad Carlotta, stopping people in the street to ask, 'Where is my child?' 'Have you seen my child?'

The sophisticated allusions to Demeter may have been inspired by the mythic references in Pierre Boileau's and Thomas Narcejac's *D'entre les morts* (1954) which Hitchcock adapted. There,

Roger Flavières, the lawyer and former detective, was a fan of mythology. Rather than use the name Renée, once he began to fall in love with his client's wife, he called her Eurydice. His gift to her of a golden cigarette lighter with a card inscribed *A Eurydice ressucitée* plays a significant role in the crime novel, but not in the film. The Boileau-Narcejac crime novel used extensive free indirect discourse to portray Flavières as a bitter, rather cowardly sleuth who resents the task he accepted from his old friend, Paul Gévigne. The setting, in Paris at the start of WWII, with Gévigne as a war-profiteer, is pure noir, in contrast to the sunny exploration of sites in the film's tour of Santa Cruz and San Matteo counties.

For the length of a normal film, Hitchcock engages us in a tragic version of the Bridey Murphy situation as if it were a repetition of the myth of Demeter and Persephone. Then the film takes its twist. In recovery, back in San Francisco, Scotty obsessively revisits the places he saw Madeline, repeatedly mistaking women on the street for her until he meets the working-class Judy Barton, who resembles Madeline to a remarkable degree. At this point Hitchcock, boldly breaking the pattern of *D'entre les morts*, reveals that Judy had been Elster's girlfriend. He drew her into a plot to impersonate his absent wife, Madeline. Knowing Scotty could not follow her up the tower, he waited there with the body of the true Madeline, whose neck he had broken, then threw it off. Scotty was the perfect witness for the false suicide. (The novel holds this information for the ending.)

Of course, Hitchcock knew that Madeline was a version of Magdalen, the name of the holy whore of the New Testament. She bore a place-name, coming from the town of Magdala on the Sea of Galiliee. If Hitchcock also knew that the etymology of Magdala was rooted in the Aramaic word for 'Tower,' there would be a further link between her false name and her elaborately contrived death. Presumably, Boileau and Narcejac knew that. They signaled her 'resurrection' not only in the gift card of the cigarette lighter, but by giving her 'real name' as Renée (the reborn woman) Soulanges. Hitchcock disguised that by changing the character to Judy, while smuggling in the association with the Biblical Judith who symbolically castrated Holophernes.[2]

Hitchcock and his screen writers (Alex Coppel and Samuel Taylor) invented, or rather drew Midge out of the character of Boileau and Narcejac's Madeleine (sic), who was herself an amateur painter in *D'entre les morts*. In the film her affection for the protagonist complements the erotic triangle at the core of the mystery. 'Midge' is a nickname for Margaret, Michelle, or Miriam. If the character had been born Miriam, she would have had the name of Moses's prophetic sister. In the psychodynamics of *Vertigo*, she treats the protagonist as if she were a jealous but good-humored older sister. From the start, she is practical and rational: in the first scene where we encounter her, she is drawing an advertisement for a new style brassiere; she jokes about Scotty's familiarity with the object, saying in her motherly tone: 'You're a big boy now, Johnny-O.' There is nothing mysterious or romantic about Midge. As her nickname suggests, she is the diminutive opposite of the voluptuous Madeline and her sensuously earthy counterpart, Judy. The casting of Barbara Bel Geddes as Midge and Kim Novak as Madeline/ Judy plays up the opposition; the trope of the cantilever bra underwrites the difference in their figures.

In the second half of the film Judy, still in love with Scotty, reluctantly allows him to make her over in Madeline's image. But after she finally dyes her hair and wears it in Madeline's style,

---

[2] In *The Philosophical Hitchcock: Vertigo and the Anxieties of Unknowningness* (Chicago, University of Chicago Press, 2017), philosopher Robert R. Pippin also notes the allusion to Mary Magdalen (in his footnote 78). He not only catches the play on Proust's "madeleine" as a mnemonic tool but reinforces it by deriving the name "Elster" from that of the painter – Elstir – of *À la recherche du temps perdu* (note 79). It is apparent that Pippin did not know the version of this chapter published in *The Hidden God*, ed. Bandy and Monda (New York, Museum of Modern Art, 2003). Now I would supplement Pippin's onomastic insight by pointing out that Hitchcock's change of the name of Boileau-Narcejac's Gévigne to Elster supports the notion of his covert Proustian allusion. Pippin attributes his recognition of the Proustian allusion to by Richard E. Goodkin's rather excessive "Film and Fiction: Hitchcock's Vertigo and Proust's *Vertigo*" in *MLN*, Vol. 102, No. 5 (Dec., 1987), pp. 1171-1181.

she inadvertently puts on the necklace Elster gave her, a necklace he had claimed was the heirloom of Carlotta Valdez. Realizing the fraud, Scotty forces her to return to the scene of the murder. He manages to drag himself and her up the tower where, hearing someone enter, Judy falls to her death in fright. It was merely a nun from the mission who tolls the bells and has the last word: 'I heard voices...God have mercy!'

By unveiling the murder scheme and debunking the mystery of Carlotta's reincarnation as Madeline, Hitchcock immediately jolted his film out of one genre and into another. Once the plot is revealed and the supernatural theme shown to be a hoax, Scotty looks utterly different, even though many of the subsequent shot-countershot exchanges mimic those from the earlier part of the film. Whereas in the earlier shot-countershot exchanges his gaze had been transparent, a vehicle reflecting the curiosity of the viewer, in final third of the film Scotty becomes the object of our gaze, without quite effecting of the reciprocal shift of identification with Judy. We come to witness the effects of his insane love of an illusion; for 'Madeline' is the ultimate Hitchcock MacGuffin. The quest for a phantom brings him to the brink of perversion, making him a necrophile, and virtually a rapist in the brutal ascent of the tower. In that climax, the repetitions that had previously been a structural principle have their verbal coefficient. Scotty works himself up to violence, as if coaxing himself to an orgasm, by forcing a confession from Judy using phrases about his rival Elster over and over:

> You're my second chance, Judy. You're my second chance... He made you over, didn't he? He made you over just as I made you over, only better... Did he train you? Did he rehearse you? Did he tell you exactly what to do and what to say? You were a very apt pupil, weren't you? You were a very apt pupil!...Why did you pick on me? Why me? I was the set up. I was the set up. I was the made-to-order witness.

At the climax of this displaced rape, he realizes that he has reached the top of the stairwell with a final repetition: 'I made it! I made it!' The story of Scotty and Judy repeats that of Scotty and Madeline, just as Madeline was said to repeat Carlotta. At this moment Scotty also realizes that he has replicated Elster in his make-over of Judy.

Stripping away the hoax of reincarnation and the myths of eternal recurrence, Hitchcock reveals his protagonist as a man caught in obsession, enraged by erotic rivalry, and capable of finding satisfaction only with an imaginary woman. He brings Judy to the brink of her death, heedlessly repeating Elster's treatment of the actual Madeline.

The last part of the film forces us to reconsider the earlier mystery, to retrace Scotty's decisions and affections. Now it is apparent how bad he was at his job. Only Inspector Clouseau rivals his ineptitude as a detective. He uncovered nothing but what Elster had planted for him. It was Midge who knew how to find out Carlotta's story; she brought him to Pop Liebl. But far more serious than his failure as a sleuth was his violation of professional ethics. As far as he knew he was hired by a profoundly worried husband to protect his wife. Despite that, he fell in love with her, hid his feelings and their consequences from the husband, and transported the wife to the site of her suicide.

The moment when Scotty and Madeline fell in love with each other is a vertiginous ellipsis in the film. As soon as he pulls her out of San Francisco Bay, the scene shifts to several hours later in his apartment just before the telephone rings. Clearly, it is Elster calling. Scotty tells him 'It's alright' and promises to call later. The telephone has awakened Madeline from a nightmare. She shows wonder and alarm to find herself in Scotty's bed, apparently naked. A pan past the kitchen had revealed her dress and underclothes drying there; Scotty sheepishly offers her his red robe: 'You'll need this,' then leaves for her to dress. She walks out of his bedroom with a slow studied walk that we will see only once more in the film; at its erotic climax, when Judy emerges from the toilet of her hotel room, finally made-over completely as

Madeline, she has the same studied walk. This time Hitchcock filmed her walk through a misted lens. (In fact, he shot the two scenes in tandem.)

In retrospect, we realize that when Scotty removed all of her clothes, dried her naked body, and lifted it into his bed, she was shamming unconsciousness. The necrophilic passion her limp and defenseless naked body aroused in him, in turn kindled her love for him. It is a situation of exquisite perverseness, which means one thing for Scotty and another for Madeline/ Judy. Of course, she knew that Elster had a wife whom he planned to murder; she was his lover and part of the plot. The birth of her love for Scotty puts her not only in a vertigo of conflicts, but endangers her life. But Scotty believes he has just stripped Elster's *wife*. From this moment he progressively pursues an adulterous course, which the filmmaker is at pains to underplay.

Hitchcock has so brilliantly crafted the film that viewers are made to sympathize with Scotty's passion and overlook the professional and moral implications of his transgression, even though they too, at this point in the film, know only what he knows, believe only what he believes. In the enchanted, pagan world of eternal recurrence the sacramental bonds of marriage dissolve.

If the first part of the film suggests a mythopoeic model for the romance of Scotty and Madeline, the second part replaces it with a psychoanalytical subtext. With her acute, intuitive understanding of Scotty, Midge recognized the psychodynamics of his breakdown. In the hospital she tried to reassure him, saying, 'Mother is here.' But just as her good-humored self-portrait as Carlotta failed to jolt him from his fixation of Madeline, her recognition that the necrophilia of his passion is thoroughly Oedipal does neither her nor him any good. He is doomed to reenact the scenario with Judy until, playing a version of Elster's role, he virtually forces her to her death.

Just before the fake suicide of Madeline Scotty kissed her for the first time, and they declared their love for each other. He insisted, 'We're in love. That's all that counts.' To this romantic declaration of the insignificance of her (supposed) marriage and the irrelevance of her traumatic possession by a ghost, she told him repeatedly it that it was 'too late.' When she broke loose from his embrace, telling him 'I want to go into the church – alone,' he demanded to know 'Why?' Without an answer, his glance at the tower provided a premonition of her suicide; so, he followed her into the church.

This was not the first time Hitchcock filmed Scotty in a Roman Catholic Church. In his initial trailing of Madeline he had to pass through the sanctuary of Dolores Mission to reach the graveyard. Catholic theology asserts that the Real Presence of the Body of Christ resides in the eucharistic bread of Communion. The hosts not consumed during a Mass remain in the tabernacle of the altar, objects of veneration, to be used in subsequent rites. Catholics are taught to halt and kneel before the altar every time they cross the tabernacle in acknowledgement that they are in the actual Presence of the Incarnate God. As a non-Catholic, Scotty passes the altar without genuflecting. In pursuit of his quarry he misses the opportunity of the momentary epiphany of the Real Presence. It is as if his entanglement with Madeline-Judy required this initial and repeated obtuseness to God's Presence.

At the mission of San Juan Battista where he has taken Madeline to show her the sources of her delusions, Scotty plays the psychiatrist unraveling the web of her confused associations and memories, when he is actually being led each step of the way by the diabolical scheme of Elster. In retrospect, of course, we realize the inadequacy of the psychological strategy Scotty, at this point, thinks will cure Madeline of her unconscious possession. Overwhelmed by his adulterous love and convinced of his psychological diagnosis of her dementia, he cannot imagine why she would want to go into the church. The possibilities of prayer, veneration, meditation, and confession never occur – to him or us as viewers – in the moment before the shot of the tower intimates her suicide. Thus, nothing is further from his – or our – mind than the Real Presence when he rushes into the sanctuary to stop her. Hitchcock carefully shows him momentarily halted before the Baroque altar, puzzling out which way she turned. When he glances in one direction, a countershot shows the baptismal fount, and a painting of the Baptism of Jesus by John, the patron saint of the mission. The sacramental meaning of this option is cancelled instantly as he turns to the other side seeing the staircase to the tower, the trap Elster has so carefully baited for him.

When he returns at end of the film, Judy resists, saying, 'I don't want to go in there,' as he drags her to the scene of the crime. This time, we do not see the altar. Our previous acquaintance with the scene assures us he must again pass the Real Presence to get to the tower, but by now he has lost even the illusion that he possesses a love that is 'all that counts.' It is Judy who desperately hopes their passion for each other is 'all that counts,' while Scotty is driven to recover and understand the past – an ironic echo of what the pseudo-Madeline sought. In a grim parody of his earlier imitation of a psychiatrist, he ominously tells her he must force her into the church and up the tower because 'When it's done, we'll both be free.'

In *Vertigo*, Hitchcock suggests that the freedom psychoanalysis proffers is another false idol. As David Sterritt recognized, the film is about falling, including the Fall into sin.[3] Hitchcock does not represent revealed religion as a viable alternative to the deluded compulsion to repeat falling into sin; rather, it is the nearly invisible backdrop against which the falling occurs. In the more mundane lives of us viewers that compulsion takes the form of going to the movies.

---

[3] See David Sterritt, *The Films of Alfred Hitchcock* (New York: Cambridge University Press, 1993).

Vertigo (Alfred Hitchcock, 1957)

Alfred Hitchcock (A.I. Visions).

7

Nomen Est Omen: Stan, Georges, and Harry

For indeed, as Walter Shandy often insisted, there is much, nay almost all, in Names. The Name is the earliest Garment you wrap round the earth-visiting ME; to which it thenceforth cleaves, more tenaciously (for there are Names that have lasted nigh thirty centuries) than the very skin. And now from without, what mystic influences does it not send inwards, even to the centre; especially in those plastic first-times, when the whole soul is yet infantine, soft, and the invisible seedgrain will grow to be an all overshadowing tree! Names? Could I unfold the influence of Names, which are the most important of all Clothings, I were a second greater Trismegistus. Not only all common Speech, but Science, Poetry itself is no other, if thou consider it, than a right *Naming*. Adam's first task was giving names to natural Appearances: what is ours still but a continuation of the same; be the Appearances exotic – vegetable, organic, mechanic, stars, or starry movements (as in Science); or (as in Poetry) passions, virtues, calamities, God-attributes, Gods?

Thomas Carlyle: *Sartor Resartus*

In the late 1980s the opposing epicenters of avant-garde cinema in Boulder, Colorado were Stan Brakhage and Harry Smith. Brakhage had long been wary of the Naropa Institute before Harry Smith became its 'shaman-in-residence' in 1988. Although they were two of the most prominent American avant-garde filmmakers of the time, and both autodidacts, they were polar opposites in important ways: Brakhage called Smith 'a black magician' while he considered his own artistic practice related to 'white magic;' Brakhage was the most prolific filmmaker of his generation, making more than three hundred films; he was obsessed with their proper preservation. Smith may have made thirty films, but he lost or destroyed half of them; he claimed preservation a waste of money that ought to be spent on developing a time machine that could retrieve anything from the past. Brakhage was heterosexual, fathering seven children across two marriages; Smith homosexual and perhaps celibate. Smith read widely and possessed an encyclopedic memory; Brakhage focused his attention on poets of the 20th Century. Most crucially, they differed on the epistemological status of language. Brakhage based his view that artistic seeing requires a disengagement of the all-pervasive linguistic function on his personal experience and artistic practice, but Smith was committed to understanding the relation of the human brain to linguistic systems as philosophers, anthropologists, and biologists had formulated the issue since the Middle Ages. There is no record of any serious conversation between them, although Brakhage did write to R. Bruce Elder, who told me:

> On July 22, he wrote me to report on the visit [to New York] (which seems to have exhilarated him). Among his comments was, 'We had long marvelous conversations with... Charles Boultenhouse... Sidney and Bernice Peterson... Allen Ginsberg and Harry Smith (Allen having just saved Harry from another 'near death', Harry having been over in the Bronx recording the dying statements of derelicts in the burned-out bldgs. and gutters, ending in the hospital with pneumonia himself).'

Some thirty years before the encounter Brakhage described to Elder, both filmmakers had completed epic films of cyclic mythopeia; several years in the making. Brakhage's *Dog Star Man* (1961-64) – a Prelude and four Parts, corresponding to the seasons – was a silent seventy-minute-long work with an expanded version – *The Art of Vision* (1964) – running two-hundred-and-fifty minutes, also silent. Harry Smith's *No. 12* (ca. 1955-1960) is said to have been originally six hours long, but only an hour-long version survives: a black and white animated film with an elaborate soundtrack of synchronous and asynchronous 'effects.' It was to have been projected through specially designed color filters in a 'magical' theater wired to allow the restless movements of the audience to contribute to the rhythms of film projections and filter changes. The imagery involves a version of the myths of Dionysus and Osiris, with figures and objects emerging from and returning to an Egyptian sarcophagus, after innumerable dismemberments and recombinations.

At the heart of Smith's enterprise was a vision of a universe of correspondences. He had made paintings keyed to major jazz compositions. His *No. 10* and *No. 11* combined hermetic and alchemical symbols with familiar magazine cutouts. *No. 11* was meticulously synchronized to Thelonious Monk's "Mysterioso", but he showed *No. 10* with the Beatles first album virtually slapped onto a reel of his early films. He did that in the sincere belief that the simultaneity of music – any music – and rhythmic cinema would create a productive fusion in the viewers' minds.

There has been very little scholarship and interpretation devoted to Harry Smith's *No. 12* [the so-called "Heaven and Earth Magic" or the Magic Feature] since I published *Visionary Film* in 1974. Before that, there was almost nothing written on the film: Jonas Mekas had mentioned it in his *Village Voice* columns; I had published an interview with Smith in *Film Culture* in which he described, often cryptically, how the film was made; and he himself had crafted an even more cryptic note for the *Filmmakers Cooperative Catalogue, no. 4* (1967).

Rereading my discussion of the film, I think my central contribution was the explication Smith's note which I will now quote:

> A much expanded version of *No. 8*. [lost] The first part depicts the heroine's toothache consequent to the loss of a very valuable watermelon, her dentistry and transportation to heaven. Next follows an elaborate exposition of the heavenly land in terms of Israel, Montreal and the second part depicts the return to earth from being eaten by Max Müller on the day Edward the Seventh dedicated the Great Sewer of London. (Approx. 50 min.)

Characteristically, Smith leads us back, from the very start, to an earlier point of origin, the now lost *No. 8.*, which he had described thus:

> Black-and-white collage made up of clippings from 19th Century ladies' wear catalogues and elocution books. The cat, the dog, the statue and the Hygrometer appear here for the first time. (approx. 5 min.)

Reading Smith's note in the light of the interview of 1965 and other clues he had provided for me over several years, I proposed a scenario – a plot summary – for the film and listed a few of its sources: Max Ernst's collage novels (*Une femme cent têtes* [1929], *Une semaine du bonté* [1934]), Schreber's *Memoirs of My Nervous Illness* [*Denkwürdigkeiten eines Nervenkranken* (1903)], and Daniel Gottlob Moritz Schreber's *Medical Indoor Gymnastics* [*Die ärztliche Zimmer-gymnastik* (1855)]. I glossed Israel with Mac-Gregor Matthews's *The Kaballah Unveiled* (1887), and Montreal with Wilner Penfield's and Herbert Henri Jasper's *Epilepsy and the Functional Anatomy of the Human Brain* (1954). The Victoria Embankment Sewer was officially opened on July 13, 1870. At that time Müller was the Oxford Professor of Comparative Philology. A German-born Sanskritist, he wrote and edited popular books on comparative religion as well as scholarly studies.

However, I had not noticed the publication dates of the English language editions of most of the crucial sources. Little, Brown brought out the Penfield and Jasper book in 1954; Ida Macalpine and Richard Hunter translated, edited, and provided an introduction and notes to Schreber's *Memoirs of My Nervous Illness* in 1955. These two books, along with Carl Stormer's *The Polar Aurora* (1955) and Linn Cooper's *Time Distortion in Hypnosis* (1954) probably came into Smith's hands just before he started the film. The latter two are mentioned in conjunction with the film in the A.J. Melita interview [(1976;) first published in *Think of the* Self Speaking (1999).] A frenzy of book buying and eclectic reading seems to have preceded the initiation of Smith's long projects. At the very least we can now conjecture that *No. 12* was begun in 1955 or shortly after.

It is possible that reading MacAlpine and Hunter's edition of Schreber's *Memoirs*, or their notes on it, led Harry Smith to the work of Schreber's psychiatrist – and in his delusions, his tormentor and 'soul murderer' – Dr. Emil Paul Flechsig. His inaugural lecture, *Gehirn und seele* [*Brain and Soul*] (1894), contains a diagram of his topological analysis of the human brain. That and the portrait of Fleichsig, sitting in front of an enlarged image of a human brain in the first plate of MacAlpine and Hunter's volume might have led Smith to the work of Penfield. Curiously, Daniel Paul Schreber shared one Christian name – Daniel – with all of his distinguished male ancestors and another – Paul – with Dr. Fleichsig. Despite Smith's having named Stormer's and Cooper's books as sources for *No. 12*, I have not been able to see their relevance to the film.

Although there is very little on the film in *American Magus: Harry Smith – A Modern Alchemist* edited by Paola Igliori, (New York: Inanout Press, 1996), a careful reading of its interviews provides several interesting clues. There, Lionel Ziprin indicates that Smith read aloud to his mother on her deathbed a chapter written by Karen Horney on sadism. I presume that was the twelfth and final chapter, "Sadism," (before the Conclusion) of

Horney's *Our Inner Conflicts: A Constructive Theory of Neurosis* (Norton, 1945; the date is plausible). There Horney emphasizes the sadist's compulsion to control and play on the emotions of another person, to exploit, disparage, and humiliate them, often having 'spells of an almost insane rage.' The idea of a deathbed reading of such a text apparently seemed to characterize Smith in Ziprin's mind, and so struck the interviewer that she repeated it to Dr. Joseph Gross. Was Smith trying to tell Ziprin something about his mother's nature? We cannot exclude the possibility that Smith, who frequently flew into self-destructive rages, was reading this passage in an effort of self-explanation to his dying parent. In any case, it is one of many confirmations of Ziprin's claim that Smith was widely read in psychoanalytical literature, particularly at that time. MacAlpine and Hunter, the translators of Daniel Paul Schreber's *Memoirs*, were psychiatrists revising Freud's pioneering work on Dr. Schreber: "Psycho-Analytic Notes on an Autobiographical Account of a Case of Paranoia (Dementia Paranoides)" (1911). In their revision, they pointed out the implicit sadism of the 'educational' devices invented by Dr. Schreber's famous father, whom Freud had treated rather simplistically as a venerable man. However, the filmmaker furiously rejected Freud's interpretation of Schreber's book and that of MacAlpine and Hunter. (Now I regret I did not ask him to expand on that reaction.) Although Smith denigrated their analysis, I suspect it was the commentary that led him to acquire a copy of Daniel Gottlob Moritz Schreber's *Medical Indoor Gymnastics* [*Die ärztliche Zimmergymnastik*] which would furnish the fundamental figure for his animated film. I believe Smith considered *Memoirs of My Nervous Illness* a document of Revelation rather than of paranoid madness. Schreber wrote in the "Preface" to the book's publication:

> It is... in my opinion of little importance whether, in view of the relationship contrary to the Order of the World which arose between God and myself, ideas which I formed at the time were more or less faulty. A more general interest can in any case be claimed only for

those conclusions which I arrived at in consequence of my impressions and experiences about the *lasting* conditions, about the essence and attributes of God, the immortality of the soul, etc. In this respect I have no reason whatever, even after my subsequent personal experiences, to make the very slightest alteration in the basic ideas... of the Memoirs.[1]

Linguistic affiliations abound in the *Memoirs*: birds speak without knowing the meaning of their messages, the nerves of the human body – the locus of the Soul according to Schreber – have a language of their own; the Sun spoke; and living and dead Souls spoke to him as 'voices.'

Furthermore, in addition to these documented references, I recall Smith's recommendation to me to read Geza Roheim's *The Gates of the Dream* (New York: International Universities Press, New York, 1952), which he said was one of the sources of *No. 12*, particularly noting the associations of bed wetting and myths of the flood. We might recall here that *No. 12* is just a fragment of a film that was to include Noah's Ark, and the Raising of the Dead.

Smith's familiarity with psychoanalytical literature is particularly interesting in the light of Annette Michelson's discussions of *No. 12*. Her fullest version, "The Mummy's Return: A Kleinian Film Scenario", appears in *Meaning in the Visual Arts: Views from the Outside, A Centennial Commemoration of Erwin Panofsky (1892-1968)*, edited by Irving Lavin (Princeton: Princeton University Press, 1995). Michelson offers a psychoanalytical reading of the film informed by Melanie Klein's work on infant development. Here is Michelson:

> ...*The Magic Feature* as the representation of an elaborate working through, in the form of a prodigally generous form of reparation offered by artistic practice, of the spectrum of infantile development through paranoid-schizoid and depressive positions. And our first step toward that reading will entail an account of the initial image of the film which I note, with more than casual interest and amusement, neither of the exegetes cited above [myself and Noel Carroll who read the film as a model of the Humean mind] troubled to include in his

[1] Daniel Paul Schreber, *Memoirs of my Nervous Illness*, Trans. Ida Macalpine and Richard A. Hunter (New York Review Books, New York, 2000), pp. 4-5.

own reading: that of the Homunculus who sets in motion the epic of repeated slaughter and resurrection by introducing (literally carrying onto the screen or scene) the other member of the primordial dyad, whose name we read as in a rebus: 'Mummy.'[p. 343]

That critical insight is so brilliant it whets our appetite for further revelations, say, of the meaning of the watermelon, the dog, the strawberry, the elevator, to flesh out the Kleinian scenario she so provocatively initiates.

I doubt that Smith ever read Jacques Lacan's writings on Dr. Schreber, since the readings he first proposed of Schreber and paranoia in the mid-Fifties were not translated into English until at least thirty years later. Lacan did not make the case the central focus of a study until the following decade. It is merely a coincidence then, and consequently an irony, that just when Harry Smith was making *No. 12*, Jacques Lacan was lecturing in his Parisian *Seminaire* on the use of Schreber's *Memoirs* as key to the nature of the unconscious as a language.[2]

Lacan was a fierce opponent of Melanie Klein. I invoke him here merely to suggest that Smith intuitively shared his emphasis on the centrality of the symbolic father's function – where Klein focusses on the mother – in hallucinations of The Woman. If there is a 'primordial dyad' in the film it is father/ son rather than son/ 'Mummy.' The 'protagonist' of *No. 12* is the cutout figure of a man, manipulating all the figures and objects of the film. His gyrations derive completely from animating the illustrations in the originally best-selling exercise book of Judge Schreber's father, Daniel Gottlieb Moritz Schreber, *Medical Indoor Gymnastics*. The entire hallucinatory scenario might be seen to be under the control of the father who shared a surname and a baptismal name with his son. Lacan came to call this symbolic function 'the name-of-the-father.'

Brakhage and Smith even had opposing attitudes toward literary, anthropological, and psychoanalytical references. For

---

2 *The Seminar of Jacques Lacan: Book III – The Psychoses, 1955-1956*, ed. Jacques-Alain Miller, trans. Russel Grigg (New York: Norton, 1993)

Brakhage they constituted what he called "Margin Alien" (alienated 'marginalia') in his first theoretical book, *Metaphors on Vision*, which he wrote, avowedly, to liberate his sensibilities from linguistic references and academic or 'professional' disciplines. In his films, he eschewed all traditional symbols. Smith spoke repeatedly of his bibliographic sources and the hermetic emblems he often used in his films in a conscious effort to dispel the cultic aura of initiation and secrecy encouraged by occultists

In the second half of his life Brakhage taught film theory and history for a living. By the time Harry Smith arrived in Boulder, Brakhage was a professor at the University of Colorado. Since his first permanent teaching appointment at the School of the Art Institute of Chicago in the 1970s, he had been lecturing on important filmmakers, imagining their lives from the evidence of their films. He was so taken with Gertrude Stein's reflections on the force of names in *Four in America* (1947), that he used first names as keys to the imaginary biographies of great filmmakers in his book *Film Biographies* (New York: Turtle Island Foundation, 1979), on Georges Méliès, David Wark Griffith, Carl Theodore Dreyer, Sergei Eisenstein, Charlie Chaplin, Stan Laurel & Oliver Hardy, Buster Keaton, Jean Vigo, Fritz Lang, F.W. Murnau and Alexander Dovzhenko. As early as the "Poetry and Grammar" essay in her *Lectures in America* (New York: Random House, 1935), Stein had laid out the naming principle *in nuce*:

> …A name is adequate or it is not. If it is adequate then why go on calling it, if it is not then calling it by its name does no good.
> People if you like to believe it can be made by their names. Call anybody Paul and they get to be a Paul call anybody Alice and they get to be an Alice perhaps yes perhaps no, there is something in that, but generally speaking, once they are named the name does not go on doing anything to them and so why write in nouns. (p. 210)

Etymologically, 'Harry Smith' means the 'Commander who fabricates metals,' even though the verb 'to harry' means almost the opposite: to destroy, or in diminutive modern parlance, to harass. The name and the verb aptly describe the contradictory character of the artist/ alchemist himself. However, Brakhage said nothing of Smith's name in the School of the Art Institute of Chicago lecture he devoted to his work, but he mined the interview I did with Smith in the *Film Culture Reader* to construct an even more outrageous childhood for him than the one Smith dubiously concocted to tell me. But for Brakhage's Griffith, Dreyer, Chaplin, Keaton, Hardy, and Murnau nomen *was* omen. The first biography of his book, that of Georges Méliès, never explicitly associates the boy he calls 'George' – he usually referred to the filmmakers by first name to underline the centrality of their childhood for understanding their work – with the eponymous Saint, but he describes him as a dragon slayer of 'The Hydra… a singularity we all… share amidst a tangle of dangerous angel hair – that electrical thought-glass which cuts instinctual nerve to pieces…' (p. 17)

The phrase 'nomen est omen' was first formulated by the Roman comic playwright, Plautus, in his *Persa* as a gag about the value of a female slave named 'Lucris.' Carl Jung takes the notion more seriously in his *Synchronicity – An Acausal Connecting Principle* (trans. R.F.C. Hull, London: Routledge and Kegan Paul, 1972), where he noted that the driving theories of three major psychoanalysts, Freud, Adler, and himself, can be traced to their surnames: 'Freud [Joy], he observed, asserted the pleasure principle, Adler [Eagle] the will to power, and he Jung [Young] the idea of rebirth…' (p. 15) Earlier German psychologists had focused on surnames as determiners of trades and professions. Wilhelm Stekel called it the 'obligation of the name' and Karl Abraham even speculated that it may be a genetic inheritance from the ancestor who originated the family name from his trade. "On the Determining Power of Names" (1911), Abraham's brief essay of less than a thousand words, quickly alludes to the indication of neuroses, character traits, the choice of objects of emulation and love in first names and pseudonyms as well.

Thus, 'Harry Smith' might have descended from a line of

blacksmiths. His fascination with alchemy might then be attributed to the principle of nomen est omen. Etymologically the Christian name 'Harry' derives from 'Henry.' Yet Brakhage would not have known that Harry Smith bore the name of his father's father, not a nickname. There would have been an indirect precedent for speculating on 'Henry' from *Four in America* (New Haven: Yale University Press, 1947), where Gertrude Stein imagines U.S. Grant as a religious leader, Wilbur Wright as a painter, Henry James as a general, and George Washington as a novelist.[3] In that book she always refers to Henry James by both Christian and surname:

> *Volume XXIV*
> Let me tell the history of Henry James simply tell the history of Henry James which bring me and us back to names.
> I have nothing to say about names even if I make a mistake.
>
> *Volume XXV*
> A name is a name by which someone reads something or not then when does he does she not.
> And if he does if she does, does it make a moon.
> A moon is no name.
> James is no name.
> Henry is no name.
> Why is no name.
> Shares is no name.
> Blinded is no name.
> Predicate is no name.
> This is no name.
> Henry James if you say so Henry James was a name.
> You can think of a name or not a name. It is very easy to think of

---

[3] Brakhage's follow-up book on filmmakers, *Film At Wit's End* (1992), bears a tangible, but even more remote kinship to Sigmund Freud's *Der Witz und seine Beziehung zum Unbewußten* (1905) [*Wit and its Relations to the Unconscious*] than *The Brakhage Lectures* (1972) and its expansion into *Film Biographies* had to Freud's case histories. One sign of the change is the shift from the rigorous use of first names for Jerome Hill, Marie Menken, Sidney Peterson, Maya Deren, Christopher MacLaine, James Broughton, Bruce Conner, and Ken Jacobs. in the former. In the later book, he always refers to MacLaine by his surname and alternates between James and Broughton. There, he nearly abandons *nomen est omen*, using it, erroneously, only to characterize the 'shyness' of the affable Peterson: 'You could almost see him as the little boy called 'Sidney'... cursed as are all boys named Sidney, who was bookish and somewhat shunned by his fellow students, though in maturity developed a tremendous power of intellect.' [p. 50]

> Henry James as not a name. When a boy is a general that is to be is going to be a general being the son and the graduate of one and another one and either of them have been a general they may say to him you cannot be afraid. And he may say but I am I am afraid, I am often afraid, I am afraid when I see something and it turns out to be a horse then I am afraid. But then how can you come to be a general. But a general is on a horse and on a horse it is not on a horse that there is any way to be afraid. And beside that any general is not where there is any danger to be a general in any danger as a general oh no not indeed not for a general. So that is it.
>
> Henry James if he was to be a boy was then to be a general oh yes if not then if not why not a general. But he is a was to be a general… (pp. 153-54)

Although he was under the influence of Gertrude Stein, Brakhage's lectures on filmmakers were much more didactic and straightforward than this typical passage from his great model.

In *American Magus* we also find Bill Breeze's hermetic insight that the salamander (which he identifies alchemically as a 'fire elemental') occurs with a fire engine sound. Again, we hope such conjunctions might be systematically explored, perhaps by the anthology's contributor Harvey Bialy, who claims that the film would offer 'multiple hermetic scenarios.' But nothing in *American Magus* takes us as far as Michelson's interpretation. Yet, as I read it, I was reminded of the daring, speculative meditation of Stan Brakhage almost twenty years earlier:

> Brakhage: ['Harry'] then – already defeated by some-such creatures as we can begin to imagine on the barren planet of his foetal mind… completely overwhelmed, torn to pieces before what-we-would-call his 'birth' – begins as a child to invent a spirit-of-himself which will revenge him… a hero who will FREE the wickedly enchanted – or otherwise destroyed – pieces of his actual being […] [young 'Harry'], perhaps later then, begins to imagine a heroine who will restore him, a woman who will sew together or otherwise remember his actual being […]
>
> ['Harry'] himself decides to become just such a magician; but first he must make the hero of his invention a magician. As he is *imagining* the woman… she will always be the victim of this magic – subject to the transformations of it: thus young ['Harry'] hopes to have power over her equal to her necessary ability to remember and, as Mother

then, to restore him. He must also manage some ultimate magic for his actual being which can defeat the magic he gives the hero-of-his-invention; and he begins therefore to create a demon-self (of himself-imagined-restored) who can tear his hero to pieces as he foetally once was. (pp. 17-18)

I am cheating, of course; for Brakhage was not projecting this version of the Kleinian scenario onto Harry Smith (and his *No. 12*) in 1977, but onto Georges Méliès (and all his films), and where I inserted 'Harry' Brakhage wrote 'George.' It is an irony that the online recording of Brakhage's lecture on the films of Harry Smith at the School of the Art Institute of Chicago, a wildly fabricated and grossly inaccurate 'biography,' begins with a screening and discussion of Brakhage's own autobiographical *Sincerity (reel one)* [1973].

I changed 'George' to 'Harry' because, for my part, I wanted to pounce on a memory Jordan Belson offered Paola Igliori: 'He had some interesting books around. He had a book on Méliès, for example.' I'll bet that this was Maurice Bessy's and Lo Duca's *Georges Méliès, mage* [Paris: Prisma, 1945, 205 pages, with illustrations, some of them in color.] This was the sort of expensive, lavish, hard-to-get-book Smith could hardly ever resist.

Brakhage's recuperation of Méliès, the prestigitator, as an Oedipal magician neatly coincides in this one instance with Smith's hermetic archeology of popular culture. Consequently, I shall try to chart the ways in which *No. 12* could be viewed as an homage to Méliès.

Méliès hand-colored many of his films, producing a more vivid intensity of hue than later photographic color processes could match. Similarly, Smith colored *No. 12* with a series of masks, filters and jells, hand operated as he projected the film through a contraption of his own design (which he flung in a rage from the third-story window of the Film-Makers Cooperative on Park Avenue South in the mid-Sixties. Mercifully no one was injured.) The mechanism resembled some of the devices Méliès invented to create his filmic effects.

These interesting but superficial similarities pale beside the remarkable echoes of images and structures found in Méliès' corpus and Smith's *No. 12*. The play between flatness and depth exemplified by the photograph of the watermelon recalls a continual inspiration to Méliès, as *Le livre magique* (1900) illustrates. The evocation of Egyptology and the imaginary projection of women are a part of both the Méliès and Smith fantasmagoria. Even Méliès' transformation of bodies into skeletons becomes a favored trope for Smith, as do extraordinary shifts of scale.

The dismemberment and reconstitution of the human body is even more central to both. I presume Méliès's most famous trick film, *Le Mélomane* (1903), would have especially appealed to Smith who spent so much of his life exploring the visualization of music. Furthermore, I presume that the original sound of Le *Mélomane* would have been a live orchestra's rendering of the notes for "God Save the King," evoked by the sparagmos of the composer in the film, who removes his own head again and again to heave it on the telegraph lines above him, transforming them into a musical staff. The elaborate variations on the dissection and transformations of Smith's woman lead to her ascent into the heavenly zones. At one point she is multiplied, like the heads of the *Mélomane*.

In *Voyage à travers l'impossible* (1904) and A *la conquête du pôle* (1914), a large monster consumes without killing a group of explorers. Deliverance by consumption, a version of Jonah and the whale, also appears in Méliès' *Le royaume des fées* (1903). These comic versions of Polyphemus's horrendous meals in *The Odyssey* find their correspondence in the turning point of *No. 12*, where a large human head (that of Max Müller, the popularizer of comparative mythology and religions, Smith tells us) ingests all the animated figures, only to defecate them in the penultimate moments of the film.

The final descent of the elevator in *No. 12* entails a

splashdown in the sea – indicated by the sound of water rather than imagery – and a re-ascent to the surface, following the pattern of the space-rocket in Méliès' most famous film, *Le Voyage dans la lune* (1902). Finally, Méliès' *Hydrothéropie fantastique* (1909) plays with the explosion and reassembly of a human body – the central act of *No. 12*. In Méliès's fantasy an obese man, seeking weight reduction, is placed by a quack in a faulty machine for hydrotherapy. It explodes scattering his body parts, which the quack assembles and drops back into a repaired machine, from which the man re-emerges, thin and happy.

• • •

Smith called his *Mahagonny* an interpretation of Marcel Duchamp's "Great Glass". He probably was unaware of Michel Carrouges' *Les machines célibataires* when it was published in 1954; but he certainly learned of it when Harald Szeemann revived the notion of bachelor machines in his exhibition *Le macchine celebi/ Bachelor Machines* (Kunsthalle Berne), for which Rizzoli, published the catalogue in 1975. He would have owned the catalogue because Szeemann included *No. 12* in the exhibition. I believe that catalogue was the impetus for the ironic subtitle of *Mahagonny*. In that vein, I would now call *No. 12* an interpretation of the work of George Méliès.

When I invited Harry Smith to be the guest on my monthly radio show on June 2, 1977, he began the session with a bibliographical catatog:

> The only preliminary thing I would like to say is that.... The assumption is that the radio audience is familiar with the works of Lévi-Straus, regarding the Stop sign and the Go sign, the raw and the cooked, animals being cooked and eaten by men. I particularly suggest page 96, and then you can throw away *The Raw and the Cooked* [*Le Cru et le Cuit* (1964)]. Always knowledge of Chomsky is necessary, although in that case, after you have thrown away the little bit of Lévi-Strauss and skipped the middle [undecipherable] etcetera... Chomsky should, at least be looked at enough... *Aspects of the Theory of Syntax* [1965], which is his doctoral thesis, which is probably the most brilliant one Harvard has had since 16-something;

and then, of course, a little about Wittgenstein. In that case it's not necessary to take the cellophane off the book [there is no complete or selected edition of Wittegenstein's writings in a single volume] before you throw it away... If you would ask a few questions... but, please, explain first that the answers have no connection with the questions unless the Up and the Down is binominally [word slurred, perhaps 'posed'] but mispronunciations being the raw/ cooked part; in fact, as you leave your home tonight, examine the fire hydrants to see if they are still painted red and green the same way they were.

Thus, with characteristic sarcasm at the start of that radio interview about his then film-in-progress *Mahagonny*, he mentioned the perusal of three authors. In essence, he was telling us that three general notions permeate the theories of the mind of and of language informing all of his films. From Lévi-Strauss, we might consider the anthropological applications of Saussure's binaries, from Chomsky the innate human propensity to generate the syntactical structures of every language, and from Wittgenstein the ideas of fundamental language games or pictorial references. (By naming the Austrian philosopher, rather than one of his books, Smith may be suggesting that both the picture theory of the early *Tractatus Logico-Philosophicus* (1921) and its repudiation in the idea of 'language games' and 'grammar as a form of life' in *Philosophical Investigations* (1953) ought to be taken into account.)

All his life Smith explored systems of symbolic organization, freely synthesizing his vast reading in linguistics, psychoanalysis, anthropology, hermetica, and natural science with his passion for music and ethnomusicology. For instance, following the example of Aleister Crowley, Smith did elaborate research into the "Enochian language" as it had been revealed to the Elizabethan occultist John Dee. It was supposed to be the sacred language, before Babel, in which the patriarch Enoch spoke to Yahweh. Angels 'revealed' it to Dee through his assistant William Kelley in 1581-82.

Near the end his life, as shaman-in-residence, at the Naropa Institute, he proposed a lecture in Naropa's Jack Kerouac School of

Disembodied Poetics on "The Rationality of Namelessness." Unfortunately, by the time he was to deliver the lecture, he forgot the topic, instead speaking as if it were to be a talk on Surrealism, and never once mentioned names or namelessness in his confused (and probably drunken) ramble.

"The Rationality of Namelessness" was to be followed on succeeding Saturdays by "Is Self-Reference Possible?", "Communication, Quotation, and Creation," and "The Grammar of Awareness." According to Rani Singh, Smith always meticulously prepared his lectures then immediately lost the topic once he began to speak. What can we conclude from this? Little more than that Smith continued to speculate on the relationship between mind and language until his final years. But his thoughts about names and self-reference remain unknown. However, in the rant that took place instead of the lecture on "The Rationality of Namelessness" he offered a rationale for his propensity to insult both his hosts and his auditors (that is 'to harry' them excessively) as a 'definition' of Surrealism: 'Surrealism cannot be discussed… It is a specialized way of bring people into unity with one another through the medium of insults and arbitrary interactions between them.'). In this extraordinary paean to insults Smith may have recalled Daniel Paul Schreber's *Memoirs* where the judge had described the insults God directed at him as 'sublime' and 'pure.'

Stan Brakhage

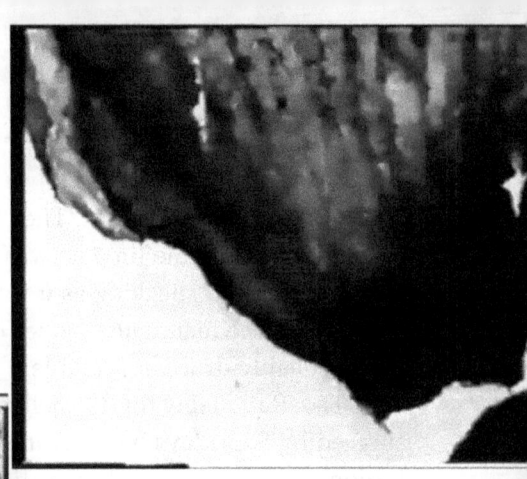

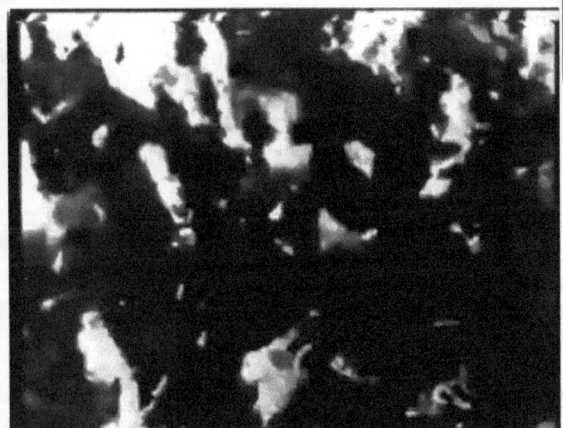

Mothlight (1963).

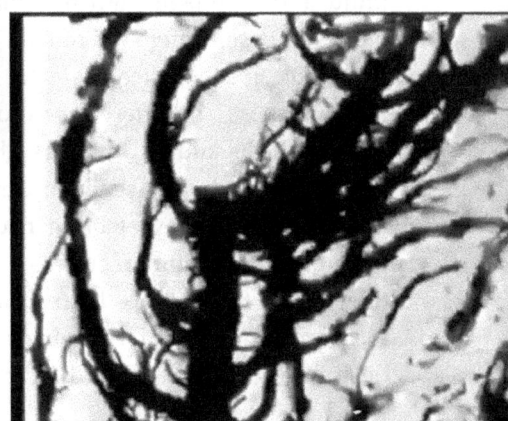

Dog Man Star (1961-64).

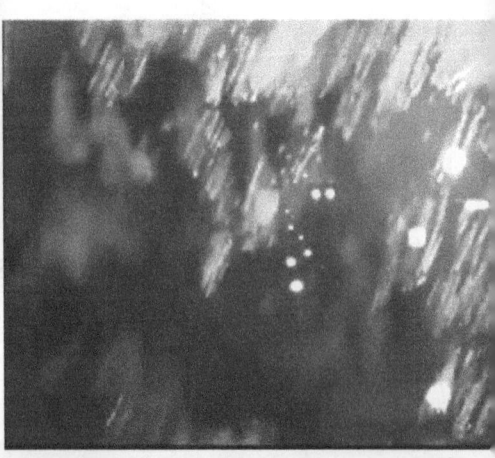

Harry Smith, No. 12 ("Heaven and Earth Magic")

8

Dropped Names

Michael Snow's longest film, at four hours and fifteen minutes, has, congruently, the longest of his titles: *Rameau's Nephew by Diderot (Thanx to Dennis Young) by Wilma Schoen* (1974). It contains a composer's name, a translation – the film is subtitled 'For English speaking audiences' – an author's surname, an acknowledgment that is also a covert dedication by means of a parenthetical inclusion of a full name, and an anagram. Dennis Young (whose two names invokes a new or 'young' god of tragedy and comedy – Dionysus), the curator of modern art at the Art Gallery of Ontario, had given Michael Snow an English translation of Denis Diderot's *Le neveu de Rameau*. The film is actually, or literally, dedicated to the inventor Alexander Graham Bell, whose felicitous surname and conqueror's first name might be construed as an omen of his invention of the telephone, although being born of a deaf mother and an elocutionist father may have overdetermined his fate.

Wilma Schoen is an anagram of 'Michael Snow'. It is the first of many anagrams of his name to appear. 'Schoen' is the German word for 'beautiful.' The letters of 'Wilma' are left over when *schoen* is extracted from 'Michael Snow;' so, the filmmaker may not even know that the name means 'resolute protector.'

Nevertheless, the feminized author of the film is the resolute protector of what? Of Beauty? Or is she the beautiful and resolute protector of Diderot's book? Or even of Michael Snow's barely hidden identity, and of his status, comparable to that of Diderot or the composer, Jean-Philippe Rameau? Wilma is, by accident or on purpose, appropriately a Germanic name, since for decades the French text of *Le neveu de Rameau* was misplaced and the book was known only in the German translation Goethe made of it.

However, the title sequence, larded with outrageous anagrams, is far from the first thing we see in this long film. That would be Michael Snow whistling into a microphone, shot from several directions. One of the functions of this opening is to generate a rebus whose meaning will be suspended until the final shot, of a snow-covered truck, from which we might derive that the entire work is framed by the name of 'Mike... Snow.' Before we come to the long roll of titles, read by a man with a speech impediment and corrected by the voice of Snow himself, we see a temporarily blurred FOCUS card (over a German voice reading from Diderot's text) and, after the FOCUS card actually comes into focus, a shot of Mother Snow at a grand piano reading aloud from a Spanish translation of Diderot's Mennippean satire.

Under the long scroll of credits, prolonged further by those interwoven anagrams made from the author's name, we see a freight train passing. Its seemingly interminable sequence of boxcars symbolize the paratactic assembly of scenes that will make up the film. The anagrams suggest that for each member of the extensive cast there is an encrypted version of the author. They are 'translations' of his name, just as the barking of a dog in a later episode is 'translated' by the artist, Denis Burton, as 'Whorf', the surname of the distinguished amateur linguist, Benjamin Lee Whorf, who argued a major theme of the film: that the language one speaks shapes one's thought.

Over the past half-century I have written on Snow's films so often that I shall not attempt new interpretations here. What I had to say about *Rameau's Nephew...* can be found on pages 383-386 of the third edition of my *Visionary Film*. A much more ample examination of the complexity of that masterpiece might be read in the book by Ivora Cusack and Stéfani de Loppinot accompanying Re:Voir Video's DVD edition of the film (see Ivora Cusack and Stéfani de Loppinot, *Rameau's Nephew by Diderot (Thanx to Dennis Young) by Wilma Schoen*, Trans. Pip Chodorov (for English speaking audiences) [Paris: Exploding and ReVoir, 2002]). It is well summarized online by Jan Philip Müller's "Sync Sound / Sink Sound: Audiovision und Synchronisation in Michael Snow's Rameau's Nephew by Diderot by Wilma Schoen" (*Zeitschrift für Medien- Und Kulturforschung*, 2014 [5]).

Instead, I shall briefly write of the two scenes Snow recorded of me for the film. I appear, visually and audibly, in the longer of the two very near the end of that serial work; audibly only in an earlier sequence. At the time of filming, I had no idea of what the former scene meant or why Snow asked me to recite the script he gave me. In profile I enumerated the four variations on the homophone /fôr/, as a number (4), the word for the number (four), the conjunction and preposition (for), and a prefix (fore-). Snow did *not* have me include the etonym /-phore/, as in *metaphor*. The academic exercise of counting the instances of the homonym in this epically long film was, of course, a send up of my tedious procedures as a critic. Just as Frampton had tricked Snow into apologizing to himself for making a poor advertisement for a show of his art when he got him to read the 'autobiographical' text he wrote for the soundtrack of *Hapax Lefiomena: (nostalgia)* (1971), and George Landow would further parody that film by having Snow read a takeoff of it in *Wide Angle Saxon* (1975), I was skewering myself. Snow turned the brief film clip into a canon by superimposing it on itself and repeating it, four times (of course!).

When Babette Mangolte had finished filming me that evening, something struck me as funny. In those days I was capable to falling into nearly uncontrollable fits of laughter. Snow picked up on that, and got me going again as he recorded an extended explosion of my guffaws. Later he overlayed it on an image of the microphone placed in front of the vinyl yellow chair in his studio, suggesting that the chair couldn't stop laughing its ass off. That was an even more pointed jab at my critical folly; for that very chair stood prominently against the back wall in Snow's *Wavelength* (1967). I had written of the film with gushing enthusiasm and even constructed around it my most notorious article, "Structural Film." It caused more controversy than anything I had attempted earlier or achieved later; for I took *Wavelength* to be the emblematic instance of a sea-change in the aesthetics of the American avant-garde cinema, comparing it to films by Hollis Frampton, Joyce Weiland, Paul Sharits, Stan Brakhage, Gregory Markopoulos, and George Landow. All hell broke loose (a tempest in a teapot). The filmmakers I included were all offended to be 'lumped together.' Those I didn't mention were even more annoyed. Academics decried my use of the adjective 'structural' because of its potential (mis)association with French Structuralism, and film scholars complained I had misrepresented the collective phenomenon – for which they all proffered improved taxonomies, of course. From the filmmaker's point of view, the chair, the last three-dimensional object one sees in *Wavelength,* couldn't stop laughing.

Cusack and de Lipponot cleverly observed that in uttering and defining the term 'foramen' while mouthing Snow's script, 'Sitney confers his final blessings on *Rameau's Nephew*... with a robust 'for-amen.'' (p. 114) More pointedly, they probably did not know, but Snow would have known, that I alone of that small community was a regular church-goer as a practicing Roman Catholic. Yet again, the joke was on me who never 'heard' myself saying that *amen* until I read it in their book. Although my name appears wedged in among the seemingly endless credits, there is nothing to indicate that I am the one acting as the reciter of the /fôr/ words. Nor is the woman reading Spanish at the piano identified as the filmmaker's mother or even named in that scene. It is a characteristic of Snow's wit to play with such covert allusions. It is also typical of the exegesis of Snow's films to point out these connections and to draw conclusions from them.

Accordingly, now I am struck by an absence amid all those 'fore-'s: nowhere in that film, nor in any other Snow film to my knowledge, does Richard Foreman's surname appear, even though the filmmaker so admired his writing that he asked him to provide a text for an ultimately unfilmed scene of people talking in *The Central Region/ La Région centrale* (1971), unless my uttering 'foramen' be taken as the dramatist's name with an anaptyctic vowel /a/ inserted. Foreman's absence is an offstage 'presence' near the end of *Wavelength*, although a viewer would not know that from the film itself.[1] If one knows anything about that film, one knows it all takes place in a loft, filmed through a zoom lens, that proceeds from the back of the room to a wall all the way at the street end, between the two large windows. In a way that *Rameau's Nephew...* is *about* the autonomy of the soundtrack and the variety of sounds the body (and nature) produces, *Wavelength* is *about* the zoom lens.

The zoom lens was adapted to filmmaking in the late 1920s to facilitate a quick change from a long (telephoto) to a short (wide angle) lens or vice versa. That made it possible to get a close shot of wildlife in the field without losing time by having to move the camera. In 1951 Pierre Angénieux refined the focus mechanism so that the camera could easily film while the lens was changing its focal length. That made 'zooming' possible. While traditional

---

1 See Michael Snow, *The Collected Writings of Michael Snow* [The Michael Snow Project] (Waterloo, Ont.: Wilfrid Laurier University Press, 1994), p. 44: "Think it's great too and was happy that Richard Foreman, Ken Jacobs, and Andy Warhol thought so when [*New York Eye and Ear Control* (1966)] was first shown at (the Filmmakers') Cinematheque." Amy Taubin sent me (email, April 12, 2020) the following passage from an interview she had recently conducted with Snow:

In 1964, Richard Foreman and I (then married) were introduced to you and Joyce Weiland (then married) by Ken and Flo Jacobs (still married) outside the Astor Place Theater where your first major film, *New York Eye and Ear Control*, was about to screen.

Your reminiscence caused mine: I'm honoured to have known such wonderful people as you, Ken and Flo Jacobs, and Joyce Wieland. The theatre of Richard Foreman is the greatest that I have experienced. I was lucky to be the sound person in the presentation of one of his plays.

(*Film Comment*, online [https://www.filmcomment.com/], May 1, 2020).

camera movement, or tracking, maintained a consistent focal length, giving the impression of what a subject sees while moving, the mechanical property of the zoom, instead, often suggested a dramatic act of attention, rather than physical movement. The zoom lens is really two lenses. The outer one fixes and focusses an image, while only the inner one moves a few millimeters toward (or away from) a detail in the former.

Oddly, *Wavelength* is not quite the 'continuous zoom' Snow claims when he wrote:

> *Wavelength* was shot in one week Dec. '66 preceded by a year of notes, thoughts, mutterings. It was edited and first print seen in May '67. I wanted to make a summation of my nervous system, religious inklings, and esthetic ideas. I was thinking of, planning for, a time monument in which the beauty and sadness of equivalence would be celebrated, thinking of trying to make a definitive statement of pure film space and time, a balancing of "illusion" and "fact," all about seeing. The space starts at the camera's (spectator's) eye, is in the air, then is on the screen, then is within the screen (the mind).
>
> The film is a continuous zoom which takes 45 minutes to go from its widest field to its smallest and final field. It was shot with a fixed camera from one end of an 80 foot loft, shooting the other end, a row of windows and the street. Thus, the setting and the action that takes place there are cosmically equivalent. The room (and the zoom) are interrupted by four human events including a death. The sound on these occasions is sync sound, music and speech, occurring simultaneously with an electronic sound, a sine-wave, which goes from the lowest (50 cycles per second) note to its highest (20,000 c.p.s.) in 40 minutes. It is a total glissando while the film is a crescendo and a dispersed spectrum which attempts to utilize the gifts of both prophecy and memory which only film and music have to offer. (Michael Snow, [in the catalogue of the] *Fourth International Experimental Film Competition* [Brussels, Cinématheque Royale de Belgique 1967] p. 66; reprinted in *Film Culture*, no 46 (Autumn 1967), p. 1; and in *The Collected Writings of Michael Snow*, p. 40.)

Wavelength's zoom is actually *dis*continuous. Its movement is anything but smooth. It pushes forward in tiny increments, halts, moves a little forward again as color filters change, or even as color negative shots of the room intervene. Sometimes the zoom recommences from a fractional distance behind its previous limit of progress. Ironically, in his frequent and fierce denunciations of the film as a mechanical operation, Stan Brakhage seems to have been responding more to the description than to the film itself; for there is more split-second optical manipulation of the color, textures, and light tonalities in *Wavelength* than any other comparable film of its period, aside from those of Brakhage himself and Robert Breer.

Snow did not shoot the film in the sequence we see. He began at night with the intruder. That, like all the other sections of the film, was made in a three-minute increment using a roll of 16mm film, one hundred feet long. Each roll was of a different film stock. The filmmaker shot both during the day (when we can see the street sign of the hardware store opposite) and at night (with the unshaded windows opaquely black). He often used filters to color the light waves and he made a separate montage of intermittent pure colors, sometimes in brief flashes, to superimpose over much of the finished film. He even had to recenter and to move the camera closer to the windows in the final quarter of its screen time, in order to get near enough to the black and white photograph of ocean waves he wanted to be seen at the very end.[2]

Originally Snow supplemented the soundtrack of the live room with an autonomous sine wave generator. But to distribute the film, he sacrificed a degree of the ear-piercing pitch of the generator to put a mixed soundtrack on the film. The human activity is concentrated near the beginning of the film and near the end (that is, in the five minutes before the generator starts again). Some minutes after a figure staggers into the room and falls suddenly to the floor, a young woman enters, looks back to where the body had collapsed and makes a telephone call. By that

---

[2] See Elizabeth Legge, *Michael Snow Wavelength* (London, UK: Afterall Press, 2009), pp. 18-22 for details of the production. Legge aptly notes that Snow's catalogue description of the film "streamlines the account" [p.20]. In *Visionary Film* and elsewhere I have been guilty of similar streamlining, as Bruce Jenkins pointed out in "The Case Against Structural Film" (*Journal of the University Film Association*, vol. 33, no. 2 [Spring 1981]).

point the pitch of the continuous sine wave permits her words to be heard.

The title of the film alerts us to the varieties of light and sound emitted by the film and permeating the space it represents. The sine wave is outside of the diegesis of the visible action, but invisible waves of sound within the room allow a radio to translate music (the Beatles' 'Strawberry Fields') to us; the 'realistic-live' sound of moving a bookcase and the breaking of wood and glass by the intruder provide an alternation of on-screen and off-screen noises; and finally, Alexander Graham Bell's invention translates the young woman's plaintive voice into electrical impulses, presumably to be retranslated into those same tones and words to the receiver of the call. He is named Richard, etymologically 'a strong king.' We never hear his voice. The woman says:

> 'Hello, Richard. It's Amy. I just got here and there is a man lying on the floor, and I think he's dead… No, I don't know how he got in. He doesn't look drunk; he looks *dead*. What should I do?… No, I don't want to do that. Could you come over? *Please*… Alright; I'll wait downstairs.'

The actress is Amy Taubin. At the time she was married to the dramatist, Richard Foreman.

After she departs, Snow superimposes silent black and white fragments of the scene, as if a reverberating echo of her dramatic moment hovered, ghostlike, in the room. But because the zooming frame has inched a little closer toward the back wall and its photograph, the superimpositions no longer quite 'fit' the space in which we originally saw them; for the zoom lens not only generates the illusion of forward movement in a fixed space, it transforms the depth and width of the space with every change of focal length.

In its final moments, it becomes apparent that the color film will end on the black and white photograph of the waves frozen in time; dead, as it were. Snow presents us with a superimposition of the photograph pinned on the wall over the photograph filling the whole frame. A dissolve seems to move closer into the photograph itself. But what is a filmic dissolve? The light fades on one image just as it increases on the other, in superimposition. When the two are spatially proximate, the mere simultaneous exchange of luminosity registers as a slight movement forward (or backwards).

After a long hold on the photograph, as the sine wave reaches its highest pitch, the image whites out. This turns out to be the function of focus. By turning the lens to its utmost limit, the image blurs, goes completely out of focus, and then disappears until nothing but white light comes through. Thus, in *Wavelength* the world of rooms, things, and people become functions of focus, mere filterings of the white light of the projector and the ambient light bouncing off of matter in front of the camera.

In this film of sound and light only two proper names are spoken: Amy (etymologically 'beloved') and Richard. Their ontological status is nothing more than that of the flux of sound waves, just as are the footsteps of the men moving the bookcase, the music from the radio and the intruder's breaking of glass and wood. The personal names are focal devices, unnecessary but helpful in juicing up the narrative that brings together the Fallen Man with the future arrival off-screen of the so-named Strong King, to console and assist the shaken Beloved. Their first names are stylistic markers of the eruption of 'realism' in the film.

Things, too, have *names*. Often the ambiguous words for things remain latent puns in Snow's film. Of *Wavelength*, one might recall that the Latin word 'camera' means room. The slippery nature of the names of things is the source of a gag in the concluding scene (before the Erratum and Addenda) of *Rameau's Nephew...*: there Snow shows and identifies three objects for the painter, Reg Holmes (unnamed). The first, a cymbal, has a punning name; the second, an orange, bears a name that is both a noun and, when naming a color, an adjective; but for the third, a banana, Snow switches gears, as it were, saying 'yellow' before he laughs. What is he laughing at? Us viewers? Because our expectations have been fooled? At the oddity of the ways language names things?

However, the primary locus of significant names, and perhaps even more significant omissions, in Snow's filmography would be *So Is This* (1982). It is a forty-five-minute film of nothing but printed words in white, appearing on the screen one at a time, for varying periods, against a black background. It begins with a fib: 'This is the title of this film.' The initial fib is glossed in the second paragraph:

> In 1979 Drew Morey made a film titled This is the title of my film. Since this is not his film and the "this" in his title is not the title of this film and hence the author (Michael Snow) of this film decided to retain this title and include the foregoing reference to issue in this film. This is still the title of this film. So is this.

Morey and Snow are not even the first proper names to appear on the screen. Before mentioning them, the flashing words of the film thanked Anna Pafomow for 'placing the words on the screen.' In that same second paragraph Snow also cited John Kamevaar for giving him a bronze cast of the word 'This.'

Yet it is the third paragraph that deserves our closest attention, and consideration of both the names that *are there*, and which ones *are not*. In it we find:

> Next there have been several films or videotapes that concentrate on texts, for example Richard Serra, Tom Sherman, Su Friedrich, John Knight, and Paul Haines have made excellent use of texts. The author would like to have been the first but it's too late. Priority is energy. In some respects this is first. Obviously this is not the first time that this has been used for the first time. This belongs to everybody! This means this, you think this, we see this, they use this, this is a universe! So what is important is not this, but how this is used.

The first four names Snow cites as examples were artists who posed no threat to his preeminence as a filmmaker. Serra already had a greater reputation as a sculptor than Snow, but he frequently and publicly acknowledged Snow as the prime inspiration for his films. Tom Sherman is a Canadian artist, known at that time for his music videos. John Knight may be the Canadian installation artist whose work would become known two decades later. (I know of no films or video works by anyone of that name.) Likewise, Paul Haines may have been the poet and jazz lyricist who began making video tapes around the time *So Is This* was released. Finally, Su Friedrich would become a major figure of the American avant-garde cinema only after her fourth film, *The Ties that Bind* (1985), drew attention to her earlier oeuvre. It was prescient of Snow to recognize the importance of her text-based dream diary, *Gently Down the Stream* (1981). Its inclusion in this litany gives away Snow's familiarity with avant-garde cinema and therefore underlines the serious omissions of the achievements of major filmmakers for which the names of Serra, Sherman, Knight, Haines and Friedrich are substitutes or evasions.

The prolific James Broughton never made a film showing texts, but in his *This Is It* (1971) he recites a poem he had written much earlier, playing extensively and wittily on the words 'this' and 'that.' More to the point, would be Marcel Duchamp's *Anémic cinema* (1926) and Paul Sharits's *Word Movie* (1966). In so far as Friedrich's text-based film mixes words with images, George Landow's *Remedial Reading Comprehension* (1970) would be an apt candidate for mention. However, the most startling omission is the name of Hollis Frampton, Snow's friend, who enacts the role of the dying intruder in *Wavelength*. The central section of his *Zorns Lemma* (1971) alternates words found in the city environment with those imposed by the filmmaker. Yet his *Hapax Legomena: Poetic Justice* (1972) is a thirty-one-minute long film, composed entirely of hand-printed pages of a script. It is the third part of a serial film; the first part for which Snow spoke the voiceover.

I understand this evasion to be a case of poetic or artistic rivalry, hastening to add that such competitiveness (nearly ubiquitous among major artists) is not a moral deficit in character.

Snow happens to be a good-humored, generous man, who idolized the work of Duchamp and acknowledged his great influence, maintained friendly relations with Frampton and Sharits, and spoke well of Landow's work. His restraint in the face of Stan Brakhage's public polemics against his films was admirable.[3] Brakhage was notoriously ferocious toward filmmakers who challenged his preeminence within the avant-garde cinema, e.g. Jack Smith and Warhol, before Snow. As far as I know the only reaction of Snow to Brakhage's taunts came indirectly within the tea party sequence of *Rameau's Nephew....* where all the participants recited their lines backwards as they commented on an explosion of flatulence – Cusack and de Lipponot tell us that the episode was based on the one embarrassing meeting Snow had with Duchamp, his wife Teeny, and Joyce Wieland (then Snow's wife) – as one tea drinker asks about the odor, 'noisiv fo traf eth sith si?' in a crude allusion to Brakhage's longest film *The Art of Vision* (1961-1965).[4]

The glaring omission of Frampton's name here may actually have been triggered by Frampton's assiduous efforts to position himself as the principle figure associated with 'structural film' in the half-decade following the dramatic unveiling of *Wavelength*. He completed more than thirty films and embarked on a twenty-four-hour film cycle he would not live to finish; he published a brilliant series of articles making him the most important theorist

---

[3] For an example of Brakhage's attacks, see his "Selected Film-Talks – 1970s: Some Arguments, November 4th, 1977" *Millennium Film Journal 47/48/49* (Fall/Winter 2007-08), pp. 65-74.

[4] Evidently Snow thought he was making a good-natured joke on Brakhage's title. In 1993 he told Mike Holbloom:

> I remember seeing *The Art of Vision*, which really knocked me out, but there were things about it that clarified my wanting to make work with a total shape, wanting the camera, not the maker, to be the story… I never wanted my work to talk about me. I want my work to exist on its own, to be self-reliant, so you can have a dialogue with it. The expressive use of the instrument, which was what Brakhage was doing, and which I still think is one of the most radical things that ever happened in the arts, was something I didn't want for myself. His strength clarified my own way of thinking. That's what was wonderful about being in New York — there was so much powerful work that it was really a sink-or-swim thing. I had to ask what I could do."

("Michael Snow: Machines of Cinema (Interview)," http://mikehoolboom.com/?cat=407)

of the avant-garde cinema since Brakhage; and less admirably, he eagerly solicited articles from critics, providing stills and documents to guide them in the interpretation of his films. Most egregiously, he seems to have publicly snubbed the screening of *La Région Centrale* at the massive festival of recent avant-garde films Jonas Mekas curated in New York at the Elgin Cinema in February 1972 to curry favor with Brakhage, in whose company he entered the theater as they took seats in the front row in the final minutes of the première of Snow's film. In "On Hollis Frampton" Snow paid obituary tribute 'to the memory of a great friend, great artist, and great talker' in 1985, praising both *Zorns Lemma* and *Poetic Justice*, and mentioning Landow and Sharits kindly, but not the Elgin Theater incident (which he may not have even noticed). (See *The Collected Writings of Michael Snow*, pp. 241-48.)

If indeed, '[p]riority is energy' the text of *So Is This* recoils from the energy of the great text-based films made a decade or so before Snow issued his. When he goes on to claim 'So what is important is not this, but how this is used,' he speaks of more than just the demonstrative pronoun in an effort to reclaim his originality. In other words, he is claiming that *this* film – *So Is This* – *uses* language on screen more extensively, more self-referentially, and more self-consciously than any film made before it. If the others used words on the screen, this one is *about* words on the screen.

After a very significant use of ellipsis, the one political 'name' mentioned in the film occurs in a witty figure of apophasis:

> Remember the old saying: "Sticks and stones may..." etc. There'll be not one word about El Salvador no mention of Trudeau and no political commitment whatsoever.

The 'old saying' is a rhyme: 'Sticks and stones may break my bones/ but names will never hurt me.' The 'names' in this cliché are specifically insulting epithets, or metaphors, not simple proper names. To 'call someone names' is to reduce them to a despised type. Yet, the ellipsis suggests that another sense of 'names' lurks behind the citation, as if saying Duchamp, Broughton, Landow, Sharits, and Frampton in *So Is This* would indeed hurt 'the author' by undermining his authority, sapping his energy, and questioning his originality.

By deliberately substituting the names of lesser filmmakers at the early moment when his originality is at stake, he is saving the 'big names' for the end. The sixth paragraph switches midway to French, where he mentions Magritte:

> Ça fait penser l'auteur au tableau bien connu de Magritte: Ceci n'est pas une pipe. C'est vrai ici aussi. L'auteur aime beaucoup le mot "ceci".

> (That makes the author think of the well-known painting by Magritte: This is not a pipe. That is true here as well. The author really likes the word "this.")

Magritte and Trudeau pose no threat to Snow as a filmmaker; nor does the giant of Greek philosophy in his *Phaedrus*, the master text about writing; for the film concludes thus, with the biggest names of all:

> Flashback. Writing in the 4th century B.C., Plato has Socrates say: "You know Phaedrus that's the strange thing about writing which makes it truly analogous to painting. The painters' products stand before us as though they were alive, but if you question them they maintain a most majestic silence".

Even the word, 'flashback' has more than one meaning here. Of course, it states that long before *So Is This,* even before Sharits made his *Word Movie* or Broughton wrote 'This Is It,' Plato articulated the parameters of written language; at the same time, it flashes back to *Rameau's Nephew...*; for, in the very lengthy hotel scene near the end of the film, the sculptor Royden Rabnowich, playing 'Jack,' destroys a table as a lesson in ontology. When the 'real table' reappears in superimposition it can no longer support household objects. Unmentioned, the tenth book of Plato's *Republic* inspired this comedy. There Socrates used the examples of a table and a bed to demonstrate the physical manifestations of his theory of Ideas or Forms. In that same episode, Snow makes a parallel play with a bed, both with and without superimposition. He even expands it to complimentary sequences of fingers playing a piano synchronized to the sound of a female orgasm and an image of genitals copulating, as if generating piano music. The picture to picture and the sound to picture relations throughout the hotel episode constitute a *reductio ad absurdum* of Plato's idealism.

Snow's decision to omit the presence of people and of language from *La région centrale* is as much indicative of his sense of the focal organization he gave to each of his films as it is of the secondary importance of speaking in a film. The focal organization of his films alternates between complexity and formal isolation. (I never saw the first one he made, the silent animation, *A to Z* [1956], described in the *Film-Makers' Cooperative* as 'A cross-hatched animated fantasy about nocturnal furniture love. Two chairs fuck.' The title alone reveals the consistency of Snow's fascination with alphabets, words, and writing.) *New York Eye and Ear Control* (1964) might be called 'dialectical' in its complexity. It plays off the two-dimensional silhouette of a sculptural figure (his "Walking Woman" outline) against the visual depths of the city and the acoustic rhythms of jazz. It marks the artist's transition from his central practice of sculpture and playing music to cinema. Presumably, the first five words of the title come from the signs for the New York Eye and Ear Hospital seen in downtown Manhattan. The substitution of 'Control' for the final noun names the power cinema gives the maker for determining spatial and auditory relations, even when the one 'thing' he fully controlled in the filmic field was the cutout figure of the Walking Woman. Curiously, the style of the film is so unique that its relation to Frampton's *Zorns Lemma* would pass unnoticed – probably unnoticed by either filmmaker – since the long, silent, middle section of Frampton's film alternates between signs found in the New York streets with words superimposed by the filmmaker over city views, for a parallel articulation of flatness and depth.

Snow's third film is a clear-cut case of the isolation of a filmic technique. *Standard Time* (1967) concentrates on the counter-clockwise circular motion of a camera on a tripod in a small interior space. *Wavelength*, was his next film; it is complexly 'dialectical': because it explores the illusions inherent in the use of the zoom lens when it is situated in a 'realistic' environment that entailed minimal aspects of narrative and speech; so minimal in fact, that only two names are briefly used. Between *Wavelength* and *Rameau's Nephew by Diderot (Thanx to Dennis Young) by Wilma Schoen*, five of the six films he made have no language. <–> (also known as *Back and Forth*) (1968-69), *La Région centrale*, and *Breakfast (Table Top Dolly)* (1972-76) wordlessly concentrate on varieties of camera movement, while the silent *One Second in Montreal* (1969) and sound film, *Side Seat Paintings Slide Film* (1970), were composed of static images. The former employs only black and white photographs – one-second-long exposures – of sites for potential sculptural installations in Montreal; Snow isolated the static images to emphasize the quality of cinematic duration. The latter, a slide presentation of the filmmaker's paintings filmed from an extreme lateral angle, offers an exception, as Snow recites the titles of his works and names the photographers who took the slides. A year later Hollis Frampton would enrich and ironize this principle in *Hapax Legonema: (nostalgia)* by making an oblique autobiography from a chronological sequence of photographs he took, accompanied as they burn, one by one, on a hotplate, by an asynchronous commentary he got Snow to recite as if the photographs were his own works, or as if he were Frampton.

Admittedly, proper names have never been central to Snow's cinema. In fact, I might never have joined together dispersed thoughts I had on the three films I concentrate on here were it not for the ideas generated by writing the previous chapters of this book. The range and roles of spoken language in cinema – not just names – becomes the manifest subject of *Rameau's Nephew...* and of written words in *So Is This*. Between them he made *Presents* (1980-81), a three-part film exploring the nature of a mobile stage set, a violently destructive subjective camera, and for two-thirds of its ninety minutes, the relationship of montage to handheld camera movements. Its use of speech, in the opening section, is even more minimal than *Wavelength*'s, and without names, as far as I recall. *Presents* is Snow most mis-estimated film. He was at the top of his game when he made it but the *zeitgeist* was against him. The centrality of female nudity in it brought down a barrage of feminist criticism precisely at the moment when feminism was emerging as the most important dimension of both avant-garde film criticism and filmmaking. Very brief images of female genitalia caused the Ontario Board of Censors to prohibit temporarily the exhibition of *Presents*. He humorously attacks those censors in the fourth paragraph of *So Is This*:

> Anyway there are apparently some things that this just can't say. Perhaps we will be classified Adult by the time you are reading this. Or perhaps you are reading this elsewhere. If this is appearing in Ontario, Hello Censors, Hi Mary. This film is clean as a whistle Ha Ha Ha Ha. (Hollow laughter).

'Hi Mary' is the most enigmatic instance of a proper name in the corpus of Snow's cinema. Is she one of the censors? In that case, the inclusion of her name would be an ironic taunt. Or, less likely, did she help him in his ultimately successful fight to get both *Presents* and *Rameau's Nephew...* shown in Toronto, making that greeting an acknowledgment of thanks? Despite the inclusion of 'dirty words' in the same paragraph, *So Is This* was not censored.

It took the astounding success of *Wavelength* to engender a critical reevaluation of *New York Eyes and Ear Control*. The proper appreciation of *Presents* may never come. In its version of the complex 'dialectic' characteristic of some of Snow's most ambitious films, it sets dramatic play-acting on a blatantly artificial stage against the location shooting in Europe and the Canadian north, where 'tracking' and 'hunting' are among the latent puns. The hour-long exercise in montage rigorously refuses any obvious connection between more than two shots in a row. It is as central an exposition of the ontology of montage as *Zorns Lemma*, or Brakhage's *The Riddle of Lumen* (1972), but its contribution has been ignored, or rather, wiped out by attacks on its putative 'sexism.'

In the three films on which I have concentrated, names take a broad spectrum of forms – a rebus, anagrams, a salutation, a self-identification, in citations, apophasis, and quotations. In *Wavelength* the names give weight to a cry for help. In *Rameau's Nephew...* they chart the disguise of authorial presence. But in *So Is This* the omission of the names of significant contemporaries (especially those associated with the concept of 'structural film') betray a degree of anxiety that the monumental achievements of *Wavelength*, <->, *La Région centrale*, and *Rameau's Nephew...* would be diminished by perpetuating that context. Those names, '*This*' implies, would be better left 'in a most majestic silence.'

Wavelength
(Michael Snow, 1967).

9

Dubious Terms and Names: Structural Film Redux

Fifty years ago my essay "Structural Film" first appeared in *Film Culture* 47 (published in early 1970 as the Summer 1969 issue of the journal). Nothing I have written since has been so widely read; nothing as 'successful.' Yet it would be an egoistic distortion to claim its 'success' was due wholly to me or to my ideas; the controversy it created, first among filmmakers, later among scholars, bolstered its prominence for nearly twenty years. Now that a half-century has passed and the controversy is only of antiquarian interest, I wish to elaborate on the conditions under which I wrote it, and respond to the most astute of the criticism it elicited. Almost all of its critics made one or more salient points, yet most of them got carried away by the antagonistic spirit of revision. I would like to acknowledge those corrections and yet again reiterate my position, or at least, what remains worth maintaining of that position.

I have had to invent several unique terms for the clusters of avant-garde films I had been discussing since 1962. It seems a transparently innocent and harmless gesture, hardly any different from employing already familiar terms. In fact, for many years I thought Parker Tyler had been the first to use the term 'trance film' to describe the genre of avant-garde cinema that dominated the 1940s. When I scoured Tyler's writings to footnote his first use of the phrase, I first suspected. and eventually had to conclude, that I had 'coined' the term from many astute observations about the tradition of entranced figures Tyler had made in several books, especially in *The Three Faces of the Film* where he illustrated the concept with stills from *The Cabinet of Dr. Caligari* and *Meshes of the Afternoon*. By doing nothing more than using Tyler's noun 'trance' as an adjective, I had 'invented' a name for a genre. Yet that coinage and that genre aroused no controversy. It was barely noticed for a decade.

Imagine my surprise and discomfort when a few years later, 'structural film' met with a storm of protests, both terminological and substantial, that lasted even longer that the gap between my first use of 'the trance film' and its first innocuous notice.

Between June 1967 and August 1968, I had travelled to eight European countries with some forty hours of American avant-garde films. In the middle of that stretch of time – from Christmas until New Year's Day – I attended the Fourth International Experimental Film Competition, sponsored by the Cinématheque royale de Belgique at Knokke-le-Zoute where Michael Snow's *Wavelength* gained the grand prize. As soon as I returned from that extended tour of the Third International Exposition of the New American Cinema, Jonas Mekas and I awarded Snow's film *Film Culture*'s Ninth Independent Film Award.

For the fourth time since its inception in 1955, the journal changed its format. For the first time it had no images, no stills, not even a cover. The Independent Film Award was on the first page, where the cover would have been. On the same page, readers would encounter the invaluable program note for the film Snow submitted to the Competition in Belgium and "Conversation with Michael Snow" by Mekas and myself.

While I was abroad three issues of *Film Culture* had come out without any input from me. *Number 43* was a 'special issue' devoted to Expanded Cinema, designed as a foldout newspaper by George Maciunas, who contributed his own encyclopedic graph of the evolution of performance art (*avant la lettre*) with 'expanded cinema' as a subcategory of it. Professor Steven P. Hill organized most of *Number 46* around the films of Lev Kuleshov, to which Mekas added material by several of the usual contributors, Herman Weinberg, Gregory Markopoulos, an interview with Peter Kubelka by Mekas himself, and material about Len Lye, Bruce Connor, Carl Linder, and Barbara Rubin. Finally, the *45th* issue was devoted mostly to the cinema of Andy Warhol (with contributions Gerard Malanga collected as the guest editor) supplemented by discussions of the Kuchar brothers, Ron Rice, Gregory Markopoulos and, significantly for the argument of this chapter, a letter from poet Jackson MacLow to George Maciunas.

Mekas always made the final decision on layout and contents of *Film Culture*. Three times before he had restrained from supplementing the issues of a guest editor: Seymour Stern's volume on Griffith's *The Birth of a Nation* (*no. 36*), Andrew Sarris's volume on American Cinema (*no. 28*), and Stan Brakhage's book, *Metaphors on Vision* (*no. 30*). After I had completed my work on *no. 29* in 1967 – the first issue Mekas had handed over to me to devote to avant-garde films – he decided on his own to give the Fifth Independent Film Award to Jack Smith for *Flaming Creatures*, putting that and several articles relating to Smith at the front of the issue, with a still from Smith's *Normal Love* (then called *The Great Pasty Triumph*) on the cover. The cover image of Smith's film-in-progress rhymed ironically with the previous cover, selected by Sarris for his American Cinema volume, from a Busby Berkeley musical.

For most of 1969 I had been preoccupied with organizing the institution that would become Anthology Film Archives. During that year I was very excited by seeing a great many of the films that I had missed while I was travelling in Europe. The avant-garde cinema, and the other advanced arts that might be seen and heard in New York, seemed at a high peak. That October the

Metropolitan Museum of Art opened Henry Geldzahler's massive show of *New York Painting and Sculpture 1940-1970*. One Sunday afternoon, probably in November 1969, after visiting the show at the Met for the third time and having read through its catalogue, I sat in my living room to write about the achievement of *Wavelength* and the emerging sensibility it brilliantly exemplified. I had been thinking about the topic for a few months, and arguing with colleagues who tended to link Snow's film to those of Warhol.

In three astounding years (1963-1966) Warhol had made the most essential contribution to the American avant-garde cinema since Stan Brakhage 'invented' the lyrical cinema in the late 1950s and early 1960s. In 1964 *Film Culture* gave him the Sixth Independent Film Award for *Sleep* (1963), *Haircut* (1963), *Eat* (1964), *Kiss* (1963), and *Empire* (1964). But his important film work was over long before I wrote "Structural Film." Although there were many important aspects of Warhol's cinema that I came gradually to understand only in the decades after his death in 1987, I believed then, and still believe, that his collaborations with Paul Morrisey after he survived being shot by Valerie Solanas in 1968 marked a rapid degeneration of his art.

Shortly after that time, I began to think of *Sleep*, his five-hour film of Jean Giono sleeping as a phenomenological repudiation of the oneiric psychodramas of Deren, Peterson, Harrington, and Anger; I suggested that in the "Structural Film" chapter of *Visionary Film* in 1974. But it took the destruction of the World Trade Towers to bring home to me the prophetic politics of *Empire*, his eight-hour concentration on what was then the world's tallest building. Not only was he celebrating the biggest phallic erection on earth – and the United States's misplaced and unconscious pride in it – but by filming through the night until 'the dawn's early light,' he was substituting the Empire State Building for the Star-Spangled Banner in the very twilight of the American 'empire;' for, already plans were afoot to raise the World Trade Towers higher, while the myth of the *pax Americana* was bursting throughout the world. Similarly, his phenomenological approach to sex acts in the *Kiss* series and *Blow Job* put the lie to the eroticism of avant-garde films as they were slyly promoted by the Cinema 16 screenings of the previous decade.

The only film I had seen him shoot was *Taylor Mead's Ass* (1964). I reported that Warhol walked away from the running camera, while Mead improvised with a few props at hand. Later Callie Angell justifiably took me to task, for implying that such indifference was Warhol's usual practice. The use of the zoom lens, in most of Warhol's films from 1965 and 1966, ought to have alerted me of the error of my generalization.

The first critics of "Structural Film" were filmmakers themselves. Peter Kubelka sincerely believed that he, alone and isolated, had invented a new way to compose cinema in the late Fifties with *Adebar* (1957), *Schewechater* (1958), and *Arnulf Rainer* (1960) – he called them 'metrical films' – and that, a decade and more later, other filmmakers – those I identified as making structural cinema – began to work in the mode he pioneered. Kubelka publicly objected to the critical elevation of his fellow Austrian, Kurt Kren, in the late 1970s by European practitioners of structural cinema, claiming that Kren had been his student and imitator, who predated his first films to imply an historical priority over Kubelka.

The conceptual artist and founder of the Fluxus movement, George Maciunas, made a graph to debunk my essay. When I noticed him photocopying it at Anthology Film Archives, I asked if I might publish it as addendum to my revised essay in the *Film Culture Reader* (1970). He generously let me have it. He was the first that I knew of to object to the term 'structural film,' when he wrote:

> The term *Structural Film* is semantically incorrect, since structure does not mean or imply simple. Structure is an arrangement of parts according either to simple or complex design, pattern or organization.

With his encyclopedic knowledge of conceptual art, Maciunas listed an array of merely conceived films (such as his idea of an unmade tree film imagined by Jackson MacLow that the poet had attempted, in vain, to dissuade him from declaring as a genuine antecedent to Warhol's cinema in his letter in *Film Culture 45*), and other very rarely shown and unavailable Fluxus films to highlight the 'cliquishness and ignorance' of my essay. He deliberately misread my aim as seeking to define and historically contextualize what he called 'monomorphic' films.

Soon I had to face a more troubling objection to my terminology. I had not realized that the Structuralism of Lévi-Strauss, Lacan, Barthes *et al* had gained ascendancy in the humanities programs of many US universities in the year I had been out of the country. A day after I received by B.A. from Yale in 1967 I flew to Rome to take over the film exposition from Jonas Mekas. I did not return for fourteen months. If structuralist thought and methodology had gained a foothold in the American academic world even earlier, we never heard about it in the classes in Greek, Latin, and Sanskrit that occupied my studies. However, many of the more sophisticated readers of *Film Culture* were puzzled by what they thought might be my application of such Structuralist thought to new films. Some even mocked me for failing to understand Structuralism properly.

I recall that I had not been thoroughly happy with the term 'structural film' when I hastily wrote about the new sensibility I perceived emerging in American avant-garde cinema. At that time, I was particularly impressed by Michael Fried's essay "Shape as Form: The New Paintings of Frank Stella" that Geldzhaler included along with texts by Greenberg, Rosenberg, Rosenblum, and Rubin in the catalogue of *New York Painting 1940-1970*. I filched the word 'shape' from it, when I wrote: 'The structural film insists on its shape and what content it has is minimal and subsidiary to the outline.' That sentence became even more prominent when Mekas opted to print "Structural Film" on the front page of the coverless *Film Culture 47*.

In writing the article, I was trying to delineate a sensibility I found in some recent films of Conrad, Baillie, Markopoulos, Landow, Brakhage, Weiland, Sharits, and above all in Snow's *Wavelength*. Although *Wavelength* (1967), *The Flicker* (1966), *All My Life* (1966), *Gammelion* (1967), *Bardo Follies* (1967), *The Film that Rises to the Surface of Clarified Butte*r (1968), *Song 27: My Mountain* (1968), *Sailboat* (1967), and *N:O:T:H:I:N:G* (1968) did not look at all similar, I felt strongly that they shared a sensibility different from the more obvious analogues to the films of Warhol and Kubelka. Then I was trying to name the new *genius temporis* from which *Wavelength* and several other powerful films issued. I tentatively proposed a four-fold taxonomy based on their technical modes of production: fixed camera position (*Wavelength, All My Life*), Flicker effects (*The Flicker, Gammelion, N:O:T:H:I:N:G*), rephotography of projected images (the two Landow films), loop printing (*Sailboat* which I misperceived at the time as a loop, and some earlier Landow films). Of *Song 27*, I noted the fragility or inadequacy of this taxonomy:

> The extreme concentration in Brakhage's film upon the mountain as durable energy – it survives several seasons, persistently emerges from engulfing clouds – creates a kind of tension and a sense of potential comparable to the most dynamic structural films, *Wavelength*, Landow's *Bardo Follies*, Markopoulos' *Gammelion*, and Sharits' *N:O:T:H:I:N:G*.

But none of the critics of the essay seem to have paid much attention to the presence of Baillie, Brakhage and Markopoulos in it, apart from the latter two filmmakers who objected strenuously. In fact, Brakhage campaigned against the very idea of structural films and against many of the films themselves for years, while Markopoulos maintained a general disdain for American avant-garde cinema, its institutions and its exegetes, from 1967 until his death in 1992.

Once I had envisioned the four-fold taxonomy I realized that Ernie Gehr's films *Wait* (1968) and *Morning* (then called *Moments* by the filmmaker) (1968) were relevant to my argument. In the subsequent revisions of 1970 (*Film Culture Reader*) and 1974 and 1979 (*Visionary Film*), I repeated the taxonomy while extending its scope to include films made after 1969, even nuancing and qualifying it, when the films challenged the boundaries of those four dominant techniques.

In 1976 filmmaker Peter Gidal (an American making films and writing in the UK) published *Structural Film Anthology*, at first, as the catalogue of an exhibition he curated at the National Film Museum in London. His own fierce polemic, "Theory and Definition of Structural/ Materialist Film," opened the volume, followed by an excerpt of fellow filmmaker, Malcolm LeGrice's then forthcoming book, *Abstract Film and Beyond* (1977). Twenty filmmakers are represented by contributions to the anthology. Eight of them were among those I discussed in the first two versions of "Structural Film;" ten others worked in Great Britain (including Gidal and LeGrice); and the two Austrians, Kubelka and Kren, were there, presumably to give credence to the editor's contention of European antecedents for structural cinema.

I found myself in agreement with Gidal's characterization of my position (despite his contemptuous tone):

> [The] romantic base of much American Structural film has been elucidated by P.A. Sitney. Visionary filmmaking is precisely the post-Blakean mire that Structural/ Materialism confronts, whether this confrontation is articulated or not. 'Unconsciously thought' processes define themselves in practice. One must go on after Warhol, not revert to a reinvigorated pre-Warholian stance; one ought to be, by now, tired of expressing the same old thing ... 'trying to express when there is nothing to express'. To ignore the ideological function of Sitney's exegesis of a 'new romantic affirmation in recoiling against the tremendously crucial aesthetic attack that Warhol made' is precisely to be embedded in dominant ideology as located in the specific area being discussed: film. (*Film Culture*, Spring 1972 [sic], P.A. Sitney.)[1]

Although Gidal cited with approval Louis Althusser's call for the necessity of precisely correct terminology early in the essay,

---

[1] pp.14-15; *Flare Out: Aesthetics 1966-2016* (London: the Visible Press, 2016), p. 66.

he failed to account for the inclusion of 'Structural' in his manifesto for the 'Materialist' cinema he practiced. I assume he wanted to piggy-back the definition and theory of "Materialist Film" on what was by then the institutional acceptance of any number of versions of Structural Film.

LeGrice's book (rather than the excerpt in Gidal's anthology) is much more explicit (and inclusive) in its argument for the centrality of European structural cinema:

> So, whilst the American underground has had an undeniable influence on contemporary European film-makers, the formal direction of much recent European work was already initiated before the American influence, and certainly before Sitney's American structuralists were heard of in Europe. In many respects, the formal basis of post-war European work can be considered a continuation of the search for new cinematic form begun in the twenties, even though it was not a direct reaction to the films themselves which, like the American underground films, were not seen until the new movement was underway... In tracing the development of this new formal tendency, I shall accept the broad divergence of the experimentation, and instead of seeing those factors which Sitney refers to, like flicker effect, loop printing, and rephotography, as identifying characteristics of a category, I shall see them as concerns or directions of inquiry in a broad formal tendency. I shall add to them a number of other concerns, like celluloid as material, the projection as event, duration as a concrete dimension. I shall also modify Sitney's characteristic of a fixed camera in favor of a more general exploration of camera-functioning and the consequences of camera-motion or procedure in their various forms.[2]

'Concerns or directions of inquiry' is admirable. I wish I had written something of that sort prominently in "Structural Film;" *that* might have avoided some of the aberrant evaluations of my argument. However, taken together Kubelka, Maciunas, Gidal, and LeGrice seem to agree that the phenomena I observed in 1969 was real, but that I misnamed them, misunderstood their historical context, excluded some of the most important instances and included irrelevant ones, and devised the wrong taxonomy. Their disagreements occurred when they attempted to replace

---
2 Malcolm Le Grice, *Abstract Film and Beyond* (Cambridge: MIT Press, 1977), p. 88.

those 'errors.'

Gidal implied in the 2016 "Introduction" to *Flare Out* that every history is a rhetorical gesture toward a specific end. I have almost no disagreement with that; In fact, as I shall eventually note here, I agreed with the same point when Keith Sanborn made it forcefully thirty years earlier, in regard to histories of the avant-garde cinema. Furthermore, even when the end appears to be self-serving, the alternative history that frequently culminates in the polemicist's own films is usually irradiated by unique insights the filmmaker generated from the intense clarities attending the creation of his or her films. For instance, a late critique by Luis Recoder ("The Death of Structural Film: Notes Toward a Filmless System," *Spectator*, 2007), insightfully notices the prevalence of images of destruction in several widely discussed structural films, along with the representation of the ruin and mutilation of the film material itself. But, lo and behold, it turns out that the climax of that revised history is the 2006 installation, *Light Spill,* a large heap of film in a gallery by Sandra Gibson and Luis Recoder himself. Like all of the filmmaker critiques this one too made salient points despite the self-serving motive it might betray.

However, these attacks on my article or chapter, not only pointed out factual errors, inconsistencies and lapses of logic, they too frequently faulted my taxonomy for failing to account for films made later, and to which no one (aside from the authors of the criticism) thought to test their failure. I have read only one critique – R. Bruce Elder's – that admits that that taxonomy was offered as fragile and incomplete.

Le Grice made that anachronistic argument when he takes Snow's <–> (1969) and *La région centrale* (1971) as examples of the inadequacies of 'fixed camera position' and 'shape.' But not only is *La région centrale* the closest Snow (or any of the other filmmakers I discussed) ever came to Brakhage's *Song 27: My Mountain,* even the equatorial mount he commissioned to supplant the vertical and horizontal limitations of a conventional tripod (both fully explored in <->), inscribed in his film the tropes of filming its shadow, the coming of dawn, and the dance of the moon that may allude to Brakhage's *Anticipation of the Night* (1958), where unrelenting camera movement became an index of the filmmaker's selfhood. Snow's equatorial mount and its remote control deny the representation of that selfhood.

The academically-trained authorities on avant-garde cinema tended to make the same mistake, even the best of them: Paul Arthur, Regina Cornwell, and Bruce Jenkins. Starting with the last to be published and working backwards, I note that Jenkins, in "A Case Against 'Structural Film'" (*Journal of the University Film Association* of the 33.3, spring 1981), confessed that his disparagement of "Structural Film" began when he tried to apply the four-fold schema to Hollis Frampton's *Autumn Equinox* (1974) section of his uncompleted *Magellan* (ca. 1973 – Frampton's death was in 1984). I would have been shocked if Jenkins had succeeded with that tool. In fact, if it had worked, it would have been a strong argument that the schema was so porous anything could be accommodated by it.

He corrected my faulty description of the two early Gehr films, and devoted several paragraphs to nuances of inadequate descriptions of other films, including *Wavelength*. For a long time, I had been troubled by my persistently following the extraordinary program note of Snow in calling *Wavelength* a continuous zoom movement from a fixed point of view. That is indeed so imprecise that it obscures the rich subtleties of the moment-by-moment visual phenomena that make the film a masterpiece. My imprecision was pointed out by Jenkins and other critics of "Structural Film" (generally without also blaming the filmmaker's program note). However, throughout the Seventies I ignored the cavils of professorial attacks (as mere 'nitpicks') while I responded to those of filmmakers (for I took them more seriously). Recently, in the chapter "Dropped Names" of this book, I finally tried to correct that deficiency in regard to *Wavelength*.

Of course, a gap of twelve years and the acquisition of prints of avant-garde films by academic institutions abetted Jenkin's admirable scrutiny and exactitude. Moreover, the strength of his critique derives from the cleverness with which he accounted for, and distinguished, the three successive versions of "Structural Film." He identified them as: first, criticism, then, theory, and finally, history. The first and last were quite fair assessments. It seems to me extravagant to label the revision of 1970 a work of, or even an attempt at, 'theory' just because the word appears *once*, in a justifiable context, and because I quote a passage from Viktor Shklovsky to illuminate the processes of Ken Jacobs's *Tom, Tom, The Piper's Son* (1969), a filmic masterpiece that had not been available to be seen when I wrote the first version, but which plays a central role in the revisions. Perhaps he wanted to suggest that I did not know my place and my limitations as a critic. But the real punch came when Jenkins called my 'leap from the space of criticism into the temporal domain of history' 'a sleight-of-hand.' By the time chapter 12 of *Visionary Film* appeared, in 1974, the structural cinema had indeed passed into history, without any stage-magical assistance from me. It turned out to have been a brief moment in the late 60s and early 70s, that became avant-garde mainstream in Europe by the 70s. Nearly all of those filmmakers I had mentioned moved beyond that mode by the time Chapter Twelve – "Structural Film" appeared, revised yet again, at the end of the first edition of *Visionary Film*.

Wieland, Landow, Conrad, and Sharits were making films of a different sort. Frampton's shift away from structural cinema is recorded in his massive serial film, *Hapax Legomena* (1971-72); later, he was totally engaged with making *Magellan*, which sometimes manifested aspects reminiscent of structural cinema, but not in *Autumn Equinox*. Snow's *Rameau's Nephew...* was made in 1974. No one would call it a structural film. Paul Arthur accurately identified the 'heyday' of structural film as '1968-1972.'[3] If in 1969 I was trying to name the emerging sensibility

---

[3] Paul Arthur, *Line of Sight* [Minneapolis, University of Minnesota Press, 2005], p. 80.

shared by many of the most original avant-garde filmmakers in America, by 1974 that *genius temporis* had morphed into an historical phase, and the name I had given it, for better or worse, had stuck.

Most of the first artificers of structural films tended to build their new films on the experience of their earlier efforts, moving away from a mode and/or redefining it, each in his or her own direction, thus scattering the brittle cohesion of my initial taxonomy. Overriding shape was perhaps the first aspect to be discarded; flicker went quickly after that. The initially peripheral concentration on a place as a source of multiple energies, as in Brakhage's *Song 27: My Mountain,* and *La region centrale,* acquired centrality, animating the best of Ernie Gehr's films, for instance.

Even Regina Cornwell's potentially useful approach in "Structural Film: Ten Years Later" (*The Drama Review,* Sept. 1979) via a chronology, stopped in 1969 unfortunately leaving out the five years of filmmaking and writing on structural cinema before *Visionary Film.* Beginning in 1963, by comparing the effect of seeing Brakhage and Warhol, she charted year-by-year the important films and programs of Gehr, Snow, Weiland, Sharits, and Landow, and later Frampton, asserting quite rightly that 'There was never a movement, nor was there a school involving these individuals.' (She might have noted that I had never used the words 'movement' or 'school.') Cornwell terminated her chronology with the release of *Tom, Tom the Piper's Son* before launching into her attack on "Structural Film" and *Visionary Film.* She faulted both versions for lacking 'the rigor of structuralist method' even while she acknowledged that 'Sitney's critical and descriptive procedures and the way in which he defines this 'other' cinema have nothing to do with structuralism as a method and discipline.' I take it that having 'nothing to do with structuralism' was not the virtue in her mind that it was in mine.

In her critique she referred to several films by Paul Sharits and to his essay "Words per Page" that appeared after her chronology ends, in a German translation in 1971 and the English original a year later. Had she extended the chronology to include all the films she mentioned, with a level of analysis and insight comparable to what she showed in the first eight annals, the careers of Frampton, Gehr, Gidal and Le Grice (as well as the vicissitudes of *Film Culture, Millennium Film Journal,* and *Artforum* in the Seventies) ought to have enriched her perspective, and perhaps even softened her criticism of me.

She might not have known of the efforts Hollis Frampton made after the publication of "Structural Film" to promote his subsequent films, providing potential critics with stills, plans, and keys for each new work. As soon as he made *Artificial Light* (1969), a loop printed with different scratches, marks or optical variations in each repetition, he offered me the layout of stills I used to illustrate the 1970 revision of "Structural Film" in the *Film Culture Reader*. All those stills provoked a gentle complaint from Michael Snow that Frampton had unjustly come to dominate my structural film thesis.

Sharits too sought out critics to publicize his work. He regularly sent us his writings. Thus, Cornwell promoted his "Words Per Page" as a preferable counter-text to "Structural Film" because she found it

> quite the opposite of the visionary and romantic attitudes indicated in Sitney's "Structural Film." Intention or artist's intention in the vernacular way used by Sitney and connected with the "Intentional Fallacy" has absolutely no place here. Nor do purely intuitive, non or anti-intellectual, or emotive/ expressive attitudes have a place here within the art-making and theory that promotes liaisons with the social and physical sciences.

Cornwell was right: for me that 'emotive/ expressive' attachment must always come first. I only write about the films I love. After that, I would seek out anything that illuminates the film, including the artist's program notes and declarations of intent.

George Landow's *Wide Angle Saxon* (1975) escaped mention in

Cornwell's summary critique. There would have been no reason that Cornwell ought to have known, or cared, that in 1972 I lectured at the Art Institute of Chicago on the influence of Duchamp on Hollis Frampton's cinema, even if she had brought her chronology all the way up to 1974. As part of the lecture, I screened two of the filmmaker's recent autonomous parts of *Hapax Legomenon: (nostalgia)* (1971) and *Poetic Justice* (1972) – both variants on filming from a fixed camera position. The only reason to note that event is that George Landow saw those films for the first time then, and that screening set in motion what would become the most delightful of all the critiques of "Structural Film": Landow's *Wide Angle Saxon* where an innocent, polite viewer decides to convert to Christianity while sitting out a boring likeness of *(nostalgia)*, purportedly made by the fictive Al Rutcurts, whose name is nearly a palindrome of 'structural.'

I always admired Paul Arthur's enormous appetite for seeing films and his heroic efforts at contextualizing them. His essay "Structural Film: Revisions, New Versions, and the Artifact: Part Two" was both the most exhaustive and the most insightful commentary I read from a fellow professor, before I saw the essay by Bruce Elder I discuss in the 'Postscript' here. (But I never quite understood what Arthur meant by 'Part Two' unless my original article was Part One). Arthur was slightly more sympathetic to the film studies community than I, but he happily shared a greater allegiance to the film-makers than to the academics. (To a somewhat lesser degree the same might be said of both Cornwell and Jenkins. Who else would risk an academic career quibbling about structural film?)

His article was published in *Millennium Film Journal*, from a crucial avant-garde institution in New York whose print organ had rapidly drifted into academia, by depending on the writings of graduate students at NYU's Cinema Studies Department. So did *Artforum*, where Annette Michelson enlisted her NYU students to write for the special film issues she edited. In *Number 4/5* of *Millennium Film Journal* (1979), where Arthur's essay appeared, two of the three editors came from NYU Cinema Studies, and at least 16 of the 27 contributors (including Arthur himself) were graduate students in that Department; and two or three of the others were NYU faculty.

Arthur practically began his essay by asking himself why to expend his energy on the 'dilatory' subject of my formulations and the 'perhaps premature' one of Gidal's. To the three versions of "Structural Film" that I published he added two more: a debate with Le Grice and a lecture I gave at the Museum of Modern Art, but he did little to distinguish one iteration of it from another. Yet all through his article he displayed his abundant knowledge of avant-garde and European films, as well as painters, photographers, and issues of film theory.

His impressive scholarship made his essay the most exhaustive and useful criticism of "Structural Film" to which he was more charitable than most other antagonists. Early on in the lengthy essay, he presented the most exacting critique of my 'sloppy' terminology – especially 'structure,' 'shape' and 'form' – demonstrating, even to my conviction, how I helped to bring on myself the confusion of 'structural film' with Structuralism. Yet, he was prone to praise me with one hand and take it away with the other, as when he wrote:

> These are minor contradictions, certainly, but they suggest both a sloppiness of articulation and a gradual process of simultaneous expansion and attenuation. For instance, where, in F[ilm] C[ulture] R[eader], Frampton is presented as the 'most critical case of the ambiguity of the definition of structural film,' (to my mind, an accurate assessment) by *Visionary Film* he is safely ensconced within the canon.' (p. 122)

'safely ensconced within the canon' would be, by 1979, merely a negative rhetorical flourish. But rhetoric aside, Arthur turned a blind eye to the films Frampton made between 1969 and 1973 that resolved that early ambiguity and, more significantly, contributed to the simultaneous expansion and attenuation of the range of structural cinema.

The elisions of the different versions of "Structural Film" in these academic destructions prompts me to lay out the actual motives and the sequence of the revisions. The mechanism that stimulated the sequential revisions of "Structural Film" was overwhelmingly the creation of new films by the artists who had worked in that domain before 1970. In reprinting and expanding the essay for *Film Culture Reader*, I naively expected to clarify my position in the face of the objections of Kubelka and Maciunas, but much more important to me was the incorporation of new films to the argument. I saw John Cavanaugh's *Dragon's Claw* (1965), Conrad's *The Eye of Counter Flickerstein* (1967), and Sharits' *Peace Mandala* (1966) for the first time and re-saw Snow's *New York Eye and Ear Control* and Landow's early films, but my primary objective was to account for the flood of new 'structural films': Gehr's *Reverberation* (1969) and *History* (1970), Sharits' *T,O,U,C,H,I,N,G* (1968), films by sculptors Robert Morris and Richard Serra, Snow's *<->* (1969) and *One Second in Montreal* (1969), Jacobs' *Soft Rain* (1969) and *Tom, Tom, the Piper's Son* (1970), Weiland's *Reason over Passion* (1970), and especially Frampton's *Artificial Light* (1969). Most of the refinements and modifications of my initial thesis came from the effort to assimilate those films into a more malleable schema.

With the first publication of *Visionary Film* in 1974, I attempted to expand and further refine the notion to accommodate the striking innovations of Snow's *La region centrale* (1971), Frampton's *Zorns Lemma* (1970) and Landow's films of the early seventies. The publication of Stephen Koch's *Stargazer: Andy Warhol's World and His Films* (1974), from which I quoted, helped me to understand and solidify the aspects of Warhol's cinema that foregrounded structural cinema. Likewise, quoting from Annette Michelson's "Toward Snow" (*Artforum*, June, 1971) allowed me to enlarge my discussion of *Wavelength*.

My first editor at Oxford University Press did not expect *Visionary Film* to be as successful as it was. (Neither of us anticipated the adaption of the book by courses in American avant-garde cinema.) He was counting on the translation of Christian Metz's *Film Language* to carry his film list and compensate for such losses as my book might have accrued. But the mystique of Metz, the French Structuralist film theorist *par excellence*, evaporated once American academics who couldn't read French realized what he was claiming. Thinking there would never be another edition or a reprinting of *Visionary Film*, OUP had agreed to Gregory Markopoulos's demand that the chapter on him be excised from any paperback or future edition. But by 1969 my editor had forgotten that promise when he asked me to prepare an expanded edition of the sold-out book. By removing the Markopoulos chapter, reluctantly but with the consolation that the films were practically invisible because the filmmaker had withdrawn them all from circulation in America, the addition of a new chapter became economically acceptable to the publisher.

Rather than introduce yet another technological mechanism into the taxonomy of structural cinema to accommodate the linguistic shaping-agents innovated by Landow and Frampton in the Seventies, or to consolidate loop printing and rephotography once the workshops, such as Millennium, and the art schools and universities that hired filmmakers, made 16mm optical printers available, I decided to treat the expansions of the structural film sensibility by those filmmakers who originated it, in the two revisions of *Visionary Film* in a new chapter.

For the second edition, I concentrated on writing on "The Seventies", where I placed Landow's *What's Wrong with the Picture?* (1971-72) and his later *New Improved Institutional Quality* (1976), *Thank You, Jesus, for the Eternal Present* (1973), and *Wide Angle Saxon* (1975). In that chapter I folded-in substantially rewritten observations on the peculiarities of autobiography in recent avant-garde cinema that I had contributed to *Millennium Film Journal* when it was founded in 1978. In much the same way, I had incorporated earlier texts from "Structural Film" into the chapter of that name in 1974. Aside from relocating the material on *Tom, Tom, the Piper's Son* from "Structural Film" to the previous chapter, "Recovered Innocence," where I discussed Jacobs' earlier films, "Structural Film" remained largely unaltered in the second edition of *Visionary Film*. "The Seventies" also allowed me to discuss Hollis Frampton's impressive theoretical writings on film and his seven-part *Hapax Legomena* as well as Yvonne Rainer's turn from dance to cinema. I used the autobiographical theme to expand on the then recent work of Stan Brakhage, whose prolific outpouring of films alternated between autobiography and abstraction in the Seventies and James Broughton, who had returned to cinema after a long absence with *Testament* (1974), his filmic autobiography. In "The Seventies", I introduced Joel Singer and Robert Beavers as promising younger filmmakers and wrote on Gehr's breakthrough film, *Serene Velocity* (1970), which the Oxford designers chose for the new cover on the first paperback edition.

By then it seemed to me that the hubbub about "Structural Film" was over. But the controversy wasn't dead; it had migrated into the academic arena, as the critiques of Arthur, Jenkins, and Cornwell show. I paid them no attention, aside from noting down a few factual errors that I ought to correct if there were ever to be a third edition. Perhaps the return to print of *Visionary Film* in that second edition reignited the antipathy to my "Structural Film" formulations.

It wasn't until the new millennium that the second *Visionary Film* sold out. My new editor at Oxford University Press insisted that if I were to restore the Markopoulos material (which his heir, Robert Beavers, authorized providing I corrected some errors), and add another update, which I felt indispensable, I would have to cut as many words from the second edition as I was adding in the new chapter. The availability of digital copies of many of the films eased those excisions: they had made much of the descriptive prose redundant. I cut lengthy descriptions of such films and many other paragraphs I felt could be spared. The new final chapter, "The End of the 20th Century", introduced the category of a cinematic Menippea, but neither the filmmakers (whose works I discussed under that rubric, such as Snow, Rainer, Child *et al.*) nor the cinema studies academics raised any objections. As far as I can tell, they never even noticed.

In the matter of the definition and criticism of structural cinema, I now recognize my difficulty in adjusting to changing times and methods of work. Just as today, I have no interest in seeing digital cinema, then I persisted in the working methods and intellectual concerns that I had been developing since the early Sixties. I confidently shrugged off academic film studies just as I had ignored Structuralism and its descendants, once I became familiar with them. I assured myself that they would soon pass from relevance, unaware that I too would pass along with them.

My arrogant indifference to the criticism of academics stemmed from several factors: in the first place, I did not want to fan the fires of a 'structural film' controversy. I did, nevertheless, agree to publicly debate filmmaker and critic Malcolm Le Grice on the subject at the Millennium Film Workshop. My performance in that December 1977 spectacle during which Le Grice graciously endured my jibes, now printed in both the *Millennium Film Journal* (*nos. 16-18*, 1986) and Le Grice's *Experimental Cinema in the Digital Age*, ought to be characterized as sit-down humor (I was intoxicated to the point of making stand-up unfeasible). My disdain for academic film criticism, especially of avant-garde cinema, had also been fueled by my experience as a teacher of graduate students in the Cinema Studies Department of New York University, from which I resigned in 1976. (Although I returned to academic appointments after that, I would never again serve in a film studies department or train graduate students.)[4]

---

[4] Lest over-diligent 'scholars' want to waste time refuting this assertion, I must add that greed and pity got the better of me in two cases; once I gave a summer course (for the extra money!) in film studies to Princeton graduate students in literary disciplines who were paid to take it; and several years later, I gave a graduate course in French cinema (for no extra pay, that time) when a professor from another institution cancelled his visit to Princeton after students had signed up for his seminar.

What does all this tell me? For sixty years I have been fascinated by avant-garde cinema until digital production became dominant, because I was captivated by a series of often puzzling works of genius. As I became more and more familiar with them, through repeated screenings, I kept on finding patterns of genre that presented me with an historical morphology. By writing about the films, those patterns, and their historical sequence, I partially satisfied my need to come closer to the films. But only once, in the evolution of that writing over at least forty years, did the recognition of a pattern and the term with which I identified it, escape into a troubled life of its own: Structural Film. In naming it, I had stumbled upon an overcharged adjective, and in describing the phenomena I had disturbed many sensitive vested interests that entailed what Keith Sanborn would later call 'competing and overlapping histories.'

In 1988 Sanborn, a natural polemicist and no friend of my critical enterprise (although subsequently a personal friend of mine, I must add), had fired off a polemic ('Let's set the record straight') signed by seventy-one filmmakers that only indirectly debunked my work:

> We challenge the official History promoted by the International Experimental Film Congress to be held in Toronto this Spring. The time is long overdue to unwrite the Institutional Canon of Master Works of the Avant-Garde. It is time to shift focus from the History of Film to the position of film within the construction of history. The narratives which take up this new task must respect the complexity of relations among the many competing and overlapping histories which make up the activity within the field.

It hardly matters that, from the little I know of it, the Toronto Congress would never have endorsed my criticism nor the 'canon' of films I loved and frequently discussed. Filmmakers and critics of the avant-garde cinema have been challenging the taste of Anthology Film Archives, *Film Culture,* and my writings since 1970. With significant variations and deviations, the major art museums and cinematheques of the western world endorsed that so-call 'Institutional Canon' and, in doing so, apparently made the morphological sequence I described into 'the official History.'

However, artistic canons are necessarily flexible and continually subject to challenge. They are established, reinforced, and revised by artists who make new works in response to them, not by critics or historians, who merely follow and attempt to give labels to what the artists have deemed important.

POSTSCRIPT

I thought I had finished this chapter after completing a revised draft of it, when I discovered the existence of a Brazilian volume devoted to Structural Film. But since I can read only a little Portuguese and that with great difficulty, I cannot take account of Theo Duarte's rather lengthy contribution on the criticism and the films. However, I was very surprised to find in his bibliography a reference to an essay in English of which I had never heard: R. Bruce Elder's "The Structural Film: Ruptures and Continuities in Avant-Garde Art" in *Neo-Avant-garde*, edited by David Hopkins.[5] Elder kindly and promptly responded to my request to see the essay. The volume in which it appeared is virtually inaccessible because of its rarity and its expense. I was astonished by what he sent me; it contradicts most of what I have written about my critics of the essay in this chapter.

Elder is a prolific filmmaker who has also written more (and more useful) books and essays on avant-garde cinema than anyone else. He never construes film history as a teleological event leading to his own films. His scholarship and his film production are admirably distinct. That is demonstrated, yet again, by the objectivity and insight with which he assessed

---

[5] *Avant-Garde Critical Studies 20*, ed. Klaus Beekman (Amsterdam-New York: Rodolphi, 2006), pp. 119-142.

"Structural Film." He wrote:

> Today [2006], the appearance of "Structural Film" is commonly regarded as one of the cardinal moments in the discussion of films made outside the context of sponsored films. When it appeared, however, it was subjected to an inordinate number of attacks. The phenomenological description of structural film's defining feature, its insistence on its shape, was the ground of some of the fiercest rejoinders. (p.121)

In the first place, he confined his remark to the 1970 version of my text as it appeared in *Film Culture Reader*. He alone observed that my four-fold taxonomy was never posited as a universal schema for structural cinema. But more amazing to me was his identification of Michael Fried's "Form as Shape" as the crucial influence on my use of that term.

Furthermore, Elder takes account of the attacks of Maciunas, Gidal, Le Grice, Jenkins and Arthur (but not Cornwell) in his learned study; and he discusses at length Sharits' "Words Per Page" (which he reads as essentially supporting the thesis of "Structural Film"). He concluded, on the basis of the argument and the films mentioned in 1970, that 'predetermined schema' (p. 129) would be a more accurate term than 'shape' uniting the various structural films:

> Despite [Maciunas', Jenkins' and Arthur's] protests, it is reasonably clear that the tendency that Sitney was describing was that of using a form whose outline is established before the shooting or the editing has taken place, or which responds, in a systematic and predetermined fashion, to events that arise during the shooting or editing. (p.123)

Here Elder articulated, more succinctly and clearly than I ever did, the common quality of the films discussed in the 1970 text (before the central filmmakers made works that contradicted that commonality).

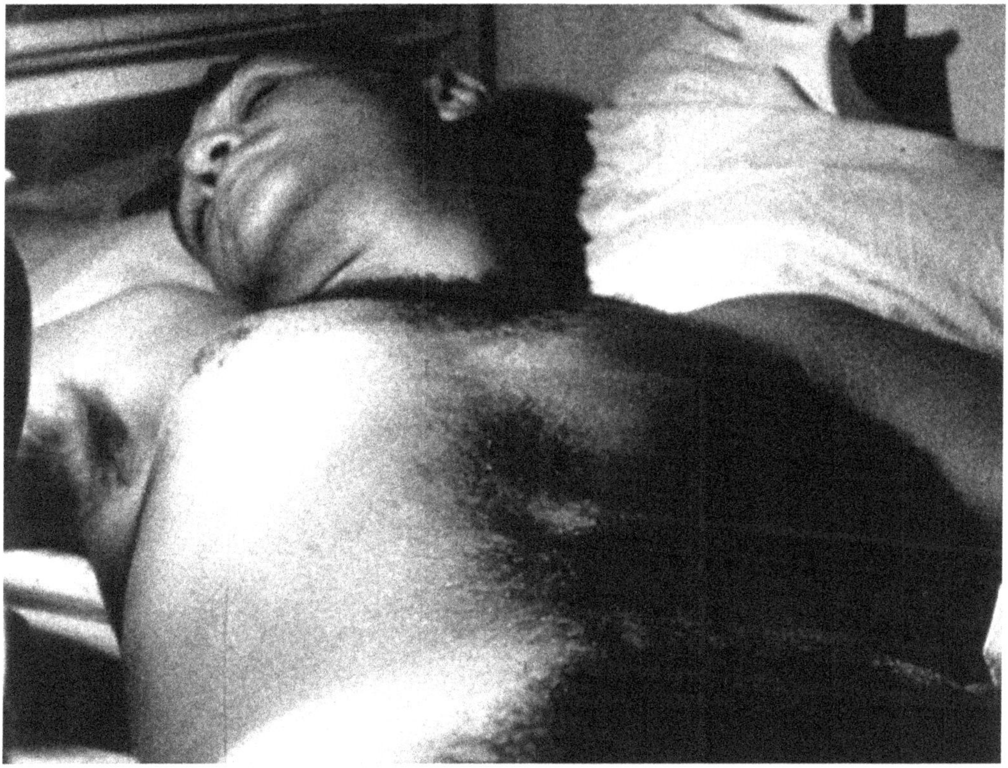

Sleep (Andy Warhol, 1963).

CRESCENT MOON PUBLISHING

web: www.crmoon.com e-mail: cresmopub@yahoo.co.uk

ARTS, PAINTING, SCULPTURE

The Art of Andy Goldsworthy
Andy Goldsworthy: Touching Nature
Andy Goldsworthy in Close-Up
Andy Goldsworthy: Pocket Guide
Andy Goldsworthy In America
Land Art: A Complete Guide
The Art of Richard Long
Richard Long: Pocket Guide
Land Art In the UK
Land Art in Close-Up
Land Art In the U.S.A.
Land Art: Pocket Guide
Installation Art in Close-Up
Minimal Art and Artists In the 1960s and After
Colourfield Painting
Land Art DVD, TV documentary
Andy Goldsworthy DVD, TV documentary
The Erotic Object: Sexuality in Sculpture From Prehistory to the Present Day
Sex in Art: Pornography and Pleasure in Painting and Sculpture
Postwar Art
Sacred Gardens: The Garden in Myth, Religion and Art
Glorification: Religious Abstraction in Renaissance and 20th Century Art
Early Netherlandish Painting
Leonardo da Vinci
Piero della Francesca
Giovanni Bellini
Fra Angelico: Art and Religion in the Renaissance
Mark Rothko: The Art of Transcendence
Frank Stella: American Abstract Artist
Jasper Johns
Brice Marden
Alison Wilding: The Embrace of Sculpture
Vincent van Gogh: Visionary Landscapes
Eric Gill: Nuptials of God
Constantin Brancusi: Sculpting the Essence of Things
Max Beckmann
Caravaggio
Gustave Moreau
Egon Schiele: Sex and Death In Purple Stockings
Delizioso Fotografico Fervore: Works In Process 1
Sacro Cuore: Works In Process 2
The Light Eternal: J.M.W. Turner
The Madonna Glorified: Karen Arthurs

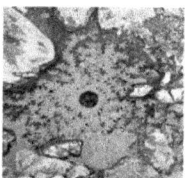
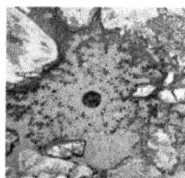

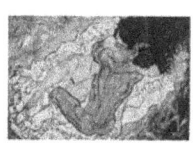

LITERATURE

J.R.R. Tolkien: The Books, The Films, The Whole Cultural Phenomenon
J.R.R. Tolkien: Pocket Guide
Tolkien's Heroic Quest
The *Earthsea* Books of Ursula Le Guin
Beauties, Beasts and Enchantment: Classic French Fairy Tales
German Popular Stories by the Brothers Grimm
Philip Pullman and *His Dark Materials*
Sexing Hardy: Thomas Hardy and Feminism
Thomas Hardy's *Tess of the d'Urbervilles*
Thomas Hardy's *Jude the Obscure*
Thomas Hardy: The Tragic Novels
Love and Tragedy: Thomas Hardy
The Poetry of Landscape in Hardy
Wessex Revisited: Thomas Hardy and John Cowper Powys
Wolfgang Iser: Essays and Interviews
Petrarch, Dante and the Troubadours
Maurice Sendak and the Art of Children's Book Illustration
Andrea Dworkin
Cixous, Irigaray, Kristeva: The *Jouissance* of French Feminism
Julia Kristeva: Art, Love, Melancholy, Philosophy, Semiotics and Psychoanalysis
Hélène Cixous I Love You: The *Jouissance* of Writing
Luce Irigaray: Lips, Kissing, and the Politics of Sexual Difference
Peter Redgrove: Here Comes the Flood
Peter Redgrove: Sex-Magic-Poetry-Cornwall
Lawrence Durrell: Between Love and Death, East and West
Love, Culture & Poetry: Lawrence Durrell
Cavafy: Anatomy of a Soul
German Romantic Poetry: Goethe, Novalis, Heine, Hölderlin
Feminism and Shakespeare
Shakespeare: Love, Poetry & Magic
The Passion of D.H. Lawrence
D.H. Lawrence: Symbolic Landscapes
D.H. Lawrence: Infinite Sensual Violence
Rimbaud: Arthur Rimbaud and the Magic of Poetry
The Ecstasies of John Cowper Powys
Sensualism and Mythology: The Wessex Novels of John Cowper Powys
Amorous Life: John Cowper Powys and the Manifestation of Affectivity (H.W. Fawkner)
Postmodern Powys: New Essays on John Cowper Powys (Joe Boulter)
Rethinking Powys: Critical Essays on John Cowper Powys
Paul Bowles & Bernardo Bertolucci
Rainer Maria Rilke
Joseph Conrad: *Heart of Darkness*
In the Dim Void: Samuel Beckett
Samuel Beckett Goes into the Silence
André Gide: Fiction and Fervour
Jackie Collins and the Blockbuster Novel
Blinded By Her Light: The Love-Poetry of Robert Graves
The Passion of Colours: Travels In Mediterranean Lands
Poetic Forms

MEDIA, CINEMA, FEMINISM and CULTURAL STUDIES

J.R.R. Tolkien: The Books, The Films, The Whole Cultural Phenomenon
J.R.R. Tolkien: Pocket Guide
The *Lord of the Rings* Movies: Pocket Guide
The Cinema of Hayao Miyazaki
Hayao Miyazaki: *Princess Mononoke*: Pocket Movie Guide
Hayao Miyazaki: *Spirited Away*: Pocket Movie Guide
Tim Burton : Hallowe'en For Hollywood
Ken Russell
Ken Russell: *Tommy*: Pocket Movie Guide
The Ghost Dance: The Origins of Religion
The Peyote Cult
Cixous, Irigaray, Kristeva: The *Jouissance* of French Feminism
Julia Kristeva: Art, Love, Melancholy, Philosophy, Semiotics and Psychoanalysis
Luce Irigaray: Lips, Kissing, and the Politics of Sexual Difference
Hélene Cixous I Love You: The *Jouissance* of Writing
Andrea Dworkin
'Cosmo Woman': The World of Women's Magazines
Women in Pop Music
HomeGround: The Kate Bush Anthology
Discovering the Goddess (Geoffrey Ashe)
The Poetry of Cinema
The Sacred Cinema of Andrei Tarkovsky
Andrei Tarkovsky: Pocket Guide
Andrei Tarkovsky: *Mirror*: Pocket Movie Guide
Andrei Tarkovsky: *The Sacrifice*: Pocket Movie Guide
Walerian Borowczyk: Cinema of Erotic Dreams
Jean-Luc Godard: The Passion of Cinema
Jean-Luc Godard: *Hail Mary*: Pocket Movie Guide
Jean-Luc Godard: *Contempt*: Pocket Movie Guide
Jean-Luc Godard: *Pierrot le Fou*: Pocket Movie Guide
John Hughes and Eighties Cinema
Ferris Bueller's Day Off: Pocket Movie Guide
Jean-Luc Godard: Pocket Guide
The Cinema of Richard Linklater
Liv Tyler: Star In Ascendance
Blade Runner and the Films of Philip K. Dick
Paul Bowles and Bernardo Bertolucci
Media Hell: Radio, TV and the Press
An Open Letter to the BBC
Detonation Britain: Nuclear War in the UK
Feminism and Shakespeare
Wild Zones: Pornography, Art and Feminism
Sex in Art: Pornography and Pleasure in Painting and Sculpture
Sexing Hardy: Thomas Hardy and Feminism

The Light Eternal is a model monograph, an exemplary job. The subject matter of the book is beautifully organised and dead on beam. (Lawrence Durrell)
It is amazing for me to see my work treated with such passion and respect. (Andrea Dworkin)

CRESCENT MOON PUBLISHING
P.O. Box 1312, Maidstone, Kent, ME14 5XU, Great Britain. www.crmoon.com

cresmopub@yahoo.co.uk   www.crescentmoon.org.uk